Cybersecurity Career Master Plan

Proven techniques and effective tips to help you advance in your cybersecurity career

Dr. Gerald Auger
Jaclyn "Jax" Scott
Jonathan Helmus
Kim Nguyen

BIRMINGHAM—MUMBAI

Cybersecurity Career Master Plan

Group Product Manager: Wilson D'souza
Publishing Product Manager: Rahul Nair
Senior Editor: Shazeen Iqbal
Content Development Editor: Romy Dias
Technical Editor: Sarvesh Jaywant
Copy Editor: Safis Editing
Project Coordinator: Shagun Saini
Proofreader: Safis Editing
Indexer: Subalakshmi Govindhan
Production Designer: Shankar Kalbhor

First published: August 2021

Production reference: 1040821

Published by Packt Publishing Ltd.
Livery Place
35 Livery Street
Birmingham
B3 2PB, UK.

ISBN 978-1-80107-356-1

www.packt.com

No matter what path you've walked in life there is an opportunity for everyone in cybersecurity.

– Dr. Gerald Auger

To my fellow military veterans, a transition isn't easy – we believe this book will help you with your transition into the cybersecurity field.

– Jaclyn "Jax" Scott

To all the folks looking to get into cybersecurity – this book serves as proof that there is a place for everyone in cybersecurity.

– Jonathan Helmus

To everyone who wishes to join the fields of cybersecurity and computer science, I have done it, and so can you!

– Kim Nguyen

Foreword

We are living in a world where cybersecurity events are consistently front-page news. Events such as big-name organizations falling prey to ransomware attacks, popular websites and mobile applications leaking sensitive user data, operating systems getting hacked, and entire gas pipelines being shut down have all happened within the past 6 months, without any signs of these cyber attacks slowing down.

Now, more than ever, the cybersecurity industry desperately needs help. There are more job openings than qualified people to fill the roles and more corporations being attacked without the proper resources in place to defend themselves.

The good news is that many cybersecurity roles come with a slew of incredible perks, including high salaries, remote work, good benefits, and a good work-life balance. The even better news: there are more resources available nowadays for people to study cybersecurity than ever before. These resources are often free or cheap and can even involve self-study, without the need for college or university.

What is often lacking, however, is a clear roadmap in terms of the paths and resources available to break into the field of cybersecurity; a roadmap that is current, relevant, and can be trusted to navigate an individual through the different roles in cybersecurity, how to study for those roles, how to brand yourself, and how to eventually land a job. This book is that missing roadmap.

You are in good hands taking advice from Gerry, Jax, Jon, and Kim. I met Gerry and Jon when I was seeking cybersecurity education advice of my own. I was unsure of the next steps in my career when Jon reached out to me, introduced me to Gerry, and they both provided me with incredibly thoughtful advice. Consider that I was already a CEO of a cybersecurity company at this point in my career, and it truly drives home the fact that they can help anyone. Beginner, advanced, or anything in between.

Read this book, take good notes, study, and network with as many people as you can. I look forward to the opportunity of us working side by side in the cybersecurity field in the very near future.

Heath "The Cyber Mentor" Adams

CEO,

TCM Security

Contributors

About the authors

Dr. Gerald Auger has worked within information security since 2006 and holds a PhD in cyber operations. Gerald has helped tens of thousands of aspiring cybersecurity professionals through his "Simply Cyber" YouTube channel and is regularly interviewed for his thoughts on cybersecurity professional development.

Gerald is a full-time information security practitioner, adjunct faculty at The Citadel, The Military College of South Carolina; chief content creator for Simply Cyber; and managing director at Coastal Information Security Group.

> *I want to thank my family, especially my wonderful wife, for supporting my passion for pursuing all aspects of cybersecurity. I'd like to acknowledge all the practitioners I've had the distinguished pleasure of working with along the way who have expanded my knowledge and awareness of the nuances of this awesome field.*

Jaclyn "Jax" Scott is a tenured Special Operations Warrant Officer with nearly 18 years of experience working in military cyber, electronic warfare, and intelligence operations. She is the founder and content creator of Beans and Bytes tech blog, co-host of the cybersecurity podcast Hackerz and Haecksen, and the president of Outpost Gray, a cybersecurity consulting firm. Jax is an expert in military cyber policy and has led global development operations in cyber countermeasures to mitigate near-peer attacks. She is currently pursuing her master's in Cyber Intelligence at Georgetown University.

> *I want to thank my friends and mentors; I would not be here today if it wasn't for you believing in me and my dreams. Thank you to the Packt team for making this process seamless and enjoyable. A special thanks to our tech editor, Matthew Jones; you are meticulous in your reviews and generous in your feedback. Finally, to my co-authors, thank you for being the best!*

Jonathan Helmus ("Moos1e") is a penetration tester and professor with over 10 years of experience in engineering, information security, and information technology. Jon resides in a small town right outside Seattle, Washington, where he and his family raise alpacas on their mini farm. Currently, Jon works as a freelance educator teaching topics such as pentesting, red teaming, cloud security, and vulnerability exploitation. He also works as a contract pentester and cloud security professional for clients all around the world.

> *To my wife, Kim, who never stops believing in me, even when I fail to believe in myself. Without her support, none of this would be possible for me. Big shout out to my kids for being the main driver for just about everything I do in my life—I hope this shows that you can do anything!*
>
> *I'd also like to thank Dr. Auger for allowing me to join the team and contribute to such a fantastic opportunity to give back to the community.*

Kim Nguyen is a Software Engineer, with a broad background thanks to her B.S. in business administration and M.S. in computer science. Kim's day-to-day work focuses on software engineering of cloud-based technologies, while continuing her research into cybersecurity on the side. Kim is also an instructor at the City University of Seattle, where she teaches computer science courses. She is an active technical speaker and researcher at cybersecurity and computer science conferences. Kim holds several certificates, including AWS Certified Developer and CompTIA Linux+. Kim is the founder of Passion Sets Success, a platform that helps people identify their passion, to achieve the right career for them.

> *I want to thank my perfect mother Hai, for always supporting my dreams and passions – without you, I could never be where I am in life today. I'd also like to thank all my mentors and friends, who have been a remarkable part of my journey. Special shout out to Jax and all other co-authors, for allowing me to join this exciting ride; I couldn't have asked for a better team. Lastly, huge thanks to the incredible work from the whole Packt editing team and the technical reviewer.*

About the reviewer

Matthew Jones is a veteran information security architect with one of the nation's top-ranked teaching hospitals. With over 23 years of industry experience, his career covers federal government, state government, and Fortune 500 consulting. Aside from his current architect duties, he focuses on certification and accreditation, vulnerability management, identity and access management, cloud security, and privacy.

While not balancing risk on the tip of a needle, Matt enjoys stand-up paddle-boarding and can often be found traversing the waterways and tidal creeks of his coastal home.

Table of Contents

Section 2: Your Path into the Industry

3

Different Strokes for Different Folks

4

Exploring Certifications and College

5

Getting Hands-On Experience with No Experience

6

Time to Brand Yourself – Not the Burning Type

7

How to Land a Jay-Oh-Bee!

Section 3:
Now You're in; Time to Level Up!

8

Giving Back to Others and Yourself

Preface

Cybersecurity is an incredibly dynamic field that is in the news nearly daily. An eternal cat-and-mouse struggle rages between threat actors and cybersecurity practitioners as vulnerabilities are discovered and attack strategies are refined as quickly as patches are deployed and awareness is heightened.

Now is the golden age of getting into cybersecurity. Many resources you can use to develop yourself are free or reasonably priced, and the ability to engage in community discussion through social media has led to massive networking opportunities.

This book is a complete plan to help you decode the field and understand a direction to head in, the tools and supplies to take on your journey, and how to achieve your destination.

This book is broken down into nine chapters across three logical sections aligned with a career chronology. Section 1 shapes the space of cybersecurity and helps you answer the question, "Is a job in cybersecurity right for me, and if so, which?"

Section 2 takes the velocity from section 1 and throws fuel on the fire, showing you how to apply your knowledge, skills, and abilities in the field and how to showcase yourself to potential hiring managers.

Section 3 finishes strong by showing you how to level up your career once you're in the field and how to manage the process of setting actionable goals and accomplishing them.

Who this book is for

Cybersecurity careers are hyper-inclusive. You can be a recent college graduate, a transitioning service member, a mid-career professional looking for a different challenge, a stay-at-home parent who is ready to return to the workforce, a high school drop out, and many other unique situations. All of these backgrounds have the potential for a successful experience in the cybersecurity field.

This book makes no assumptions of your technical acumen, your prior work experience, or any socio-economic factors. If you are slightly curious or ferociously hungry about a career in cybersecurity, then this book is for you.

What this book covers

Chapter 1, New Career in Cyber... "Who Dis?", explores the current state of the cybersecurity industry and security frameworks, as well as the pros and cons of entering the industry.

Chapter 2, Which Career Field Is Best for You?, guides you in helping you to understand which area in the extensive field of cybersecurity is right for you.

Chapter 3, Different Strokes for Different Folks, explains how it's not just what role you want but also what industry and environment you want to work in. We explore multiple sectors, such as finance, healthcare, and energy, to highlight the pros and cons of each.

Chapter 4, Exploring Certifications and College, explores various approaches to certifications and their value in the field and examines the benefits of a college education.

Chapter 5, Getting Hands-On Experience with No Experience, covers how hands-on experience is a key differentiator for hiring managers when evaluating candidates to hire. It can be tough to get experience without the job first, and we explore precisely how to earn that experience through labs for various roles in the industry.

Chapter 6, Time to Brand Yourself – Not the Burning Type, explains how to best position yourself as a member of the cybersecurity community through engagement and contributions that will help you differentiate yourself.

Chapter 7, How to Land a Jay-Oh-Bee!, dives headfirst into how to find cybersecurity employment opportunities to get you excited. This is only half the battle, as we also explore tips to refine your résumé to stand out from the crowd and how to ace your interviews.

Chapter 8, Giving Back to Others and Yourself, covers how, given that the cybersecurity industry is constantly changing, threat actors are refining their craft, and Big Tech is constantly innovating market solutions, to stay on top of your game through knowledge-sharing and mentoring, and how to manage a mentally healthy balance between work and life.

Chapter 9, Trusting the Process, explores how to establish actionable goals and milestones as you embark on your cybersecurity career journey.

To get the most out of this book

To perform the hands-on exercise in *Chapter 5, Getting Hands-On Experience with No Experience*, you will need the following prerequisites:

Software/hardware covered in the book	Operating system requirements
Raspberry Pi Model B with 2 GB of RAM	NA
Raspberry Pi OS	Windows, macOS, or Linux
WebGoat	Windows, macOS, or Linux
Docker	Windows, macOS, or Linux

Code in Action

The Code in Action videos for this book can be viewed at https://bit.ly/3BMDv8X.

Download the color images

We also provide a PDF file that has color images of the screenshots and diagrams used in this book. You can download it here: http://www.packtpub.com/sites/default/files/downloads/9781801073561_ColorImages.pdf.

Conventions used

There are a number of text conventions used throughout this book.

Code in text: Indicates code words in text, database table names, folder names, filenames, file extensions, pathnames, dummy URLs, user input, and Twitter handles. Here is an example: "In this text field, input ip.addr==10.11.11.94 and hit *Enter*."

Any command-line input or output is written as follows:

```
sudo apt-get update && sudo apt-get upgrade
```

Bold: Indicates a new term, an important word, or words that you see on screen. For instance, words in menus or dialog boxes appear in bold. Here is an example: "You will have to use the **Register new user** option to begin."

> **Tips or important notes**
> Appear like this.

Get in touch

Feedback from our readers is always welcome.

General feedback: If you have questions about any aspect of this book, email us at customercare@packtpub.com and mention the book title in the subject of your message.

Errata: Although we have taken every care to ensure the accuracy of our content, mistakes do happen. If you have found a mistake in this book, we would be grateful if you would report this to us. Please visit www.packtpub.com/support/errata and fill in the form.

Piracy: If you come across any illegal copies of our works in any form on the internet, we would be grateful if you would provide us with the location address or website name. Please contact us at copyright@packt.com with a link to the material.

If you are interested in becoming an author: If there is a topic that you have expertise in and you are interested in either writing or contributing to a book, please visit authors. packtpub.com.

Share Your Thoughts

Once you've read *Cybersecurity Career Master Plan*, we'd love to hear your thoughts! Scan the QR code below to go straight to the Amazon review page for this book and share your feedback.

https://packt.link/r/1801073562

Your review is important to us and the tech community and will help us make sure we're delivering excellent quality content.

Section 1: Getting Started with Cybersecurity

In this section, you will gain a high-level understanding of the cybersecurity industry including niche areas, specialties, and growth fields, while also understanding that satisfaction and passion are key to long-term growth.

The following chapters will be covered under this section:

- *Chapter 1, New Career in Cyber... "Who Dis?"*
- *Chapter 2, Which Career Field Is Best for You?*

1
New Career in Cyber... "Who Dis?"

Cybersecurity is the hot new career field. It might even be hotter than the Kardashians. *Why, you ask?* To put it simply, technology is spearheading global growth. With new technology such as *artificial intelligence* and *machine learning* comes more cybersecurity demand. It's the whole supply and demand concept you learned in high school.

While more jobs are becoming remote, virtual, or replaced by robots, how do you think they are protected and secured? Cybersecurity is more than an IT helpdesk or the hackers you see on TV. It's a broad spectrum within all aspects of technology that has made cybersecurity an upward slope for careers, which will not change anytime soon.

What we know today will drastically change from what we know 1 year from now. We know that cybersecurity professionals make great money and get to wear hoodies and flip-flops to work. With all the positives do come some negatives you will learn about within this chapter.

During this chapter you will have me, Jaclyn (*Jax*) Scott, leading you. You are encouraged to have a notebook close while reading this chapter and following chapters to help with your data retention.

In this chapter, we will explore cybersecurity by breaking it down into the following sections:

- Learning about the current state of the industry
- Exploring the foundations of cybersecurity
- Understanding the pro and cons of cyber careers

Learning about the current state of the industry

Cybersecurity is rapidly growing because of emerging technology that is producing an ever-changing threat-scape. There is a reason for the rapid growth of technology, and it's outside of the next cool *Clubhouse* or *Tinder* app or that new self-driving car that picks up self-drinking slushies. It lies within history.

As you may have heard in history class, history educates us about our future. This is true even within cybersecurity. The world leaders are driven by one thing, what is that? Power! How has power historically been obtained? Typically, and sometimes the most prevalent example is *war*. As cyber has emerged, so has a new type of warfare called **cyberwar**, which is ongoing.

The battlespace and the soldiers have changed. As technology emerges and grows, so have the world powers seated at the *executive table*. China in 2019 was the first country to send an unmanned rover to the far side of the moon. We have self-driving cars and the prediction is that in 5 years, we could take trips to Mars. Technology is growing and maturing in unimaginable ways.

Understanding why cybersecurity is advancing in all sectors to include phone apps and smart TVs will help you grasp the projected technological growth and prepare you for a **cyber career**. It's crucial you understand the maturing threat-scape and vulnerabilities that exist everywhere.

Here are some things to consider related to the cybersecurity industry:

- Hackers are becoming more advanced.
- Tools for amateur hackers continue to get simpler.
- Cybercrime is exploding (and it's expensive for organizations).
- Automation is the future.
- Vulnerabilities are endless.

In 2020, many careers were impacted due to the global health crisis and pandemic called *COVID-19*, while cybersecurity jobs remained in demand. A primary reason is because everyone went from working in a controlled office space with secured networks and on-premises monitoring to working on grandma's 100/100 Wi-Fi with a default password that was 4 years old.

This new workforce left a lot of employees and companies extremely vulnerable to a cyberattack. There was a considerable increase in ransomware attacks during 2019-2020 because attackers exploited these vulnerabilities. This meant more job opportunities for penetration testers and cybersecurity professionals to protect the new remote workforce.

Cybersecurity is not going away because *cybercriminals* will always find more creative ways to lure their victims to "*click*", which keeps you in a cyber job long after your first marriage.

Cyber laws and regulations

Before we jump into the next section, we will cover some of the **cyber laws** that influence the overall cyber *growth* and impact this field.

As we are writing this book, cybersecurity laws and legislation are a sticky topic. Congressional leaders are uncertain on how to address them because they don't know how to manage the cyber growth and the World Wide Web. The threat-scape is changing quickly, making it very challenging to determine what to address. Many of the cyber laws we have today are reactionary laws, meaning something happened, then a law was developed and enacted trying to prevent *it* from happening again.

An example of a reactionary law is when the first significant data breach happened to Yahoo in 2016, when hackers stole approximately 500 million accounts dating back to 2014. This breach then sparked the need for data protection and next came the **Consumer Privacy Protection Act** of 2017.

The challenge is knowing what laws you need before something happens. How can you create a law to predict something that has happened yet?

> *In 2020, the average cost for a large business data breach was more than $150 million. In 2019, the average breach was only around $3.92 million.*

To understand the purpose of cybersecurity regulations, we will give you a law overview to help you better understand the current state of cyber legislation.

Quick cyber law class

The United States legislative system falls within three broad categories: *criminal*, *civil*, and *administrative* law. Cybersecurity regulation comprises directives from the **Executive Branch** while legislation comes from **Congress** designed to safeguard information technology and computer systems. The purpose of cybersecurity regulations is to force organizations to protect consumer data from being stolen and used for malicious means.

It wasn't till the **Computer Fraud and Abuse Act (CFAA)** of 1984 that the US saw any significant legislation specific to cyber law. This law covered general crimes such as malicious damage to federal computer systems of more than $1,000, trafficking of computer passwords, and modification of medical records. CFAA received its first amendment in 1994 when Congress recognized the face of computer security had drastically changed since 1984; this amendment was called the **Computer Abuse Amendment Act**.

The Computer Abuse Amendment Act considered more sophisticated actors that could target organizations through malicious code. It would allow for offenders' imprisonment, regardless of whether they intended to cause damage or not. There were more amendments in 1989, 1994, 1996, 2002, and the final one in 2008. Nevertheless, the laws was still very vague. This law also led to Aaron Schwartz's well-known case of 2009 and eventually his arrest a couple of years later in 2011. Mr. Schwartz was prosecuted for downloading many academic research papers from the *MIT* database.

> *Recently, in April 2020, the Supreme Court finally reviewed the CFAA for the first time to make it more current with today's cyber activity.*

Here is a brief list of current cyber **legislation** you will likely hear more about as you move through your cyber career:

- **Health Insurance Portability and Accountability Act (HIPPA)** of 1996: Designed to protect individual health records.

- **Consumer Privacy Protection Act** of 2017: This law was developed shortly after the large Yahoo breach in 2016 and was designed to protect customer information to avoid identity theft.

- **General Data Protection Regulation (GDPR)** of 2018: This is the European Union's most stringent privacy and security law globally, and it impacts US activities.

- **California Consumer Privacy Act (CCPA)** of 2018: This was the first US-specific bill passed to protect the consumer's rights by giving them more control of personal information shared.

In recent years, the US government also used specific bills and laws to strengthen its effort with communication and data sharing.

This includes the following bills and organization:

- **Cybersecurity Information Sharing Act (CISA)** of 2014: CISA provides a platform for information sharing through an open source platform while spreading cyber activity awareness.

- **Cybersecurity Enhancement Act** of 2014: Voluntary collaboration platform for public-private partners to improve cybersecurity through research, education, and public awareness.

- **Federal Exchange Data Breach Notification Act** of 2015: Requires health insurance to notify any individual whose personal data was subject to unauthorized access, such as a data breach.

- **National Cybersecurity Protection Advancement Act** of 2015: This was an amendment to the *Homeland Security Act* of 2002 to allow other entities such as tribal, private, and non-federal representatives within the **Department of Homeland Security (DHS) National Cybersecurity and Communications Integration Center (NCCIC)**.

The following is a message from the United States Department of Justice on who to report cybercrimes to, dated April 1, 2021:

> *"Internet-related crime, like any other crime, should be reported to appropriate law enforcement investigative authorities at the local, state, federal, or international levels, depending on the scope of the crime. Citizens who are aware of federal crimes should report them to local offices of federal law enforcement."*
>
> *– Justice.gov*

Now that you understand why cybersecurity is the trending career field and the laws that govern it, we will move into the foundations of cybersecurity.

Exploring the foundations of cybersecurity

What is cybersecurity? Cybersecurity defines processes, technology, and design frameworks developed to protect organizations' devices, programs, data, and other valuable assets from unauthorized access from a cyber threat.

This section will provide you with a basic understanding of cybersecurity, key terms such as **risk** versus **vulnerability**, and different cybersecurity frameworks, which include the **CIA Triad, NIST, ISO**, and **SOC2**.

Threats, assets, vulnerabilities, and **risks** will be covered in the following section. We will explain the fundamentals of how cybersecurity professionals protect data, devices, networks, and systems from attacks from viruses, malware, hackers, and data breaches.

Asset, vulnerability, risk, and threat

Some terms you will hear often within cybersecurity are asset, vulnerability, risk, and threat. These are key terms you should learn and know. We will cover these briefly in this section

Here are their breakdowns:

- **Asset**: This is anything in the environment that needs to be protected, such as data, people, proprietary tools, and processes essential for business operations.
- **Vulnerability**: A weakness within your organization that can be exploited, such as flaws in software code and out-of-date software.
- **Risk**: The likelihood or possibility a threat was successful in breaching your network, the risk would be the asset's total loss. The following is an example of the risk formula to identify your organization's risk:

  Risk = Threat x Vulnerability
- **Threat**: Anything that is trying to degrade, disrupt, or steal your asset is a threat. This would include cybercriminals or insider threats.

The preceding is not an inclusive list, it is the basics to help you get started. We encourage you to dig further into each of these to understand their roles within cybersecurity. Next, we will discuss the CIA Triad.

What is the CIA Triad?

The CIA Triad is not the Central Intelligence Agency composed of US government employees who provide national security intelligence to congressional leaders in America. The CIA Triad in cyber means **Confidentiality, Integrity**, and **Availability**. These are the core pillars of **information security** (**InfoSec**) a subset of cybersecurity. Throughout this chapter, we will focus on the CIA Triad three pillars as they are foundational elements of InfoSec.

The CIA Triad will be referenced throughout your career because it's the foundation in developing information security policies.

"So, what is the CIA Triad?" We are happy you asked. We will explain the CIA Triad by using the following diagram:

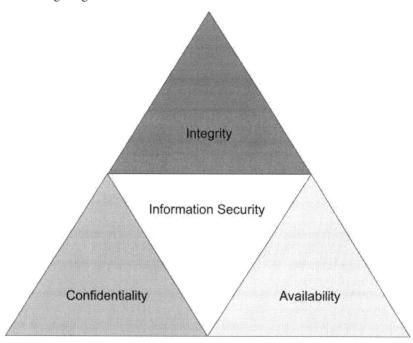

Figure 1.1 – CIA Triad

The easiest way of thinking about the CIA Triad is as a security model to help unpack various **information technology** (**IT**) security components. This model helps develop security policies to identify problem areas on a network while providing appropriate solutions. In the next section, we dissect each pillar in more detail.

Confidentiality

The best way to think about confidentiality is ensuring that only select users can access specific data. This could include encryption techniques, but there are far more ways to achieve confidentiality on a network.

Generally, all organizations have some form of sensitive information. This may include client data, company proprietary data, and customer or employee **personal identification information** (**PII**). Most companies' information systems store information that has some degree of sensitivity.

Data is the new gold and criminals target organization data in the hope of either encrypting or stealing data. Then the organization are forced to pay large ransoms to get it back. A common attack technique is a **ransomware attack**, where a criminal either encrypts or steals your data then holds it hostage until you pay the ransom using cryptocurrency.

> **Note**
> Cybercriminals will often target organizations with significantly more sensitive data because they know the payout will be larger.

An attack vector used for a ransomware attack is a phishing email. Once the threat actor has successfully breached the network, the second phase of an attack could include password stealing, credential harvesting, and data encryption.

Not all data breaches are criminal in action, meaning someone in the organization could share classified information with someone who does not have the appropriate classification to read the data. An example could include forwarding an email to the wrong Susan Smith. Instead of sending it to Susan Smith in *Countermeasure*, they instead sent it to Susan Smith in Human Resources. Another example is leaving a computer unattended and the email inbox open with PII data exposed for another employee to see.

An intentional or unintentional data breach will lead to the same result: sharing confidential data with those who do not have access.

Countermeasures to help reduce the likelihood of a data breach and increase confidentially would include the following:

- Access control list
- File and volume encryption
- Authentication through software to control access
- Administrative policies
- Continuing employee training and awareness
- Physical hardenings such as cameras and access control

The preceding countermeasures should be part of a layered security approach. It is best to have multiple security countermeasures in place to protect the confidentiality of data.

Integrity

This pillar ensures that your data stays intact and is not changed or altered. This provides data assurance, completeness, and accuracy. **Data integrity** is essential for both data at rest (stored data) and at flow (emails). Integrity maintenance starts with access control and ensuring that only authorized users have access to modify data.

Data integrity protection extends beyond malicious attacks. Unintentional alterations can occur if access controls are not maintained and the employee obtains access to a file and deletes or alters files, causing data loss or, network complications.

Try searching *Largest data breach of today*, or *Largest data breach of 2021*, and more than one article about different breaches will come up. Why? Because data breaches are becoming more and more prevalent and, unfortunately, will never go away.

Hackers are becoming more creative and finding novel ways to lure their victims into their *clickbait*. The cyberwar between cybercriminals and cybersecurity experts is a cat and mouse game. The number one thing you can do to protect integrity of data is ensure your organization's countermeasures are maintained regularly. Authentications should be robust, with access control updated regularly to help prevent unauthorized access to networks and files.

Another great example of how integrity of data is being questioned are through **deep fakes**. Deep fakes are videos or photos that look and sound like the real thing. As technology becomes better, identifying deep fakes becomes more challenging. The integrity of the document or photo is then in question and can create a myriad of other problems.

Availability

Availability ensures that the users have timely and uninterrupted access to information, systems and networks. How many times have you been working and suddenly your *cloud storage* stops working or the document you were working on is gone or corrupt? Availability ensures access to data at any time without any obstacles such as network outages or data breach.

A malicious attack includes *cyber-espionage*, where the attacker's intent is to impact the network by encrypting all the data. By denying access to the data, organizations are forced to pay the ransom or start over from scratch, which can also cost a lot of money and time. There are unintentional and non-malicious activities that impact availability that include natural disasters, bandwidth, or unscheduled software updates.

> **Important note**
> Certain individual states in the United States are proposing new laws to ban ransom payments to cybercriminal.

An example attack method that adversaries use to disrupt companies' data availability is known as **Denial of Service** or **DoS** attacks. This is an unsophisticated attack in which an attacker will flood a server with requests to overwhelm and disrupt the web service or degrade services for clients and employees.

Countermeasures to strengthen availability are as follows:

- Large organizations should consider hardware redundancies such as backup servers and data storage availability.
- Automatic cloud-scaling capabilities.
- Monitoring software such as endpoint protection to monitor the network for performance will help prevent unwanted traffic.
- Standard firewalls and routers should be updated regularly to ensure compliance.

At this point, you should have a solid foundational understanding of the CIA Triad, its purpose, and how to apply it within your organization. Next, we will cover three different cybersecurity frameworks. This is dense information, so I completely understand if you are reaching for something a little stiffer than water.

Different cybersecurity frameworks

The first cybersecurity framework we will discuss is NIST. NIST stands for **National Institute of Standards and Technology**. NIST is a framework that helps a company develop organizational controls and risk management for their information security program.

> **Important note**
> There are other internationally recognized security frameworks not covered in this book; these include IASME, COBIT, and CIS.

The NIST framework is broken into three parts:

- Framework Core
- Implementation Tiers
- Framework Profiles

Framework Core

The **Framework Core** is made up of five functions. The easiest way to remember them is to think of **Identify** and **Protect** as the organization's actions to prepare itself against a cyberattack. **Detect**, **Response**, and **Recover** are all the *things* you will do after a breach or incident occurs.

The five core functions are as follows:

1. Identify: Manages risks by correctly understanding assets, data, and other resources.

2. Protect: Protocols and countermeasures in place to protect critical infrastructure.

3. Detect: Defines what makes an event versus regular network activity.

4. Respond: Response to events through predefined actions.

5. Recover: Recovery processes for repair services and network.

If you want to learn more about NIST and download the framework's Core Function and Category spreadsheet, you can visit https://www.nist.gov/ and search for NIST Framework.

Implementation Tiers

The **Implementation Tiers** are a total of four tiers, which range from *partial* to *adaptive*. Figure 1.2 provides you with a graphic depiction of the NIST Tiers and the degree to which information is shared, and how well cybersecurity risk and decisions are integrated into the organization's broad spectrum:

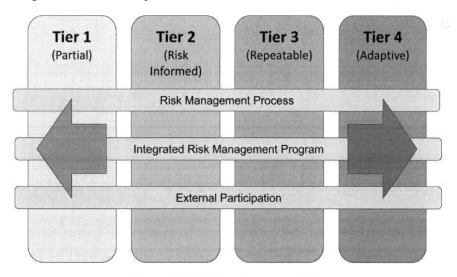

Figure 1.2 – NIST Implementation Tiers

These **Tiers** are defined by the organization requirements' objective. The organization must decide its level of risk, resources, and tools to defend against a breach.

Framework Profiles

The last portion of the NIST Framework is optional but highly encouraged because it helps an organization define its unique security posture objectives. Protection of data is essential, and companies must clearly define their risks and resources. The **Framework Profiles** are used to identify opportunities for refining or improving overall cyber hygiene. Organizations can have a current and future profile for their end state. A business may also have different profiles based on their business needs and capabilities. This process takes time and should be looked at as an ongoing and never-ending process.

Organizations should always be working on their current cyber profile to identify opportunities to increase cyber awareness and harden overall cybersecurity posture to improve security.

ISO Cybersecurity Framework

ISO 2700/27001 was created by the International Organization for Standardization. Their certifications are recognized internationally as the international standard for validation for cybersecurity programs. This standard is more risk-based focused versus technical focus.

> **Important note**
>
> Cybersecurity *risk* is an organization's probability of exposure or loss resulting from a data breach or cyberattack. When an organization takes a risk-based approach, it typically means the organization uses a methodology based on the analysis of the risk and the risk of the management framework.

This framework has over a dozen different standards for organizations to use for their security management of assets.

SOC2 Cybersecurity Framework

SOC2 stands for **Service Organization Control Type 2** and is a cybersecurity framework and auditing standard developed by the **American Institute of Certified Public Accountants** (**AICPA**) to ensure organizations are securely managing client and vendor data. NIST and SOC2 may appear to be opposite sides of the same coin; both are designed to review an organization's internal controls.

> **Note**
> NIST offers a framework for InfoSec and privacy controls while SOC2 enables organizations to obtain certifications of compliance.

We encourage you to take additional time and look into these frameworks, and the others, when you have more time. Next, we will discuss the different types of cyber attacks.

Types of cyber attacks

There are a lot of terms you will learn and need to understand to speak cyber. Terms used to explain certain **cyber attacks** are essential to know so you can understand the threat to then implement the proper countermeasure to mitigate the threat. For example, if an organization was concerned about a **Distributed Denial of Service** (**DDoS**) versus a phishing attack, the infosec team would have different countermeasures to investigate and mitigate the risk.

This section describes the top 10 most seen cyberattacks. This is basic information designed to provide a high-level context of different threats.

Distributed Denial of Service (DDoS)

A DDoS attack is achieved when an adversary targets your network and floods it with a high number of packets. This type of attack is measured by the amount of bandwidth involved. An example is in 2019 when a DDoS attack impacted *GitHub*. GitHub reported a peak of 1.35 terabits per second. At the time, this was the largest DDoS attack to date.

What happens during at attack like this is the threat actor will overwhelm the server and make it impossible to conduct **business as usual** (**BAU**). Unlike most attacks, where the attacker is trying to gain access, a DDoS is designed to degrade the company network and denial of service.

If you see a DDoS attack, it's likely an unsophisticated attack. However, recently, experts are beginning to see cybercriminals using DDoS as a secondary attack vector layered onto a primary attack. An example is when a threat actor targets a victim using a phishing lure. Once successful, they will encrypt all the victim's data. If the client refuses to pay the ransom, the threat group will conduct a DDoS on their network to disrupt it enough, making it impossible to conduct BAU. Eventually, the victim will pay or wipe everything and migrate to an entirely new server, which can be very costly with a lot of downtime.

Here are some types of DDoS attacks you may see:

- **TCP SYN Flood attack**: This happens during the **Transmission Control Protocol (TCP)** session when initializing a handshake. They exploit the buffer space and overload the system with connection requests.

- **Smurf attack**: The attack will spoof a known IP address and the **Internet Control Message Protocol (ICMP)** to overwhelm the target network. This is an echo request targeted at a select range of IPs with a response reaching back to the spoofed IP.

- **Teardrop attack**: The attacker will overlap the length and fragment fields within sequential IP, causing the system to try and fail at reconstructing the packets making the system stop working.

- **Ping of Death attack**: This attack uses IP packets to ping a target network and a large IP size. When the IP packet is not allowed, the threat actor will fragment the IP. Once the system accepts the packet, it will then experience buffer overflows and crashes.

Man-in-the-Middle

Man-in-the-Middle is when an adversary places themselves between a client and server's communication. This is when the following could occur:

- **Session hijacking**: This is when the attacker can control the client and then disconnect the client from the server. Once disconnected, the attack will replace the host machine IP address with the attacked IP address then spoof the client sequence number. The computer would look like BAU while under the control of the attacker.

- **IP spoofing**: This is when the attacker uses what appears to be a legitimate IP address to communicate with the host computer. The host machine could accept the packet from the spoofed IP and act upon it.

- **Replay**: The attack will replay an old message to obtain access to a system. This is accomplished when the attackers intercept a message to save for later use.

Mitigation techniques include using secured session tokens, time-stamping messages, and secure DNS. **Multi-Factor Authentication**, or **MFA**, and digital certificates also help to mitigate these attacks and aid in keeping confidentiality and integrity intact during communication.

> **Note**
>
> MFA is a multi-step authentication process to grant users access to specific applications. Examples of MFA include something you know, something you have, and something you are. Examples would be a password, an authenticator code, and a fingerprint.

Phishing, spearphishing and business email compromise attacks

Phishing is the most used vector for cyberattacks. Phishing attacks can be divided into three different attacks listed below.

- **Spearphishing**: Targeted attack that focus on a small group of people or organization.

- **Business Email Compromise (BEC)**: Targets higher leadership or someone who can make purchases. Typically, the lure in this attack will be about a gift card purchase coming from a trust source

- **Phishing**: Untargeted attacks sometimes referred to as a "spray and pray" attack. Spray and pray are the most common phishing attacks and they are designed to hit a larger number of emails without a specific target in mind.

Typically, the emails will come from a trusted source to lure its victims to click. They will also use emotional queues to get their victims to click, such as urgency or money tied to the message.

Most organizations have certain protocols to ensure their employees are trained to identify a phishing email versus a legitimate email.

Drive-by attack

Have you ever seen an advertisement online to win an iPad? Surprise, you never win an iPad, but you might win new malware on your computer. These attacks are called **drive-by** compromises because they lure their victims by setting *clickbait* on either legitimate websites or within a search engine.

Protection from these attacks could include spam-blocking software and maintaining an updated and patched browser. Try to avoid having too many unnecessary programs, *browser* extensions, or apps on your computer. These are third-party vendors that could be hacked and could impact you and your security.

Password attack

Attackers know if they obtain your **password**, they will likely have access to others areas of your system.

> **Tip**
> Do not use the same password for everything. Consider the strength of the password to the data you are attempting to protect. The password for your bank account should be stronger than the password you use for your video streaming platform. Both have personal data, but one has more critical data than the other.

Some of the techniques used for password hacking includes brute-force and dictionary attacks:

- **Brute-force attack** is when the attacker will rely on guessing, often through automation, and attempting as many times as possible. Typically the guesses are attributed back to the user's likes and hobbies. If your password is complex enough, it will take a long time to crack it.
- **Dictionary attack** is when the attacker attempts to use the most common passwords.

If either of these attacks are successful, the attacker will gain access to your machine and can collect or encrypt your data.

MFA helps mitigate this risk, as do timeouts.

> **Note**
> Timeout sessions are examples of when a user is logged off after idle time or after a certain period of time such as 12 hours. Then the user must re-authenticate to begin the session again.

Cross-site scripting attack

A **cross-site scripting attack** happens when a user goes to a legitimate website that was injected with malicious code. When the victim visits this website, the website will transmit the page with the attack payload in an HTML text. Then the malicious script will execute on the host machine. The outcome could be seen by stealing cookies, capturing screenshots, and logging keystrokes by prompting the user to log in again.

SQL injection attack

This type of attack is seen within a database-driven website. The attacker will input a SQL command into a database input to run the predefined SQL command. If successful, the **SQL injection** can modify or exploit data on the database, and even give a command to the operating system. To reduce the likelihood of this type of attack, ensure your access to the database is updated regularly, sanitize your variables/inputs, and configure baselines for the database management systems.

Malware attack

Malware is a fancy way of saying *malicious software*. There are many different types of malware, which can be *Trojans, stealth viruses, logic bombs, worms, droppers*, and *ransomware*. We encourage you to conduct your own research to learn more about malware.

Malware is the standard type of infection you will likely see on a system. It's essential to have a basic understanding of each type of malware and how it can infect a system. The best approach to limit possible infection of malware is by keeping operating systems patched, VPN enabled, and using an updated browser. Most successful attacks can be avoided with proper system patching and software updates.

Eavesdropping attack

An eavesdropping attack is also known as a snooping or sniffing attack. Unlike the Man-in-the-Middle attack, an **eavesdropping attacker** listens either passively or actively to the user's network. They listen to the network traffic to find data such as credit card info or passwords. The best prevention against this type of attack is MFA and overall system encryption.

Rogue software attack

Attackers have been using **rogue software attacks** since 2008. The attacker will lure its victims by making them think they have a virus on their machine. Once they have struck panic in the victim, they will convince them to pay for a removal tool that is masquerading as legitimate software.

The vector for this type of attack can be when a user goes to a website and suddenly sees a popup saying, "*Your system has been infected with malware, act now, click here to conduct a virus scan.*" Once the victim clicks, depending on the victims antivirus, the download begins. Another name for the malware used in this type of an attack is called **scareware** because the purpose is to scare the victim into reacting quickly.

The following diagram will assist you with remembering the attack names:

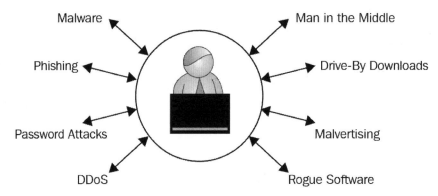

Figure 1.3 – Types of cyber attacks

As we conclude this section, we encourage you to take the time to research and learn more about cyberattacks.

In the next section, we will discuss cyber careers. I will provide you some pros and cons to prepare you for entering this field.

Understanding the pros and cons of cyber careers

Earlier in this chapter, we discussed how cybersecurity is the hot new career field and that it's not going away anytime soon. Before stepping into any new industry, it's important to know the **pros** and **cons** of that industry. This section will explain some of the advantages and disadvantages of the cyber field.

The following are subjective to the business and our professional thoughts. It is best you research and network with others in the industry to obtain a clearer understanding of this career field.

Some advantages of working in cybersecurity are as follows:

- Flexible hours.
- Sizeable salaries.
- Remote work.
- Culture varies in each workplace.
- A large diversity of positions and specialties.

- Recruiters look for you.
- You can train yourself.

Let's go into detail of each of these in the next sections.

Flexible hours

The cyber industry runs on a 24/7 clock. It never ends, which is wonderful news for those needing to work **flexible hours**. It also makes entry into the sector a little easier. As you may imagine, typically, the graveyard shifts are less-sought-after hours, meaning, if you have the ability, working a swing shift at night could be your ticket into the industry. Also, depending on the company, they may allow you to work off-hours to accommodate school or other activities as long as you still clock 40 hours. This will always depend on the organization, so make sure you talk with the recruiter on the hours and flexibility.

Great salaries

This career field pays well because of the skills and education required. Depending on your geographic location and company, many entry-level jobs will start between $70-$80. There are a lot of other factors that tie into this salary. A good rule of thumb is coming in with supporting education (either certificates or college) and hands-on experience. Then you can negotiate to a higher position. Education and the hands-on experience will be discussed in *Section 3, Now You're in; Time to Level Up!*, of this book.

Remote work life

More cybersecurity jobs are moving to **remote work** environments. This is because the companies see the benefits of saving overhead costs while allowing their employees to control their daily work life. This is not a hard and fast rule. You should verify with the employer whether they are fully remote or whether they provide a hybrid work life.

If you seek to work in an environment that requires a security clearance, you will likely be required to work on-premises 90% of the time. Again, this is something you should discuss with the recruiter to confirm the dynamics of that organization.

Cultures vary

When you have worked in one cybersecurity environment, you have worked in one cybersecurity environment. Many times, merely changing departments, not the company, is all you need. This is a pro because you may land your first job and a few months in realize you don't enjoy the culture. Fear not, you can talk with your current leadership and see about moving into another section.

From my personal experience of moving from one section to another, it was a positive shift for my professional growth. Never feel like you are stuck. If the culture does not fit your personal beliefs and values, know that it's not the same everywhere.

If you can, reach out to others in the organization to get their thoughts on the culture before accepting a job. Ask a *lot* of questions and if the company doesn't align with your beliefs, move to something else.

Large diversity of positions and specialties

Diversity of careers in cybersecurity is endless. This is very exciting because you can never get bored in this career field. Additionally, you can progress quickly through further education and training. With the appropriate certifications and degrees, you can learn your way out of your old job and into a new position.

Recruiters look for you

Once you have some hands-on experience in this field, pivoting becomes much easier. One reason is because there are more cyber jobs available than qualified candidates. This means the recruiters sometimes contact you for jobs. The best way to put yourself out there is through a proper brand and network. Branding and networking will be discussed later in *Section 3, Now You're in; Time to Level Up!,* of the book.

You can train yourself

In this career field, you don't need a formal education. The great news is you can train yourself through free online resources and certification. There are a ton of free online resources to help you learn and develop the skills you need to succeed. Take advantage of the free resources before you begin paying 3000-7000$ for a certification.

Now that we have gotten you super excited about all the positive aspects of this career, let's pivot a bit and explain the downsides or cons of this field.

Some disadvantages of working in cybersecurity are as follows:

- Entry-level has prerequisites.
- Businesses don't understand cyber yet.
- Change is rapid and learning never stops.
- Cybercriminals don't take vacations.
- This career field requires serious passion.

- Mental burnout due to high cerebral work.
- Jack of all trades and master of none.

Let's explain each one.

Entry level has prerequisites

Unlike other positions, where you can start at an entry level with a basic degree and learn everything **OJT (On the Job Training)**, that is not the case within cybersecurity. Even the entry-level **SOC (Security Operations Center)** analyst positions require a baseline understanding to triage data, research logs, and document reporting. Also, keep in mind this industry isn't the easiest to break into. You may have a college degree in computer science. Still, without hands-on experience, you could get passed up for someone who has no college but a couple certifications and 5-7 years of field experience.

Businesses don't understand cyber yet

Many organizations still think cyber is IT, there to fix their printer. Sometimes the older generation who don't understand the difference between *cyber* and *IT*. No thanks to the fantastic hacker TV shows making everyone think if you work in cyber you must be a hackers. Be patient because the change is slow. You must educate others on the difference between cyber and IT.

Change is rapid, and learning never stops

What can drain people in this field is the constant need to be reading and learning because cybercrime never stops. This can be challenging for someone who is initially entering the field in their mid to late 40s. Not only is it medically proven that learning at an older age can be more challenging, but you are learning a new skill while staying ahead of the rapidly changing threat-scape. The best advice here is to eat the cake one bite at a time. Anything is possible, but you must know this field isn't easy at first, but it does get easier.

Cybercriminals don't take vacation

Cybersecurity is rapidly changing. This is because cybercriminals are continuously evolving by updating malware variants and refining their **Tactics, Techniques, and Procedures (TTPs)**, to circumvent security protocols and breach the network. Therefore, cybersecurity professionals are trying to stay one step ahead of the adversary. This is why SOC's run 24/7 and you may find yourself working long hours. We will discuss burnout shortly, but know, in this industry, there will always be work because the cybercriminals will always be attacking you.

This career field requires serious passion

This is a con and not a pro because you will dislike this industry if you do not have passion for your job. The passion drives your desire to learn and it's because of this passion and learning that you will thrive in this industry. If you find yourself in a job with no passion, I encourage you to identify whether this is due to your external environment or possibly the position. Sometimes the passion is lacking because we are not in the right role. We will discuss the different roles available in cybersecurity in *Section 2, YOUR Path Into the Industry*, of this book. Just know, passion is key to success in field. Without passion, you will be drained and not enjoy your work.

Mental burnout due to high cerebral work

Burnout in this industry is a real thing. Before entering this field, I didn't fully understood burnout. It took me about 4 months of working 80-90 hours a week with no break when I hit a wall and couldn't get out of bed for nearly 2 weeks. The reason, which I now know, was because I was mentally exhausted. I was putting so much strain on my cerebral cortex that my body finally broke down.

Depending on your specialty, you will hear about alert fatigue, which is when you review alerting or other data daily. When you feel like you are done and cannot look at any more data this is when you reach alert fatigue. This is when you stop and move into something else to give your mind a break. This is the same with education, too much education at one time can drain you.

> **Tip**
> Make sure to take regular breaks and give back to yourself. Micro breaks during the day are just as important as longer breaks like the weekend.

Jack of all trades and master of none

Within this field, it is easy to do a certification here and there and jump around from one position to another. This is great for learning about new jobs and seeing what fits your personality and character the best. However, it is recommended that eventually you should stay put long enough to become an **SME** (**Subject Matter Expert**) in your job. Make sure to take the time to develop 1-2 excellent skills. This could be a coding language, threat hunting, or pen testing. Then you can tie that skill into other aspects of your work. Most skills in this industry will overlap with one another. Don't think because you focus on one thing that if you move to another, you will never use it again.

Ultimately, this is your career and life. Make sure to do your own research and know the organizations before taking a job. Don't be afraid to move around and make changes if you're not happy. There are a lot of companies you can work for and a plethora of career directions you may take.

Summary

By the end of this chapter, you should have a basic understanding of what cybersecurity is and where it's going in the next few years. You should also have a good knowledge of cybersecurity law and why it's a challenging topic for congressional leaders to address.

We also covered foundational data of cybersecurity, which included primers such as the CIA Triad, NIST, ISO, and SOC frameworks. We provided you with a basic understanding of the most seen cyberattacks. The final section covered the advantages and disadvantages of this industry, with recommendations before entry into this industry.

Next up, Kim Nguyen will guide you through the next chapter, where you will learn about the different types of cyber careers. She dives into the cybersecurity roadmap, top prominent cybersecurity domains, and how to choose a career. Grab something to drink and settle in because things are warming up.

Questions

1. What does the CIA in the CIA Triad mean?

2. Name three cyber threats we discussed.

3. What happened in 2016 that caused congress to enact the Consumer Privacy Protection Act of 2017?

2
Which Career Field Is Best for You?

In the previous chapter, you experienced **cybersecurity** from a bird's-eye view. In this chapter, we are going to take a deep dive into cybersecurity and learn about its different fields. As we go further, we will also be looking at varied career opportunities, and how to determine which cybersecurity field is best for you.

By the end of this chapter, you will have an overview of definitions, job requirements, and the expectations of several well-known cybersecurity positions listed in the fields of Risk Assessment, Governance, Threat Intelligence, Security Operation, Security Architecture, and Cybersecurity Education.

In addition, I will be guiding you through how to determine a cybersecurity career choice that fits you. After completing this chapter, whether you have been able to choose your favorite cybersecurity occupation or not, the tips and tricks provided can be carried on to the next chapters, which will help you continue shaping your cybersecurity path.

In this chapter, we're going to cover the following main topics:

- Introducing you to the cybersecurity roadmap
- Understanding the top prominent cybersecurity domains
- Guiding you on how to choose a career
- Which cybersecurity field is best for you?

Without further ado, let me, *Kim Nguyen*, walk you through the specializations of the cybersecurity universe.

Introducing you to the cybersecurity roadmap

As you learned in the previous chapter, cybersecurity is a general term to describe an industry where professionals manage security risks secure and defend infrastructures, systems, and applications that may be *internet-associated*. That is, indeed, what cybersecurity professionals do in a nutshell. However, the definition can sound quite vague if you are trying to decide on the right cybersecurity vocation. How and what exactly do you defend? What does "*defend*" precisely mean in the context of cybersecurity? To have a clearer view, let's break all these questions down into pieces.

Cybersecurity is no myth; you can refer to it in the same way as you think of other fields and subfields. For example, take the *hospitality industry* as an example. "*Hospitality*" refers to the service industry, and under hospitality, there are subfields, such as hotel service, lodging service, dining service, and so on. Similarly, cybersecurity acts as a broad field that contains different subfields with different focuses.

In the following mind map, several domains have been classified:

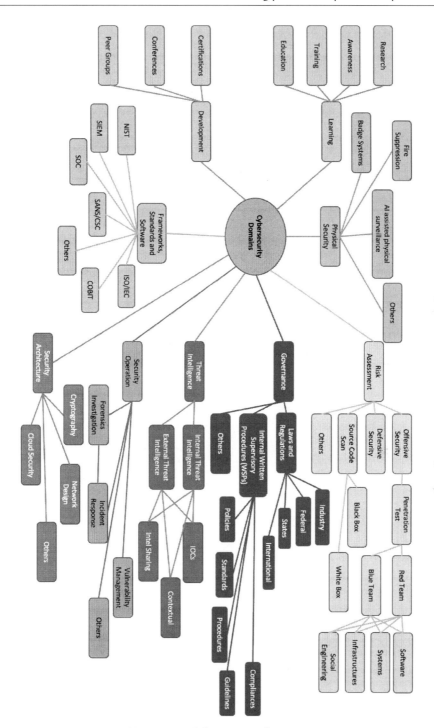

Figure 2.1 – Cybersecurity domains

As shown in the preceding diagram, **Frameworks and Standards** was introduced to you in the previous chapter. Thus, in this chapter, we will be focusing on other domains presented in the map. Let's take a look.

Understanding the top prominent cybersecurity domains

Despite the diverse number of subfields, in this book, we'll concentrate on the most in-demand areas of each **domain** shown in the preceding section, which are listed in the following table. Note that each domain has several areas that are equally in demand. However, since it is not practical to list all of them, only some have been chosen:

Domain	Area
Risk Assessment	Offensive Security
Governance	**Governance, Risk Management, and Compliance (GRC)**
Threat Intelligence	External Threat Intelligence
	Internal Threat Intelligence
Security Operation	Incident Response
Security Architecture	Cloud Security
Learning	Education, Training, and Awareness

Table 2.1 – In-demand areas of domains

Let's simplify and focus our mind map view so that it mirrors this chapter's topic, like so:

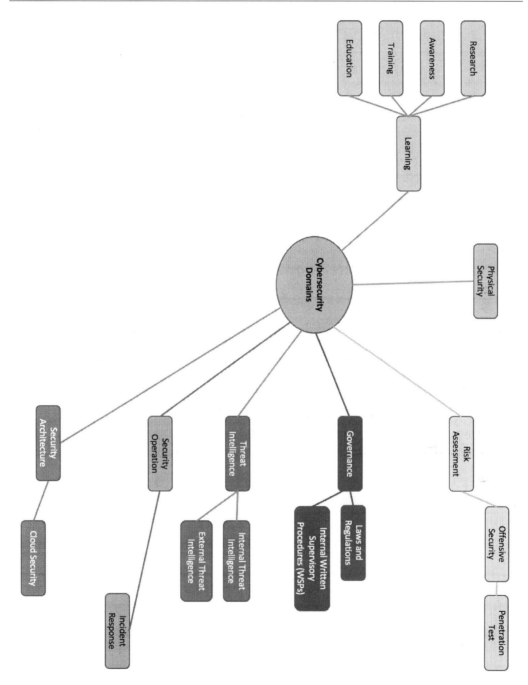

Figure 2.2 – Cybersecurity domains

In this section, we learned that cybersecurity is a broad field that contains many sub-fields of different focuses. The sub-fields we are going to work on are Risk Assessment, Governance, Threat Intelligence, Security Operation, Security Architecture, and cybersecurity Education, respectively. In the upcoming sections, each of these domains will be closely analyzed to give you an insight into the domains themselves, as well as the typical job requirements for those domains.

Risk Assessment and Offensive Security

In this section, we will be analyzing what Risk Assessment, Offensive Security, and Penetration Testing are and why they are important. Then, a detailed job description of a typical Penetration Tester will be provided. Let's get started by looking into Risk Assessment!

Risk Assessment

Risk Assessment refers to the practice of discovering and examining cybersecurity risks that might occur in an organization's business. However, *why* exactly is this process necessary?

Risks are present every day, everywhere, and in everything we do. In the cyber world, if you are using the internet, the risk is that you might get hacked. If you are using the internet with more precautions and education, such as having your online accounts secured with strong passwords, the risk of getting hacked is still there, as you might accidentally browse an infected website, and malware may be downloaded to your local machine. Even though you are being careful, there are risks you cannot think of at certain moments, and you would only find out about them after you get attacked.

In the case of a single user such as *yourself*, if your account or device gets infected, you can simply reset your password or clean up the malware in your machine using certain available applications. However, for businesses with thousands of users and employees all over the world, is it still simple to clean things up and recover after an incident *happens*? If the bank you deposited your savings in got hacked and your money was stolen, would you still trust their service, even after they have patched the vulnerability? Chances are a lot of customers would look for a better, more secured, and stable service. Thus, for many reasons, risk assessment is essential for companies to implement appropriate security controls, which can prevent unexpected exploits that can hurt their business and customers.

As mentioned previously, some risks can stay undiscovered until an incident happens, while other risks can be over evaluated. Thus, the Risk Assessment field helps businesses and companies determine how many security controls are needed and what kinds. These assessments are made based on many different factors, such as cost, effectiveness, businesses tolerance, and more. As a result, the Risk Assessment field contains many different policies, methods, services, and job opportunities to help companies apply security practices that work best for them individually.

One of the most appealing career choices in the Risk Assessment field lies in Offensive Security.

Offensive Security

Traditionally, companies tend to patch vulnerabilities after incidents have happened as they were not informed about those weaknesses in their systems, or they were informed, but had other work prioritized, which eventually resulted in serious cyberattacks that cost not only their reputation, but also their finances, and possibly other factors. As a result, over time, companies have learned that this method is not very effective to protect themselves from cyber criminals. As a result, **Offensive Security** came to the rescue.

Offensive Security refers to a proactive risk assessment approach, where cybersecurity professionals actively look for potential vulnerabilities that organizations might experience in the future. By performing Offensive Security *techniques*, companies can discover and patch their systems' shortcomings before any actual attacks occur. To do so, companies hire individuals or groups of experienced ethical hackers to hack their systems *legally* and *purposefully*, by simulating the mindsets and actions of cyber criminals. This helps address system weaknesses before they go into production, so they can implement the appropriate security protocol immediately. Offensive Security can be applied to not only systems, but also to applications, software, and more.

An important thing to note is that Offensive Security practitioners require permission from organizations to perform their job. This permission can be demonstrated through a contract, a **Pentesting Permission Slip**, and so on. Otherwise, any attacks without authorization can be deemed illegal.

For your career choice, if you are interested in Offensive Security, what job title should you look for? A very attractive answer is **Penetration Tester**, commonly known as a **Pentester**. Let's look at what they are in the following sections.

Penetration Testing and Penetration Testers

Pentesters are ethical hackers who perform penetration tests or attacks on a system to find as many sets of frangibility of the system as possible. The difference between pentesters and cyber criminals is that a pentester's purpose is to help companies protect themselves from criminals, and their work is *legally authorized*. In contrast, cyber criminals exploit systems without any permission to take advantage of businesses and possibly to carry out other destructive operations.

You now know the job title, but *what about the job description*? In other words, what tasks do pentesters perform, of course, besides hacking?

Let's look at the Penetration Testing procedure. The following diagram shows the steps in a typical pentesting procedure:

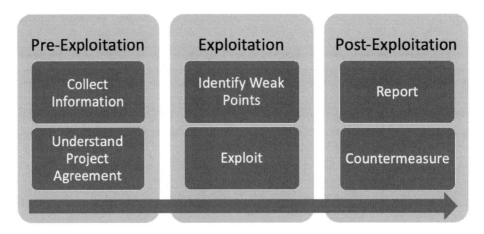

Figure 2.3 – Penetration Testing procedure

Let's look at what they are in detail.

Phase 1 – pre-exploitation

When you start a pentesting project, the first thing you want to do is gather information about the project and system you are going to work on. Specifically, you need to know what system you are testing, which part of the system or software you are testing, and what can and cannot be done. Essentially, during this phase, you will want to clearly understand the following points:

- The *agreement* between you and the company that you will perform pentesting on.

- *Technical information* about the system, which can later point your work in the right direction. For example, if you are testing a piece of software that runs on a Linux operating system, by investigating which type of operating system the application is using, you can choose the appropriate tools when you perform the exploitations. In this case, knowing the operating system is Linux-based, you can choose tools that work for Linux systems, instead of wasting your time on Windows-based tools.

Phase 2 – exploitation

During this phase, pentesters should do the following:

- **Identify potential vulnerability**: Pentesters can collect a list of potential weaknesses by performing a quick investigation or scan on the system. This process can contain activities such as looking for open ports, weaknesses in the firewalls, and so on.

- **Exploit/pentest**: Based on the result that was produced in the previous step, pentesters can then perform attacks, trying to gain access to the system by using deeper, more thorough methods.

Phase 3 – post-exploitation

After thoroughly examining the system, regardless of whether any vulnerability was found, pentesters should then create a detailed report, describing the tests they have performed and their results.

If vulnerabilities were found, pentesters have the option to recommend possible solutions to remediate the issues.

Companies can then, based on the reports and recommendations of the pentesters, determine if they want to patch their systems accordingly or perform further risk assessments. Sometimes, certain risks are affordable, and companies might not want to move forward with mitigating them right away, as there are other tasks that remain a higher priority. Afterward, whether another round of pentesting be performed or not is based on the company's decision and needs.

To sum up the *Risk Assessment* section, keep in mind that preventing risks and attacks before they happen is beneficial for organizations in many aspects. This technique is known as **Offensive Security**, and a promising job title to look for in this domain is pentester, where individuals legally and purposefully hack a system or software to find vulnerabilities before cyber criminals do. This helps prevent companies from facing cyber attacks in the future.

Governance and GRC

This section will introduce and explain the fundamentals and technical characteristics of Governance and GRC, as well as the job expectations of GRC analysts.

Governance

Organizations follow certain cybersecurity regulations and practices. To ensure that those cybersecurity laws and resources are implemented correctly and effectively, more than just a couple of IT employees are required. In fact, to have constructive and strategic cybersecurity policies implemented, involvement by a company's management is essential. This is known as **cybersecurity governance**.

GRC

The foundations of creating well-strategized cybersecurity practices is a combination of **Governance**, **Risk Management**, and **Compliance**, commonly known as **GRC**.

The following diagram captures this:

Figure 2.4 – Summarizing GRC

Now, let's take a dive into what each of these components that make up GRC are in detail:

- **Governance**: Governance has more to do with the operation of the companies' cyber regulations. Organizations have their own internal cyber rules that everyday business activities must comply with. Governance helps with overseeing the cybersecurity program as a whole for the business.

- **Risk Management**: In the previous section, you learned about *Risk Assessment*, in *Figure 2.4*. Risk Assessment shows up again as a category of Risk Management. As a GRC analyst, you will need to know not only how to assess risks, but also how to evaluate, monitor, and mitigate them, to best protect the organizations' business.

- **Compliance**: Recall from *Chapter 1, New Career in Cyber… "Who Dis?"*, in the *Cyber laws and regulations* section, that different industries have different regulatory requirements that companies must follow. At the same time, as we mentioned regarding *Governance*, each company should have their own cyber policies that fit their business activities. GRC analysts must stay informed of the required cybersecurity laws and regulations from both the government and the organization, to ensure that all cybersecurity standards are met.

Typically, GRC analysts should be on guard when it comes to each pillar of GRC when performing their jobs. Specifically, GRC analysts constantly examine the security compliances and risk management plans, proactively securing systems or software, making sure that the system functions securely as a whole. The work from a GRC analyst is often exchanged with others, such as pentesters, to help companies define the appropriate security controls to put in place. Concurrently, they should audit the business activities against the security compliances. During those processes, if any non-compliance was discovered, GRC analysts should work with other security teams to resolve the issues.

All in all, GRC analysts' work is a constant examination and improvement of the three pillars of GRC. This ultimately produces constant improvement in security compliances for organizations.

Threat Intelligence – internal and external

In this section, we will learn about **Threat Intelligence**, including its definition, importance, types, sources, and the career option of being a Threat Intelligence Analyst.

Threat Intelligence

Cyber criminals never sleep. As cyber specialists discover and eliminate existing cyber attacks, cyber criminals come up with new ways and tools to perform new attacks. Thus, cyber threats are always in existence, if not increasing. As a result, companies and Threat Intelligence Analysts need to be ahead of the game by staying posted about the most recent attacks, business trends, and even global news. This helps them analyze, predict, and prevent existing and potential cyber attacks. The practice of improving cybersecurity safeguards through sharing, learning, analyzing, and forecasting cyber threats and adversaries is known as **Cyber Threat Intel**.

The following diagram shows the main building blocks that make up Cyber Threat Intelligence:

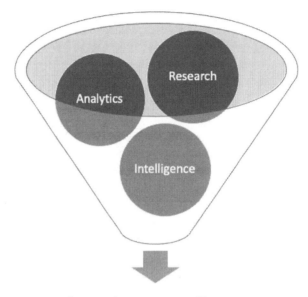

Figure 2.5 – Cyber Threat Intelligence components

Examining this more carefully, there are three types of Threat Intelligence, known as **Tactical**, **Operational,** and **Strategic**, as shown in the following diagram:

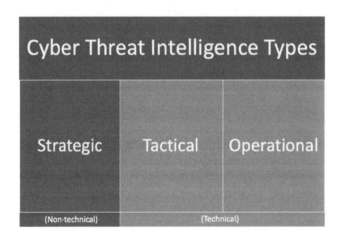

Figure 2.6 – Cyber Threat Intelligence types

Let's look at what they mean:

- **Strategic Threat Intelligence**: Strategic Threat Intelligence focuses on the non-technical aspects of the threats, which are their risks, impacts, and effects on the organizations. This is meant to help management levels with cyber defense decision making. Often, this information is exchanged with GRC analysts so that they can discuss the appropriate risk assessment and mitigation actions.

  In contrast, both Tactical and Operational Threat Intelligence are tailored toward technical audiences.

- **Tactical Threat Intelligence**: Tactical Threat Intelligence addresses the tactics of threat actors, such as the procedure of the attack, which vulnerabilities attackers are looking for, or which entry points attackers might use to compromise the system.

- **Operational Threat Intelligence**: Operational Threat Intelligence provides in-depth and highly technical details of the threat. Information can be found are the motives of the attack, the tools and techniques attackers might use, or indicators of compromises, such as IP address, filenames, type of malware, and so on.

As both Tactical and Operational Threat Intelligence narrate technical aspects of the threats, they are meant to support employees who work more closely with the attacks, such as the incident response team, risk analyst, and IT department.

Threat Intelligence sources

Despite the different focuses of threat intel types, threat intel specialists generally collect data from several sources that are classified into two groups: **Internal Threat Intel** and **External Threat Intel**. These can be seen in the following diagram:

External Threat Intelligence   Cyber Threat Intelligence   Internal Threat Intelligence
                                     Operations and Management

Figure 2.7 – Cyber Threat Intelligence sources

In detail, the two threat groups are as follows:

- **Internal Threat Intel**: Internal Threat Intel refers to the intelligence sources coming from within the organization. This could be past incidents and incident response reports and plans, security policies and practices, discovered vulnerabilities, and so on.

- **External Threat Intel**: The opposite of Internal Threat Intel, External Threat Intel is the threat resources coming from outside the organization. This includes Open Source Intelligence, Technical Intelligence, and others, as described in the following diagram:

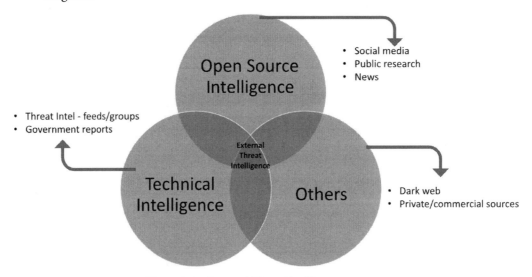

Figure 2.8 – External Threat Intelligence sources

After gathering all those resources, cyber threat intel analysts can then consolidate them with available tools to determine the severity of the threats and plan for mitigation. Fundamentally, as a Cyber Threat Intel analyst, to perform the job competently, you should constantly update and refresh your knowledge on domestic and global news, attacks, technologies, politics, and so on to gear your organization's cyber defense in the right direction.

To summarize, in this section, we learned that Cyber Threat Intelligence helps businesses and entities stay competitive with cyber criminals. Due to the diversity of Cyber Threat Intelligence types and sources, it is essential that Cyber Threat Intelligence analysts are always up to date on internal and external threat intelligence to perform their jobs effectively.

Security Operation and Incident Response

In this section, let's find out what **Security Operation** is and how cybersecurity professionals plan and react to cyber attacks. The topics we will cover in this section are Security Operations and Incident Response.

Security Operation

Security Operation is the discipline of ensuring that an organization's business is not interrupted by detecting, preventing, protecting, and responding to cybersecurity threats and attacks. There are many different sub-branches of Security Operations, such as **Security Operations Center (SOC)** and **Security Information and Event Management (SIEM)**, both of which you learned about in the previous chapter. In this chapter, we'll learn about something new: **Incident Response**.

Incident Response

So far, we have discussed how companies can plan to prevent potential cyber attacks from happening. However, the reality is that having preventions does not guarantee that you will be 100% attack-free. Thus, it is essential to also consider the worst case, where companies get compromised. In such a situation, having strategies and procedures in place to respond to the exploit and quickly recover to normal business is known as Incident Response.

As shown in the following diagram, an Incident Response plan can be broken down into three phases: **planning**, **responding**, and **aftermath**:

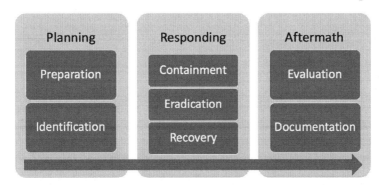

Figure 2.9 – Incident Response procedure

Let's explore each phase in more detail.

Phase I – planning

Before an incident happens, we need to plan ahead for it by doing the following:

- **Preparation**: The Incident Response team should have a structured and functional security system ready, to help prepare staff and systems to recognize and handle any potential incidents.

- **Identification**: As the security system sends out any alerts, the process moves to the Identification step, where the Incident Response team verifies whether the alerts can be verified as intrusions. If they are, identifying the kind of attack is necessary. At this step, actions must be taken immediately, bringing us to the next phase of the process: responding.

Phase II – responding

This phase is defense in action, where the following three important steps should be performed:

- **Containment**: This stage is where the Incident Response team limits as much damage as possible. Some example actions are as follows:

  - Scanning the companies' network for suspicious traffic

  - Notifying employees of unusual activities

  - Temporarily removing internet access

- **Eradication**: Now that the attack has been contained, it is time to investigate the root cause of the incident. This step normally involves the Forensic Investigation team and can be one of the most complex processes.

- **Recovery**: By using the findings from the previous steps, the Incident Response team can now apply suitable repairs to the infected system and bring the business back to usual.

Phase III – aftermath

This is the last stage of the Incident Response plan, where all the involved parties can re-examine the event without any time constraint. Any feedback and findings at this stage are exchanged between all parties to produce a well-constructed and improved incident response plan for future use:

- **Evaluation**: Although the incidents have passed, it is crucial to look back and evaluate the actions taken, to determine the effectiveness and potential improvements for the future.

- **Documentation**: Finally, documenting every detail of the incident can't be skipped. This is essential not only for reporting to management, but also for future reference and development.

To summarize, don't forget that "*incidents*" do not just refer to cyber attacks, but also physical attacks, natural disasters or data breaches, and so on. Thus, keep this in mind to provide flexible Incident Response plans. To do this, it is recommended that you use industry provided tools and frameworks, such as **NIST** or **SIEM** (which you learned about in *Chapter 1, New Career in Cyber… "Who Dis?"*).

That's it for Security Operation and Incident Response. Now, let's move on to the next domain, known as Security Architecture.

Security Architecture and Cloud Security

In this section, we will discuss Security Architecture, Cloud Security, and the job outlooks for Cloud Security Specialists.

Security Architecture

Security Architecture refers to a high-level combination of different security processes, designs, methods, and purposes to produce the overall security structure for a company's entire infrastructure. In other words, Security Architecture can be understood as a mixture of all the subfields we learned about previously, and more. Security Architecture varies from organization to organization, as each should be designed specifically based on the organization's business and objectives. To do so, Security Architects must understand the company's business drivers, in order to translate them into security objectives.

The work of **Security Architects** is to assist in designing and implementing a security program, as well as defining how security cuts across the business verticals. Security Architects help design the high-level architectures of data, security programs, software, and more. Often, Security Architects work with other architects, such as Software Architects, to decide on the big picture of the systems, software, and more that are going to production. Thus, to be a Security Architect, advanced and thorough experience is required. There are many popular frameworks available in the industry that help Security Architects perform their jobs, one of which is **The Open Group Architecture Framework** (**TOGAF**). If being a Security Architect is your interest, learning about TOGAF will be very beneficial.

Cloud Security

In recent years, the term **cloud computing** has become more and more popular among computer science professionals. Cloud computing can provide cheaper, more flexible, and more powerful computing solutions for various use cases. As the popularity of cloud computing rises, more cyber crimes and attacks are targeting *cloud-based platforms*.

Despite having attacks, cloud computing keeps expanding, and lots of futuristic opportunities are emerging with this growth, without any tendency to stop in the near future. There are many ways the cloud can be used, such as **Platform as a Service (PaaS)**, **Infrastructure as a Service (IaaS)**, **Software as a Service (SaaS)**, and much more. Besides, cloud services are very favored by both individuals and organizations. Even though cloud computing is expanding quickly, there are learning curves for end users to catch up.

As a result, cloud computing is a new and exciting land for everyone. For both cyber criminals and cybersecurity professionals, it is a great opportunity to experiment, since most people are still in the learning process, and not yet aware of many possible vulnerabilities. The difference between the two is that if cyber criminals find any vulnerabilities in the cloud, many might get attacked without even knowing, while if cybersecurity professionals discover those vulnerabilities, it would be a remarkable contribution to futuristic technologies.

All in all, cloud security is an open field with many undiscovered areas, giving lots of security practitioners the chance to join, experiment, design security architectures, research, learn, and work.

Cloud Security Specialist would be a good job title to look for. Simply put, Cloud Security Specialists help companies ensure either or both the security of *cloud-based infrastructure* and the security in the cloud of *cloud services*.

The following diagram shows some areas of Cloud Security:

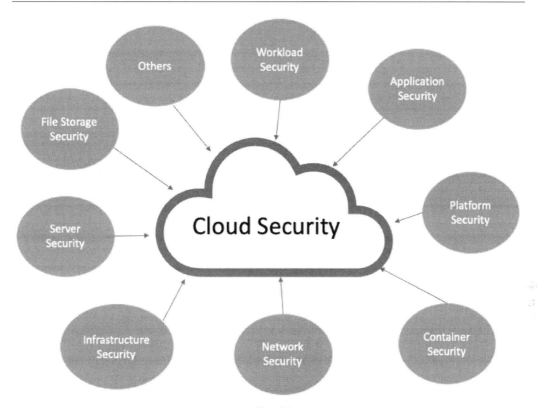

Figure 2.10 – Cloud Security areas

To sum this up, Security Architecture is a cocktail of several cybersecurity sub-domains. Under Security Architecture, Cloud Security is a futuristic area that is suitable for anyone with any experience to step into.

Learning through education, training, and awareness

Cybersecurity has always been a hot topic and has been gaining increasing attention over time. Especially during pandemics, such as *COVID-19*, cybersecurity becomes more crucial as businesses transfer to online and heavily become internet-dependent. As a result, the demand for **cybersecurity education** increases.

Generally, we can divide learning into three categories known as **education**, **training**, and **awareness**, as illustrated in the following diagram:

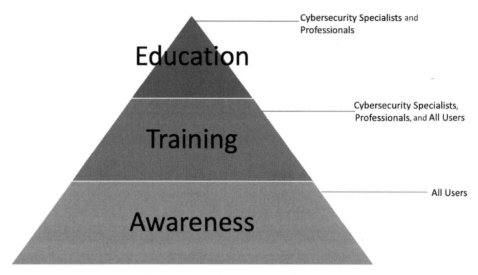

Figure 2.11 – Cybersecurity education

Many would think that training and education are both the process of learning new skills and knowledge. Even though they are similar, by nature, they are slightly different. We'll explore these three categories in detail in the next few sections.

Moving on, let's look at another attractive area of cybersecurity, that also has a lot of career potentials: education.

Education

Education refers to situations where individuals pursue focused study in order to be cybersecurity specialists. An example is to obtain academic degrees.

The education from academic degrees tends to be more theory focused, with a certain percentage of hands-on practice (this depends on each school). After graduating, students should have gained structured knowledge of the foundations of cybersecurity as a whole and deeper knowledge of the area of choice they focused on.

Another way to learn new skills is through taking online courses, bootcamps, or boot-camp-like courses. They have shorter learning times than traditional university degrees but are more intense, specialized, and, in some cases, more hands-on.

Training

Instead of learning new skills through university degrees, the other way individuals can obtain new knowledge would be through company-provided training.

Company-provided training tends to focus on specific job requirements, thus allowing the audience to be more hands-on and have the chance to expose themselves to real-world scenarios, compared to academic learning. As a result, receiving company training normally provides concentrated knowledge on specific topics, rather than a broader view of the industry.

Awareness

In contrast to training, awareness refers to reinforcing known knowledge, making it more solid and widespread to others.

To maintain cybersecurity awareness, you can apply best practices to your daily life, such as enforcing **multi-factor authentication** (**MFA**), constantly installing new software updates, and more.

To raise awareness to others, participating in cybersecurity conferences or activities is a good idea. For example, annually, in the United States, October is recognized as **National Cybersecurity Awareness Month** (**NCSAM**). During this month, companies and individuals often reinforce and share cybersecurity knowledge through public activities, social media, or even simply through casual chats with family and friends.

Besides education, training, and awareness, there are other ways to stay educated about cybersecurity, such as doing research, attending competitions, or taking industry qualified certifications. Based on the characteristics of each certificate, you will get different outcomes that serve different career purposes. We will learn about specific certificates later in *Chapter 4, Exploring Certifications and College.*

For job opportunities, don't just think of yourself as the one who receives the knowledge; instead, you can be the one who delivers that knowledge. For example, *Cybersecurity Instructor*, *Cybersecurity Trainer*, and *Cybersecurity Speaker* are several career options to consider. Finally, investing in learning is to invest in your future. Thus, never stop learning and expanding new skills.

Now, let's look at the next leg of this journey; that is, how to choose a career.

Guiding you on how to choose a career

Before deciding on your favorite cybersecurity path, let's learn how to determine if any field is right for you. The following are some recommendations to help you identify your career path:

- **Find your passion**: Believe it or not, to be successful and satisfied with any career, you need to like it first. With that in mind, find things that interest you, keep you excited, and that you can do for a long time without feeling fed up.

  For example, people who like to explore and question things tend to go for science-related fields, since the nature of those fields is to scout for new findings and discover the root causes of things.

- **Identify your strengths**: Knowing what you are good at and leveraging them is also a good way to go about finding the best fit career for you. For example, if you are not good at arts and design but very good with math, why compete with people who are masters of design? Instead, take advantage of your mathematical strength.

  Even better, you can combine your passion and strengths together. For example, if you like to explore and are also good at math, you could go for several career choices, such as Reverse Engineer, Cryptologist, and so on.

- **Create a list of dream jobs**: You do not have to make up your mind in this very beginning process. Instead, take note of several career options that attract you, with rankings showing how much you like each of them.

  Along the way, the list might change. As you are more informed and exposed to different areas, the list can help you eliminate or decide on the career path you like the most.

- **Keep exploring**: Don't stop with the list of passions, strengths, and dream jobs you have created. Instead, keep exploring new options while researching the existing ones. You never know what you may find and how they may affect your decisions.

The following diagram demonstrates the components that come into play and that you should consider when you are choosing or developing your career:

Figure 2.12 – Career components

Remember, an ideal career is built on many factors. Most people assume that only technical knowledge is enough, yet other components are just as important, including personal growth, values, interest, salary, and more.

Before moving on to the next section, spend some time drafting out lists of your passions, strengths, and dream jobs. These lists do not need to be perfect or completed right away. As you continue reading this book, you can keep editing them. We will utilize these lists more in *Chapter 7, How to Land a Jay-Oh-Bee!*.

Which cybersecurity field is the best for you?

Now, we are in the right direction to narrow down the professions that are the best fit for you. Let's summarize what we have learned about the different cybersecurity career options that were introduced in this chapter and find out which one is right for you.

Risk Assessment and Offensive Security

A good occupation under Offensive Security could be pentesting, where you can legally attack systems or software to find vulnerabilities, helping organizations prevent potential future attacks.

If you are a curious person who enjoys exploring and bringing improvements to things, and has always dreamed of being that cool ethical hacker from the movies, this could be a good career choice for you.

Governance and GRC

A GRC analyst ensures that organizations' GRC are aligned and effective. This work requires learning about certain cybersecurity laws and regulations.

As a result, if you find cybersecurity laws and regulations interesting and enjoy shuffling between different tasks, while having managing abilities, you should consider the GRC analyst position.

Threat Intelligence – internal and external

A Threat Intel analyst must stay up to date regarding national and international news, cybersecurity research, and trends, all while understanding companies' internal security situations and regulations, to provide strategic cybersecurity defense plans.

Thus, if doing research, performing analysis, and creating strategic planning is your cup of tea, *Cyber Threat Intelligence analyst* is a great profession to investigate.

Security Operation and Incident Response

Preparing for disasters to happen and how to react to them is critical to a business' success. The Incident Responder's job is a mix of planning, investigating, patching, and developing companies' procedures for Incident Response.

As incidents might happen at any time, Incident Responders should keep in mind that their availability is essential, to ensure that businesses can operate as smoothly as possible at any given hour. Therefore, if the job characteristics listed here are what you like, while working long hours does not bother you, why not try *Incident Response*?

Security architecture and cloud security

Some people are cut out to see things from the bigger picture. If you are one of those people who can integrate different focuses and areas together, which includes both the business side and technical side, then Security Architect could be your target.

However, getting a position as Security Architect does require a bit of experience, so if you have no experience, you might need to spend some time working in other positions before becoming a Security Architect.

If Security Architecture, designing and working with different architectures, is what you enjoy, a good area in this field is *Cloud Security*. *Cloud Security Specialists* help organizations strengthen their security of the cloud, the security on the cloud, or both.

The field of Cloud Security has many aspects that have remained undiscovered, so it is a good entry point for you, whether you are a seasoned security professional or a newbie.

Learning – education, training, and awareness

Whether it is education, training, or awareness, the common theme is sharing knowledge. Thus, if you find sharing, mentoring, teaching, and learning appealing, then going into education may be a good choice for you.

Shared job requirements

Although each job has its own specifications and requirements, the following are several tasks that they all have in common:

- **Teamwork**: The ability to work effectively with others is very important, as your work would support and affect the delivery of your team and other teams.

- **Cross-department collaboration**: Most of the time, your team's work will be used for other teams' work. For example, recall the GRC position: their work requires the collaboration of other teams, such as the Risk Management or Incident Response teams; or, the Incident Response team would need the help from the Forensic Investigation team to perform a part of their job. Thus, keep in mind that your career is not locked into one department – it is a diverse and collaborative work experience.

- **Effective communication**: As a requirement of teamwork and collaboration, clear and productive communication skills are a necessity. Many misunderstand that cybersecurity professionals do technical jobs; thus, communication is not important. However, that's not true – to prepare for your career, besides having strong technical skills, don't forget communication skills as well!

- **Writing**: Technical writing is another valuable skill to have, since all the jobs we have looked at all require that we document or write reports. Another common misunderstanding about being a cybersecurity professional is that you only need to do cool hacking stuff, yet in reality, documenting your findings is just as important. This is extremely useful for showcasing your work and for future improvements.

- **Research and independent learning**: One thing we see many times in this book is that cybercriminals never sleep. Hence, it is important to stay posted and ahead of the game. This would require cybersecurity professionals to constantly renew and update their knowledge. Consequently, the ability to actively and independently study and research without supervision is a must.

Career improvement opportunities

In this chapter, we have been exposed to several positions, including pentester, GRC analyst, Cyber Threat Intel analyst, Incident Responder, Security Architect, Cloud Security Specialist,, and Cybersecurity Educator. A point worth mentioning is that most of those positions are entry-level friendly positions and come with different levels, providing you with lots of room for career improvement.

Take pentester as an example: there are several levels, such as **Junior Pentester**, **Senior Pentester**, and **Pentesting Manager**.

Therefore, if you wish to move up to management in the cybersecurity field, there are most certainly several doors open for you.

Extra resources that can help you find the right career

By now, if you have not been able to create a list of your dream cybersecurity jobs, don't worry. You can still fill the list with some positions from this chapter that you feel might be interesting to you.

In the meantime, use the **cybersecurity roadmap** provided at the beginning of this chapter and keep following the next chapters to learn more about other subfields, learning resources, and options. Do not rush the process and the right choice will come along.

Summary

In this chapter, we briefly scanned the big picture of the cybersecurity field and its many different domains. After that, we investigated the leading areas and job titles in cybersecurity, including Risk Assessment, Governance, Threat Intelligence, Security Operation, Security Architecture, and Learning.

The areas we learned about were Offensive Security, GRC, External Threat Intelligence and Internal Threat Intelligence, Incident Response, Cloud Security, education, training, and awareness. Finally, the professions we learned about were Penetration Tester, GRC Analyst, Cyber Threat Intelligence Analyst, Incident Responder, Security Architect, Cloud Security Specialist, Cybersecurity Trainer, and Cybersecurity Instructor.

Thenceforth, summaries of each domain, area, and role were provided, together with guidance on how you can find your desired career. In the end, several tips and industry required skills were brought to your attention.

By the end of this chapter, you are familiar with several jobs that are entry-level to mid-level friendly. Combined with the mentioned tips and guidelines, your cybersecurity path should be on the right track. It is important to note that the positions you learned about in this chapter have many potentials for career improvements and promotions.

In the next chapter, we will keep analyzing and look at more aspects of working in cybersecurity in general, as well as in the domains we learned about in this chapter. What you learned about in this chapter will be carried on, reinforced, and built upon in the upcoming chapters.

Questions

Take a few minutes to complete the following knowledge-check questions:

1. Which of the following is NOT a step in the Penetration Testing procedure?

    A. Report

    B. Exploit

    C. Remove the company's internet access

    D. Identify the system's weak points

2. During an Incident Response event, which order is correct for executing the following actions?

    A. Plan, Report, Evaluate, Document, Eradicate, Contain, Recover

    B. Prepare, Identify, Contain, Eradicate, Recover, Evaluate, Document

    C. Prepare, Identify, Eradicate, Contain, Recover, Evaluate, Document

    D. Contain, Identify, Eradicate, Recover, Evaluate, Document, Prepare

3. Cybersecurity specialists only need to perform individual tasks; thus, communication skills are not important.

    A. True

    B. False

Section 2: Your Path into the Industry

This section provides you with information on different jobs, certs, and education styles while providing guidance on how to get hands-on experience, defining your brand, and eventually promoting yourself for a job.

The following chapters will be covered under this section:

3
Different Strokes for Different Folks

Now you know the different types of roles in the cybersecurity field, but there is another dimension to your career plan you must consider. The industry, sector, and environment will all influence the type of work and the driving mission of the organization.

In this chapter, we're going to cover the following main topics:

- Understanding cybersecurity pros and cons in several industry sectors
- Working in the public sector versus the private sector
- Introducing cloud platforms as an explosive cybersecurity opportunity growth area
- Understanding the typical organizational hierarchy structures of an information security office

The idea is, after this chapter, you will have a vibe for the various industry types and what you can expect working in any one of them. Personally, I work in healthcare and it's quite satisfying knowing the work I'm doing has a positive impact on people's health and lives.

Understanding cybersecurity pros and cons in several industry sectors

There are so many areas to work in but let's enumerate them so we can get our arms around them. The United States government's **Cybersecurity and Infrastructure Agency (CISA)** identifies 16 critical infrastructure sectors. These sectors represent the cross-section of critical assets, systems, networks, and capabilities that the United States depends on for national security and economic stability. Cyber threat-based impacts on these sectors could have a material impact on society. While this is focused on the United States government, it's reasonable to extend the importance of these sectors to other countries' societal support systems and overall stability.

These 16 sectors are as follows:

- Chemical
- Financial services
- Commercial facilities
- Food and agriculture
- Communications
- Government facilities
- Critical manufacturing
- Healthcare and public health
- Dams
- Information technology
- Defense industrial base
- Nuclear reactors, materials, and waste
- Emergency services
- Transportation systems
- Energy
- Water and wastewater systems

While these sectors each demand their own callout for their importance, there is a commonality among some of them that makes sense for this discussion. I argue that the areas for a cybersecurity professional to explore to understand each of them are the following categories:

- **Financial services**: Highly regulated and highly targeted.

- **Healthcare and public health**: Regulated, medical device considerations, and patient information confidentiality.

- **Government facilities and defense industrial base**: Government work is unique based on the large size of governments, resource availability, and it being the *public sector* over the *private sector*. This public versus private is noteworthy enough that we go into detail about it in its own section, *Working in the public sector versus the private sector* later.

- **Information technology, communications, transportation, and emergency services**: These sectors are grouped to consider traditional information technology systems that have high availability needs or have highly sensitive information. The hyper-interconnectedness of our society dictates a large number of communications and IT that directly relates to the support and upkeep of developing products for national security, emergency services (such as 911!), and transportation, including flights, shipping, and supply chain logistics.

- **Energy, chemical, nuclear reactors, materials, waste, dams, water and wastewater systems, and critical manufacturing**: These areas may seem diverse but from a cybersecurity perspective, they are related to the heavy utilization of **Operational Technology** (**OT**) that runs **Industrial Control Systems** (**ICSes**) to produce energy, manufacture plastics and metal, and control temperatures and valve openings of important and dangerous mechanical systems.

Now let's dive into each of these areas and understand what the culture and environment of those sectors look like, what the benefits are of working in those industries, and what the compromises would be.

Financial services

Financial services is the industry that handles and deals with money. Now, if you think for a moment, the value of a financial services company is based on the trust that they can extend to their customer base that they will be protecting their assets, typically their wealth. There are many different financial firms. How do they distinguish themselves to entice customers to trust their money with them? [0] It's by having effective *cybersecurity controls*!

The financial services industry funds cybersecurity well. According to a *Deloitte and Touche 2020* analysis, financial institutions are spending 10.9% [1] of their total IT budget on cybersecurity. This equals about $2,700 per employee. That is a serious investment.

Furthermore, there are many opportunities in this industry because of this high spending. According to `cyberseek.org`, currently, there are 99,948 open opportunities in the financial and insurance industry.

Figure 3.1 is a graphic taken from `cyberseek.org` and shows cybersecurity job supply and demand for the United States. The graphic is filtered on financial services jobs only but can be filtered across other sectors. I encourage you to check out this resource to gauge your geographical area and the sectors you're interested in to see what opportunities exist.

Figure 3.1 – Cyberseek.org's financial services jobs

Financial services as an industry is evolving, continuing to increase its utilization of technology to execute transactions faster, allowing *business-to-business* integrations, and offering more access to accounts and services to customer bases. This results in an increased surface that must be secured through proper configuration and routine verification.

Just as a small example, think for a moment about how many ways you can access your bank account. You can use a mobile app, a web browser, another institution's ATM, through a wire transfer, and the old-fashioned way of physically going to the bank. All of these must be properly secured to ensure only authorized access ever happens.

A cyber career in financial services can have many benefits. As mentioned, it's typical for financial service companies to take cybersecurity seriously with funding, resources, and training. An individual is likely to have access to training opportunities in various areas that can provide valuable skill sets to the individual. Furthermore, cyber teams are not one-person shops, but teams that have specialized functions. This affords the opportunity to get exposure to other cyber professionals – a great networking opportunity – and see how to execute other aspects of a cybersecurity program. This can result in you having access to lateral career movement if you find you want to pivot, for example, from compliance to incident response.

Financial services aren't all rainbows and unicorns though. 1920's bank robber *Slick* Willy Sutton answered when asked by a reporter why he robbed banks, "*That's where the money is!*". This is true today and because financial services are where the money is, that's where cyber bank robbers target.

Some of the world's most sophisticated **Advanced Persistent Threats (APTs)** and cybercriminal organizations target financial service organizations. APTs are nation-state-sponsored cyber groups that are well-funded and highly skilled. This significantly ups the level of effort and excellence in execution cybersecurity teams must operate at. The constant defending against ongoing attacks can result in burnout, fatigue, and exhaustion.

Putting this in perspective, *APT38*, a known North Korean state-sponsored group (also referred to as *Lazarus*) is primarily financially motivated. They attempted to steal $1 billion (yes, you read that correctly) from the Bangladeshi Central Bank in 2016 and almost got away with it. They were able to successfully steal the lowly sum (*sarcasm*) of only $81 million and would have got the other $919 million if not for a typo one of the attackers made.

> **A little note**
> The APT38 is a crazy-good story and to hear it in detail, check out *Darknet Diaries*, episode 72.

The point is this industry is dealing with big money with catastrophic consequences if it gets successfully compromised. As mentioned, this level of seriousness can result in fatigue and longer workdays than in some other industries.

Government (aka public sector)

Another industry that has a significant amount of opportunity is in the public sector or government space. Government can be at the federal level, the state level, or the local level. It's worth noting that the availability and opportunity for cyber jobs in this space is larger at the federal level, getting progressively smaller as the government entity gets smaller (that is, the federal level has more jobs than the state level and the state level has more than the local level). As we will see in a minute, some local governments have no capability to employ cybersecurity resources.

Federal regulation has brought forth significant opportunities for cybersecurity work in government. The **Federal Information Security Management Act** of 2002 (**FISMA**) requires federal government entities to configure and manage information systems to adhere to minimum information security requirements. These information security requirements must be implemented, audited, and managed by cybersecurity professionals. You will get a popsicle headache if you try to understand the scope of what implementing a FISMA compliant system looks like, but I assure you it is significant.

There are significant consulting and professional service businesses that serve the federal government. This is a common practice where the government hires staff at an hourly rate to do a government job instead of hiring them in the government. Many people have made a career of supporting the federal government without ever actually working for the government.

Due to this material amount of non-government staff and resources accessing and interfacing with government people, processes, and systems, in 2020 the government began requiring these businesses to also adhere to a set of minimum-security requirements under the **Cybersecurity Maturity Model Certification** (**CMMC**) [2] program.

This cybersecurity requirement indicates that finding cybersecurity work in the public sector is accessible, but also the organizations that do business with the federal government are going to have significant cybersecurity needs around the implementation, management, and audit of those controls as well.

The great thing is there is an opportunity to find a job in this sector. The range of jobs varies widely also. Not all businesses have all cyber career fields available, but government work often does.

> **Tip**
>
> As a disclaimer, the specific work you want may not be in your geo-location. I know pentesters, SOC analysts, auditors, managers and leaders, secure code developers, and tactical field operators all in the government space. It really is a buffet of job types.

There are a lot of great aspects of government cyber work. I personally worked as a consultant in the public sector for 10 years. I mentioned earlier FISMA as a *federal* standard. This standard needs to be audited annually, and as a FISMA auditor, I had the opportunity to travel to some amazing places including Chile, Antarctica (including the South Pole!), New Zealand, and several locations across the United States. In addition, as an *Information Security Manager*, I was able to manage the cybersecurity of some very amazing *Marine Corps* systems and brief Marine Corps leadership. It is wild all the interesting opportunities that a cyber career in the government space can offer you.

Another great aspect of government work is the sheer number of cyber resources available to professionals. Some individuals may find documentation cumbersome and bureaucracy burdensome, but with everything documented and readily accessible, it's easy to understand expectations, how to execute work, and how the work you are doing relates to the mission.

There are some puddles to avoid if you choose to pursue this area to work in. Actually, getting a job directly for the government traditionally is a slow-moving process. I've known individuals that were a contractor supporting a government client for years in a very specific role, and the government wanted to hire this person to do literally the exact same job, just as a civilian (the term for a non-military government employee). It took over 6 months for the candidate to go through the entire process before officially being hired.

Another seedy aspect of this world, and one that drove me out of it, is contract cycles. If you are on the contractor/professional services side of government work, then you need to understand the work you are doing is tied to a contract. The company you work for had to submit a proposal for a government request for work, it had to compete against other companies trying to win that contract, and your company had to win that work. Winning is based on several factors, including pricing, the skill of the staff that will fulfill the contract, and how it is stated the work will be conducted.

This contract could be for a short period (less than 1 year) to upwards of 10 years (note this is rare). The contract length really depends on various factors, but what I want you to know is that if you are not working on a contract, you aren't making money for your employer. If you aren't making money for your employer and you are drawing a paycheck with benefits, then you aren't really a good investment. This status is called *being on the bench* and some larger employers will let you *ride the bench* for a few weeks to find a new contract before they terminate you. Hopefully, this comes across clearly as a real anxiety-inducing situation. It's great if you don't have a lot of expenses or are very flexible in your personal life, where you can move for a new contract or other more extreme compromises to stay on contract.

I had just started a family when my last contract came up for renewal. It was a very stressful time. We weren't going to find out if we won the renewal until 2 days before the existing contract expired. I was told indirectly if we didn't win, I should be prepared to figure something out to avoid the bench. I was not sleeping and a hot mess to put it plainly.

My solution was to find a new job in healthcare outside of government work. I turned my notice in and worked my last day 2 weeks from when the contract renewal would be announced. We ended up winning the recompete, but that experience was enough for me to know I wasn't going to experience it again.

It's pertinent to share that there is a practice of a new company winning a contract and retaining all the staff except top management on the engagement. This term is colloquially known as *flipping badges*. This does introduce some risk as one cannot guarantee the incoming contract winner will retain staff, retain benefits, or retain the current salary structure.

I have mainly focused on the federal government in this section because most opportunities can be found at this level. State governments will have similar opportunities with contract work and securing systems, although they do not have to conform to FISMA. This could change as states begin to support local-level governments with statewide cyber initiatives.

State and local government is highly targeted currently by ransomware operators knowing that these organizations are critical to support communities but underfunded to properly defend. Recent examples include the cities of Baltimore [5], Atlanta [6], and Greenville [7] to name a few where ransomware operators shut down the entire cities' government and demanded money to release the keys to unlock their systems. This cost these cities tens of millions of dollars and seriously impacted citizens.

Healthcare

I have personally worked in the healthcare industry and have seen the demand and need firsthand for cybersecurity. It's not an uncommon joke at work that we have job security because there will never not be something for us to secure.

There are many factors to consider from a cybersecurity perspective. **Protected health information (PHI)** is being used in health information exchanges for big data analysis of population health, precision medicine, and to ensure individuals' medical history can follow them through life. How important would it be if you were knocked unconscious while on vacation and the hospital you went to was able to know that you were allergic to a medicine they may have administered. These are life and death type stakes.

This data exchange is great, but individuals have privacy (cyber people refer to this as *confidentiality*) rights that must be ensured. This introduces the work challenges of not just technically ensuring the exchange of data is secured through controls such as encryption, multi-factor authentication, and tokenization (a method to separate data from the person accessing it), but also through proper contractual agreements around the use, destruction, dissemination, and control of that data.

There is another major cyber objective to support when working in healthcare. There is a critical need for system availability and the integrity of those systems. Patient safety depends on life-supporting systems and having them be unavailable can have serious consequences. (Imagine for a moment a COVID patient having the ventilator that's keeping them alive get ransomware and go offline!)

In addition to this needing to be addressed as best practice, the **Health Information Portability and Accountability Act (HIPAA)** requires healthcare providers and entities that handle the PHI of citizens to maintain strict confidentiality of that PHI. This is similar to the health information exchange discussion but looking within the organization and how PHI is handled.

As a quick aside, patient privacy is a real concern. HIPAA promotes and ensures it, but beyond regulation, there can be serious human impacts if PHI is breached. Research has shown that some individuals with uncommon lifestyles or existing conditions that are shamed by society will choose to not seek medical treatment for fear of having their privacy compromised and facing guilt and embarrassment [8].

Properly ensuring confidentiality, integrity, and availability requires the data and systems that the healthcare providers and entities are handling to be secured physically, administratively, and technically. The level of security must be sufficient to both practically secure the data and to provide validation to outside auditors that the data is appropriately protected.

Figure 3.2 shows the **Health and Human Services (HHS) Office of Civil Rights (OCR)** breach portal, also known as the wall of shame. HHS OCR is a United States government entity responsible for investigating security and privacy complaints concerning individuals protected health information. You can see the most recent completed breach investigation found these entities suffered a protected health information data breach of greater than 500 records. This public record will persist in perpetuity.

U.S. Department of Health and Human Services
Office for Civil Rights
Breach Portal: Notice to the Secretary of HHS Breach of Unsecured Protected Health Information

| Under Investigation | Archive | Help for Consumers |

Archive

This page archives all resolved breach reports and/or reports older than 24 months.

Show Advanced Options   Research Report

Breach Report Results							
Expand All	Name of Covered Entity ◇	State ◇	Covered Entity Type ◇	Individuals Affected ◇	Breach Submission Date ◇	Type of Breach	Location of Breached Information
⊕	Wellness Pharmacy	PA	Healthcare Provider	545	12/10/2020	Theft	Paper/Films
⊕	26th & Lehigh Pharmacy	PA	Healthcare Provider	549	12/10/2020	Theft	Paper/Films
⊕	Diamond Pharmacy	PA	Healthcare Provider	616	12/10/2020	Theft	Paper/Films
⊕	RXN, Inc. d/b/a Lancaster Pharmacy	PA	Healthcare Provider	856	12/10/2020	Theft	Paper/Films
⊕	Brigham and Women's Hospital	MA	Healthcare Provider	882	12/08/2020	Unauthorized Access/Disclosure	Email
⊕	Hillcrest Nursing Center	IL	Healthcare	1030	11/24/2020	Unauthorized	Electronic Medical Record

Figure 3.2 – HHS OCR Breach Portal

When healthcare organizations violate these security requirements, they are financially penalized by the HHS OCR. This fine is to deter other healthcare organizations from not implementing proper cybersecurity controls and to motivate the fined parties, after receiving a financial penalty for HIPAA violations, to improve their current cybersecurity practices to avoid further penalties and reputational damage.

Adding further insult to injury, HHS OCR maintains a publicly accessible breach notification portal, often referred to as the *wall of shame*. This site catalogs all instances of healthcare industry entities that have suffered a PHI-related data breach that affected more than 500 individuals.

News outlets readily report when local healthcare organizations have large data breaches. The brand damage such breaches can cause is especially sensitive as patients may not continue to use a facility that doesn't protect their most sensitive health information.

The healthcare industry on the provider side (that is, hospitals, clinics, patient-touching operations) offers a unique challenge to cyber folks. Most providers have medical devices that are required to be certified by the **Food and Drug Administration (FDA)**. These devices take years to receive their certification, are often expensive, and are built with a very specific purpose.

This results in healthcare organizations spending significant amounts of money on these devices. Our first nuanced issue is introduced. The replacement of these devices when they go end-of-life will be an uphill battle from the business perspective. I assure you the business is not going to replace a million-dollar system they bought 6 months ago because you told them Windows 7 is no longer supported.

Furthermore, these systems are often custom systems and cannot gracefully handle being probed by a vulnerability scanner, a common tool in the cybersecurity practitioner's toolbox for finding vulnerable system configurations and missing patches. This results in literal blind spots on parts of a healthcare network that could be a juicy target for attackers.

Due to patient-safety issues and system availability, cybersecurity professionals must be creative in how system downtime is handled, what additional security controls' impact on clinical workflows looks like (literally, the number of clicks on a computer to execute a workflow is a metric that is tracked on workflows), and how to properly communicate with a clinical end user population to be effective at good cyber hygiene. Clinical professionals and cybersecurity people talking to each other can sound like people trying to speak in two different languages.

Cyber work in healthcare can be stressful. Similar to the stress financial services introduce regarding people's money, with healthcare you are talking about people's lives. The stakes don't get higher! The healthcare industry is highly targeted by ransomware actors due in part to the specialized systems, high demand for system availability, and challenges with communicating good cyber hygiene practices. It's a perfect storm of targets easy to trick, systems easy to compromise, and a business demand that is likely to pay a ransom over enduring *going to paper* for scheduling, documenting, and delivering healthcare.

At this point, you see the driving force on why there is a healthy (pun intended) market for cybersecurity work in the healthcare space. Cybersecurity professionals are needed to help these businesses properly identify their assets, protect them appropriately (at a minimum to federal standards), and adequately respond when an incident occurs.

Energy and manufacturing (cyber-physical systems/ industrial control systems)

Other industries that are significantly important regarding cybersecurity are energy and manufacturing. The energy industry represents the nation's electric power grid, oil, and natural gas infrastructure. Most of these systems are privately owned, but entire countries rely on them for heat, light, and other basic needs. A compromising attack on an energy-producing target can have catastrophic consequences.

The manufacturing industry is a critical piece of the lifeblood of commerce and society. Manufacturing is associated with the creation and distribution of metals, machinery, and transportation equipment (including automotive). Almost all other industries depend on manufacturing to produce the goods that are used to support their mission. A breakdown of manufacturing has downstream supply-chain and logistics impacts.

Energy and manufacturing are discussed in the same vein here because of their alignment in terms of people, processes, and the approach to securing systems. Key areas cybersecurity professionals are asked to focus on in this space are the integrity of cyber systems managing physical systems and the availability (aka *uptime*) of energy and manufacturing processes to continue to generate products (electricity, cars, widgets, and so on).

Another key similarity between these industries is that they utilize specialized equipment and the actual work environment operational systems control can be very hazardous to humans. These environments can include toxic gases, radiation, liquid hot metals, and high-pressure pneumatic presses. Keeping the operations running to continue revenue generation is important, but ensuring human safety is paramount.

There are some differences between these two industries that are important to call out. Specifically, manufacturing can house sensitive **intellectual property** (**IP**) and processes that need focused security in addition to the specialized operational systems.

Consider for a second how valuable the intellectual property of Tesla electric cars is right now. The whole world is trying to develop economical, practical electric vehicles and Tesla is leading the way. By hacking and stealing the IP, a country or competitor could significantly reduce (by years) the time it would take to mass-produce electric vehicles. The attacker would also save significant capital resources, not having to invest in research and development and finding and hiring the right experts. The value isn't just in the IP itself, but the market advantage it gives a competitor. This is referred to as industrial espionage and is a real cyber threat to consider.

The concern about securing and defending from insider threats is even more relevant when addressing industrial espionage. Practitioners in this space are challenged with data loss prevention through different mediums including email, USB drives, printouts, and other techniques for duplicating data. Once the IP is stolen, there is no putting the toothpaste back in the tube!

IP theft focuses on data that is stored on traditional IT equipment, such as file sharing, network servers, and databases. Energy and manufacturing have an entirely different consideration that cybersecurity practitioners need to consider, and it's a niche area: the operational systems that run the manufacturing processes themselves.

Energy and manufacturing organizations typically run legacy equipment or systems that are no longer maintained or managed by the vendor. An example would be a critical system running Microsoft Windows XP. This operating system is quite vulnerable and has not been patched by Microsoft since 2014. This is similar to the healthcare industry medical device concerns mentioned earlier, but the consequences of compromise could have an even more consequential impact. This may be an unacceptable situation to encounter in a typical business, but if this Windows XP machine is running a mission-critical application for an energy or manufacturing company, it will continue to run it. The option to simply patch or upgrade it isn't on the table. These systems are tightly coupled with industrial processes and there simply may not be a replacement for a component of a bigger system without replacing the entire system itself. At the end of the day, these are mostly revenue-driven businesses, and if a decision doesn't make financial sense it is less likely to be pursued.

So, what do you do? Hope nothing bad happens?

If you get one thing from this book, know that *hope* is not a good cyber strategy for protecting systems!

A vulnerable, end-of-life system, such as a Windows XP machine, introduces risk to that organization and requires cybersecurity professionals to help understand how to either migrate off that application/system or properly secure it through options such as isolation or other network layer controls. This would allow that application to continue to run without introducing significant risk.

As was learned in the previous chapter, a risk assessment would highlight the need for mitigating controls. With help from threat intelligence, an architect could assist in developing controls that would allow operation but reduce the risk to an acceptable level. A pentester could then be deployed to test the controls.

The energy sector is heavily regulated, especially in the nuclear space. This can be seen in a positive light because it forces the hand of these organizations to appropriately invest in cybersecurity staff and capabilities to properly secure their environments.

There are downsides to working in these industries. One of the serious downsides of working in this space is the reality of the work environment. There is a reason industrial work environments have *These many days since our last accident* signs. They can be very dangerous places to work in, with chemicals, extreme temperatures, dizzying heights, and heavy machinery physically moving (some of which is autonomous).

Another grave concern of working in the energy sector is what is at stake. We spoke of financial services being high-stress because you are protecting people's money. The energy sector provides critical power to homes. When a power grid goes down, people can be plunged into the deadly cold (as seen in Texas in February 2021 [16]) or suffocating heat (as seen with deadly impacts in Florida in 2017 [17]).

This level of life-threatening responsibility of protecting the power grid can be incredibly stressful and taxing on individuals, especially considering the likelihood of energy companies being attacked. Per a *2020 McAfee report* [9], 25% of all energy companies globally have been victims of cyber-attacks.

Additionally, it does not happen often, but nation-state capable threat actors can attack energy and manufacturing industrial control systems with devastating effects. The *Stuxnet* cyber-attack in 2010 on an Iranian nuclear enrichment facility resulted in the destruction of nuclear centrifuges, a key component in producing usable nuclear material.

Another strain of malware in this same specialized group of attacking complex operational technology is Triton. Triton can disable industrial control safety systems – the same systems that keep major disasters from occurring.

On the one hand, these malwares are truly terrifying and may cause you to think *hard pass, I'll stick to a different industry*, but some may see this as a true higher calling to take on the challenge of ensuring the security, resiliency, and safety of these environments.

It's important when talking about manufacturing and industry to cover **industrial control systems (ICSes)**, a niche space in cybersecurity. Oftentimes, when we discuss and work in cybersecurity, we are referring to securing *information technology*. This is devices such as networks, servers, workstations, and tablets.

ICS systems are concerned with **Operational Technology (OT)**. This is cyber-physical systems that control physical mechanisms such as value openings, turbine spinning speeds, gas mixtures, and so on. OT systems are like IT, being technology, but the protocols, interfaces, and controlling of OT are much different.

If you would like to learn more about ICS security, I'd encourage you to check out the training and opportunities at *Dragos*. They are a leader in the ICS security space and have several free webinars and training material on their site: https://www.dragos.com/.

We have covered quite a few fundamentally distinct industries. Each has its benefits and challenges. Part of taking control of your cyber career is identifying which industry aligns with your values and priorities.

The financial industry pays great and has opportunities, but you run a high chance of having longer hours and higher stress. Healthcare has a righteous mission to help people live healthy lives, but you must also understand policies and regulations to ensure compliance is kept in mind.

I encourage you to dig deeper if you find one particular industry that resonates with you. Jax will be giving you the inside scoop in *Chapter 6, Time to Brand Yourself – Not the Burning Type*, on how to leverage social media platforms to increase your marketability in industry, but I'll give away some of the secret sauce now.

You can leverage LinkedIn, a social media platform for business, to quickly filter down and find cybersecurity professionals that work in a specific industry. Most people in cybersecurity are happy to help the community, and by reaching out to ask them for 10 minutes to talk about cyber in their specific industry, you could quickly find the industry that will make you super satisfied with your career choice (or avoid one that would make you miserable).

We did discuss working in the public sector in general, but there is an important dimension to consider when discussing the public sector: how it differs from the private sector. Next, let's analyze and investigate the key differences.

Working in the public sector versus the private sector

We spent some time earlier talking about working for the government, specifically, we went into the federal government in depth because of all the cybersecurity requirements outlined there through FISMA and other initiatives.

It's important to call out here working in the **public sector**, which would be the government, versus working in the **private sector**, which would be with private businesses and vendors. Some of the interesting things from a cybersecurity professional perspective is when you work in the public sector, you typically get lower salaries, and you are not authorized to accept gifts from vendors (such as tickets to shows, meals, travel to vendor conferences, golf outings, and so on). Also, you may find yourself pigeonholed in your job with certain roles and responsibilities, not being able to get exposure to other areas of the field.

Public sector jobs are more stable. The government occasionally does furlough staff during government shutdown events, but for the most part, there is very little concern about losing your job in a government position.

Also, the United States federal government (and some state governments) offers pension programs to incentivize their staff to stay. Pensions are a guaranteed retirement compensation plan heavily based on years of service.

It's not uncommon for individuals to retire from their public sector job having hit their maximum years of commitment for a full retirement pension and start the next day as a contractor doing the same job. This is called double-dipping and is completely legitimate as the person then receives their pension and their contractor paycheck.

This financial and job stability afforded by public sector jobs can be quite appealing to many people.

The private sector has fewer constraints than the public sector regarding vendor gifts. Within the private sector, you can accept gifts from vendors if it's in line with your corporate policy. This will typically manifest in a vendor sending you tickets to an event, such as a security conference. If you have purchasing authority, they might send you clothes with the vendor logo on it, such as a pullover or a polo shirt. At conferences, you'll be invited to private parties with *free* food and drinks. It is worth noting that a company could have an internal policy not authorizing this, but it would be explicitly by having it as opposed to the public sector, in which it applies to all civilian and military personnel.

Why would the vendor fly me to a conference, feed me great food and drinks, and hook me up with sweet gear? The idea behind this is that the vendor is hoping that by essentially giving you gifts, you're more likely to give them your time to listen to their pitch or potentially feel obligated to move forward with a proof of concept or purchasing their solution. This is proven psychology and is a highly effective form of marketing based on social exchange theory [10].

In general, the private sector typically pays higher salaries. One study from 2013 quantified this discrepancy as private sector personnel making on average 35.2% more than their public sector counterparts. This data is a few years old, but anecdotally the private sector has better-paid jobs over comparable jobs in the public sector.

It's worth noting that in 2019, the **Department of Homeland Security (DHS)** was empowered by Congress to enact civil service reform to adjust this discrepancy in some capacity (and to adjust minimum education requirements) to retain existing talent and attract talent from the private sector [11].

You may be asking yourself *Why wouldn't I choose free stuff, better pay, and lateral career growth?* and it would be a fair question. The public sector does have its advantages.

Well, within the public sector, you can typically say that job stability is higher. The government is unlikely to lay off staff or fire staff in general. Contrast that with the private sector, which is full of revenue-driven businesses. The business may be acquired or merged with another business resulting in redundancy layoffs. Another reality is you could be laid off because the acquiring company just wanted to buy the property rights, not the people, to the intellectual property of whatever great product you were securing for your company.

In the federal public sector, the expectations are defined, and compliance is expected. Security tends to be funded and job roles are very compartmentalized. The expectation is a risk-based approach, but the reality is very framework adherence motivated. The private sector is very different, tending to be much more risk-based. You have to show the monetary value of security to the business. Often you have to convince leadership that the money spent will result in an acceptable level of risk. It seems like a subtle shift but is very impactful on your job and skillset.

Things happen, so the private sector has a little bit more volatility around the security of your job. Currently, there are a lot of unfilled jobs in cybersecurity so finding another job if you are a casualty of a layoff (through no fault of your own!) is not impossible.

Much like cybersecurity risk management, you must weigh the risks involved, how you might mitigate the risks to acceptable levels, and move forward with a decision. You see how I just related you choosing public versus private to a fundamental cybersecurity concept? Yes, I love cybersecurity.

The public sector does have fringe benefits to sweeten the deal. Fringe benefits means non-salary compensation and opportunities. Some examples of these benefits include training dollars, the ability to travel to conferences, and pension plans. The work you do in a public sector job is well-defined and it's unlikely to receive "additional duties as deemed necessary," which is a way some private sector businesses define job roles so they can pile on more work outside your existing job.

While not consistent across private sector businesses, some fringe benefits in the private sector can include performance bonuses. These bonuses are end-of-the-year financial payouts based on company performance. There may also be profit sharing or equity in the company offered as part of your compensation package. This is seen quite regularly in private sector companies. You will never see performance bonuses in the public sector.

I've seen some private sector businesses offer unlimited staff **paid-time-off** (**PTO**). That's a recent program that has seen some success. Some research has even shown that this benefit attracts high performers to organizations offering them [12].

The public and private sectors both have pros and cons. There is an ongoing increase in cyber job supply in both spaces, therefore you should have access to either, although it's worth noting, per Cyberseek.org, there are approximately 13 times as many private-sector cybersecurity jobs (484,420) compared to the public sector (37,197) currently in the United States.

You need to understand these key differences as you begin to decide where your cyber career journey will take you. Similar to choosing an industry, the public and private sector choices you must make really depend on your values and personal preferences. Stability in the government is comforting, but as somebody famously said, *Money talks!*, and there is more opportunity for that in the private sector.

Now, whether you go public or private, you have a high probability of encountering cloud technology. The cloud is significantly growing in adoption across all industries, sectors, and business sizes. Let's take a look in the next chapter at just what the cloud is, and more importantly, why cybersecurity is a golden opportunity in the cloud space.

Introducing cloud platforms as an explosive cybersecurity opportunity growth area

Let's spend some time talking about cloud security. The last 10 years have seen a massive paradigm shift in the traditional approach any business has had to support their information technology needs. Traditionally, businesses would have data centers, servers, and clients. All this (on-site) infrastructure was housed within their own environment. They'd have to hire networking staff, application staff, server administrators, database administrators, and so on in order to maintain the environment to allow their business to actually operate. The advent of the cloud paradigm has empowered organizations to migrate or offload infrastructure to these cloud providers.

As a brief primer on cloud service providers, the three big cloud service providers currently are **Amazon AWS**, **Google Cloud Platform** (**GCP**), and **Microsoft Azure**. There are different types of cloud service offerings also. There is **Infrastructure as a Service** (**IaaS**), there is **Platform as a Service** (**PaaS**), and there is **Software as a Service** (**SaaS**). The best way to understand the shared responsibility model for these services is graphically. The table in *Figure 3.3* shows which partner is responsible for what aspect of the infrastructure in these service models.

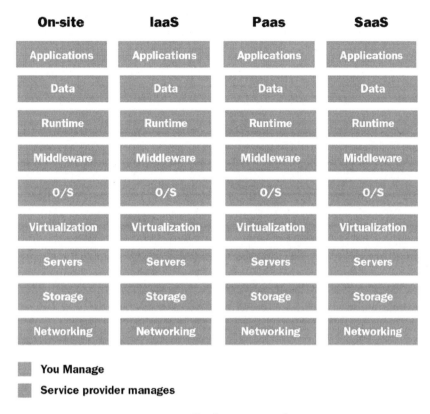

| | You Manage |
| | Service provider manages |

Figure 3.3 – Cloud service paradigms

There are some other *aaSes too, but we won't get into that right now. The important thing for you to take away is that the cloud service providers (except for IaaS) maintain the **operating system** (**OS**), the physical security infrastructure, and the patching and updating of the supporting middleware applications.

Now, this does sound good! This is a major saving for cybersecurity personnel at businesses as physical security, OS patching, and middleware maintenance are huge areas of risk that are now just taken care of by enterprise-grade service providers.

There is a lot of overhead and maintenance that the cloud service provider handles, but it doesn't eliminate the need for security; it just changes what you need to be looking at to secure. Therefore, cloud security is quite interesting and really a hot area to consider as a focus for your career. You may not think about it, but individuals like myself who have been working in the industry for over 15 years have a bit of a leg up, but the cloud paradigm and how you secure it is new to everybody.

Office 365 (**O365**) is a solution provided by Microsoft that provides an organization with Microsoft Office applications such as Word, PowerPoint, and Excel. Also, email infrastructure no longer requires an organization to maintain Exchange Server on-premises.

The O365 platform abstracts a lot of the system administration responsibilities, making it possible to administer the platform by non-technical people or small business owners that don't have server administration expertise. The functionality is related to account management and some other high-level administrative functionality.

For example, Microsoft has abstracted the layers of having to understand how things such as **Active Directory** (**AD**) work underneath the hood. When you're securing AD, now you need to start prioritizing securing the user and the user access. User access controls become critical to cybersecurity, especially since one of the attributes of the cloud is it's accessible from anywhere! Your pool of viable threat actors and attack surface just got larger.

The same can be said with file shares. If you're hosting file shares in the cloud, who can access them, who has accessed them, and the auditability of what has happened to files all become important. These audit controls are available, but along with access control, ensuring you are prioritizing logging, log aggregation, and SIEM ingestion now moves to the front of the line in terms of controls.

Some large recent data breaches were due to improperly configured AWS S3 storage containers that were left open to the world. The service has the ability to be secure, but when improper configuration management leaves the storage containers open to the internet, all your data is on Pastebin.

You have to consider audit records so you can be able to validate and understand what happened if someone accesses something or if it's configured to go from private share to public share. You also have to understand how to test those types of configurations properly to make sure that they're actually secured.

AWS holds a significant market share in the cloud infrastructure services space with Azure second and GCP third. All three of these appear in the upper-right panel of the coveted (2020) Gartner Magic Quadrant for cloud service providers, indicating their ability to execute and completeness of vision are leading the industry [13].

You can get more information and education and training around securing the cloud by using some of the following resources. These resources are provided by the cloud providers themselves and have security sub-areas to explore, but I would encourage you to get educated on the platforms and how they work in general to better identify how to secure the cloud instance while enabling the business:

- AWS: `https://www.aws.training/`
- Azure: `https://docs.microsoft.com/en-us/learn/azure/`
- GCP: `https://cloud.google.com/training`

The authors of this book have no relationship or affiliation with AWS, Google, or Microsoft. These three platforms comprise nearly all corporate cloud adoption, so spending your time and money focusing on training for these environments will easily give you the most marketable skill set if you choose to go into cloud security.

Gartner research predicts 14.2% of the total global enterprise IT spending market in 2024 will be on the public cloud, up from 9.1% in 2020 [14]. This is a massive amount of money and adoption. I would strongly advise, if you're looking for an emerging area that will have significant demand, focusing on cloud security.

Now let's move on to the next and final topic of the chapter.

Understanding the typical organizational hierarchy structures of an information security office

We've talked about different industries, sectors, and paradigms, but how is information security programmatically executed in an organization. You wouldn't have only 10 security operations analysts for a **cybersecurity office** and call it a day. You would be missing significant organizational elements. Let's explore what a typical cybersecurity program role and structure would look like. This way, you can identify the roles that *Kim* shared with how they interrelate and how you fit in.

The typical information security office organization can be seen in the organization chart in *Figure 3.4*. This structure is typical with capabilities grouped by function related to an information security program.

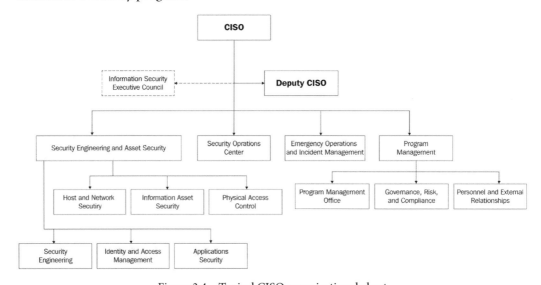

Figure 3.4 – Typical CISO organizational chart
(This chart was redrawn from the http://jcsitnet.com/journals/jcsit/Vol_7_No_1_June_2019/1.pdf research paper)

There is a traditional structure to **information security** as an organizational capability. Currently, information security typically reports through information technology or the **Chief Information Officer (CIO)** so the **Chief Information Security Officer (CISO)** will report to the CIO. The CISO is seen as a technology function within the organization.

The CISO reporting to the CIO makes sense because a percentage of information security's scope of responsibility is interacting with information technology. It's explaining to the administrators and the system owners how to properly configure their systems to be secure, why multi-factor authentication is required, who needs to do patching, and so on.

A minority of organizations have a different reporting structure for the information security office. Common alternative reporting structures include reporting to legal, risk, or even directly to the **Chief Executive Officer (CEO)**. There are pros and cons to each reporting structure, but the majority adopts information security reporting through the CIO.

An argument for having the CISO not report to the CIO lies in the mission of the CIO. CIOs of organizations are charged with ensuring IT services enable the business to achieve its mission. If a system needs downtime (being unavailable for maintenance) for security patching, this impact may be unacceptable to the business. If the CIO is the CISO's boss, the CIO can overrule the CISO on bringing a system down for security patching. You see the conflict now with this reporting structure?

Information security is not exclusively an IT function within information security offices. An information security office will have a **Governance, Risk Management, and Compliance (GRC)** function. GRC is responsible for ensuring regulatory requirements are met. GRC will help maintain and drive any cybersecurity program road map or strategic growth initiative. The GRC office is involved in policy exceptions and imposing sanctions related to policy violations. They also develop and distribute policies and procedures for the organization.

Awareness training for end user staff typically falls under the GRC function. Think of GRC as the area of information security that is doing its best to ensure that the organization is positioned to minimize the likelihood of a security incident occurring.

Another group that is common within the information security office is **security operations**. Security operations are typically where your incident response handlers, SOC analysts, and digital forensics staff work. This group of professionals is the blue team. This group is responsible for monitoring the environment using sensors and other appliances that have been previously deployed for visibility.

When an adverse or anomalous event occurs, security operations investigate it to determine whether it is in fact a security incident. This group is responsible for responding and handling it.

The **incident response** capability has a well-defined process, as seen in the *Figure 3.7* graphic. This process has two aspects to it. One is the process of detecting an incident, containing it, and returning the infected systems back to normal operations. The other is an iterative process with lessons learned from incidents feeding into better preparation and protective controls.

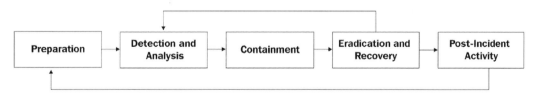

Figure 3.5 – Incident response workflow

Security operations identify a security incident, contain it to prevent further impact, and then help the organization return to normal operations. Following activities like this, they will typically investigate to identify the original cause of the incident and help prevent it from happening again.

Another area within information security that is common is **security engineering**. This group is responsible for the management of security technology solutions. These solutions help secure network devices, servers, workstations, and other endpoint-type systems. Specifically, this can mean administering the firewall, **mobile device management (MDM)**, **multi-factor authentication (MFA)**, and other tools that help secure the environment.

Security technologies, like any other technologies, must be managed, maintained, and have a life cycle. Just because it's a security technology doesn't mean that it doesn't have security vulnerabilities and needs to be patched! User access needs to be removed when it's no longer appropriate.

When issues happen or performance problems occur, somebody needs to be responsible for investigating. This is closer to a traditional IT role or function, but because it is focused on the cybersecurity space and security technologies, it typically falls into an information security role.

Identity and access management is another important area that falls under information security. It's even becoming more important as organizations move to the cloud and zero-trust models.

Any system, application, or physical area should be controlled so only authorized individuals have access. This simple concept is critical to securing systems and is the responsibility of this group. They will be responsible for creating network and system accounts, associating them with proper resources needing access, terminating accounts when no longer needed, and resetting passwords. Furthermore, this group works with application owners and third-party systems that the organization is leveraging to integrate existing network credentials for access. This provides the ability for end users to use their organization network account for logging into other systems instead of having to remember multiple usernames and passwords across systems. This is also a win for the information security office because access across multiple systems can be removed by disabling a single account.

Another area that falls within the information security office that is not common but you will see it in larger organizations and the financial services industry is a **penetration testing** or *red team capability*.

A red team testing or penetration testing is a function within information security that proactively tests and attempts to compromise the organization or service offerings of the organization. The reason for this is to identify weaknesses in a controlled manner with internal visibility and remedy them before an outside threat actor is able to realize the vulnerability and compromise the business.

An example of this is Netflix. Netflix is a complete online media streaming service provider that has millions of customers. If a threat actor was able to bring down Netflix from being able to serve media to their customer base, it would be reputationally and financially devastating for Netflix.

Netflix has an internal penetration testing team that is regularly attempting to compromise and attack Netflix. This team works closely with the incident response, security operations, and blue team in order to explain how they are attacking the environment.

This ensures the blue team is able to see malicious activity with their sensors and tools. It helps them understand and identify what that attack looks like. That way, if they're unable to completely eliminate the attack, they're able to quickly identify it because of the signatures that the attack presents.

> **Fun fact**
> This process of red and blue working is a modern term called **purple teaming**. This allows the blue team to also tune their solutions to reduce the amount of noise and fake positives they see with their tools.

There are other non-technical roles that typically fall within information security. Some organizations that are larger have people who are dedicated to awareness training. Awareness training is communicating best practices and cyber risks to be knowledgeable about to an organization's end user population.

This population can include staff, contractors, volunteers, leadership, and visitors. End users are often targeted through phishing attacks and social engineering. The activity of awareness training helps to reduce the risk of a successful compromise from these attack types.

Some organizations do awareness training through the GRC function, but it can warrant its own space. Generalized information security awareness training can be less impactful with audiences because they don't see the value in their own day-to-day activities. By focusing and tailoring training on certain user types or workflows, the training can resonate with the audience and have greater value in adjusting behavior and improving end user cyber hygiene. An example is delivering business email compromise threat awareness to accounting, finance, and leadership users. This has high value as they are often targeted with this attack type.

You may develop awareness training around risk and best practices for password management, end-of-life software concerns, and risks related to remotely connecting to systems for manufacturing line workers. These two audiences, corporate users and front-line operational staff, are wildly different, and each would find the other's awareness training less useful.

Summary

In this chapter, we looked at some technical challenges. Regardless of the industry, all businesses need cybersecurity-minded professionals that are informed about evolving threats and attacks to be able to inform the business about dynamic risk and how to best mitigate it while continuing to enable the business to succeed. It's important to know how to speak to the business side, not just IT. This is critical in the private sector especially.

We've talked about many different industries, sectors, and business types in this chapter. You can get general cybersecurity knowledge and break into any of these areas and have a fruitful career, but there are industry-focused cybersecurity certifications and educational avenues that can help you stand out as the best candidate for a job, shortcut your path to having the knowledge to perform the work in that sector, and give you the skills to have an impact.

In the next chapter, *Jon* is going to share with you exactly what you need to know to take the role you found from *Kim* and the industry/sector you got from me and get focused applied knowledge.

Further reading

- [0] Beyeler, Walter E., et al. Copy of A Model: *How Cyber-Attacks affect Brand Value in the Financial Industry*. No. SAND2012-9898C. Sandia National Lab. (SNL NM), Albuquerque, NM (United States), 2012.

- [1] Deloitte Financial Services Cyber spend report: `https://www2.deloitte.com/us/en/insights/industry/financial-services/cybersecurity-maturity-financial-institutions-cyber-risk.html`

- [2] The Department of Defense Cybersecurity Maturity Model Certification (CMMC): `https://www.acq.osd.mil/cmmc/docs/CMMC_ModelMain_V1.02_20200318.pdf`

- [4] A breakdown of the CISA critical infrastructure: `https://www.cisa.gov/critical-infrastructure-sectors`

- [5] City of Baltimore shut down by a cyber-attack: `https://www.baltimoresun.com/politics/bs-md-ci-it-outage-20190507-story.html`

- [6] City of Atlanta shut down by a cyber-attack: `https://www.wired.com/story/atlanta-spent-26m-recover-from-ransomware-scare/`

- [7] City of Greenville shut down by a cyber-attack: `https://www.scmagazine.com/news/-/ransomware-knocks-greenville-n-c-offline`

- [8] Why do People Avoid Medical Care? A Qualitative Study Using National Data `https://www.ncbi.nlm.nih.gov/pmc/articles/PMC4351276/`

- [9] What is Stuxnet? `https://www.mcafee.com/enterprise/en-us/security-awareness/ransomware/what-is-stuxnet.html`

- [10] Service providers and customers: social exchange theory and service loyalty: "Citation: `Sierra, J.J.` and `McQuitty, S.` (2005), "*Service providers and customers: social exchange theory and service loyalty*", `Journal of Services Marketing`, Vol. 19 No. 6, pp. 392-400.

- [11] DHS Cyber Pay Scale: `https://fcw.com/articles/2020/10/08/dhs-cyber-pay-scale.aspx`

- [12] (How) Do Risky Perks Benefit Firms? The Case of Unlimited Vacation

- `https://doi.org/10.5465/AMBPP.2020.18308abstract`

- [13] AWS Named as a Cloud Leader for the 10th Consecutive Year in Gartner's Infrastructure & Platform Services Magic Quadrant `https://aws.amazon.com/blogs/aws/aws-named-as-a-cloud-leader-for-the-10th-consecutive-year-in-gartners-infrastructure-platform-services-magic-quadrant/#:~:text=This%20year%2C%20G-artner%20announced%20a,and%20Platform%20Services%20(CIPS).&text=Today%2C%20I%20am%20happy%20to,furthest%20in%20Completeness%20of%20Vision.`

- [14] Cloud usage projected to continue to grow year over year. `https://www.gartner.com/en/newsroom/press-releases/2020-11-17-gartner-forecasts-worldwide-public-cloud-end-user-spending-to-grow-18-percent-in-2021`

- [15] Structuring the Chief Information Security Officer Organization: Allen, Julia & Crabb, Gregory & Curtis, Pamela & Fitzpatrick, Brendan & Mehravari, Nader & Tobar, David. (2015). *Structuring the Chief Information Security Officer Organization*. 10.13140/RG.2.1.1242.6967.

- [16] Texas power outage leads to critical health concerns. `https://apnews.com/article/hypothermia-health-storms-power-outages-texas-ffeb5d49e1b43032ffdc93ea9d7cfa5f`

- [17] Nursing home catastrophe following power outage from hurricane: `https://www.popsci.com/story/environment/hurricanes-nursing-homes-power-heat/`

4
Exploring Certifications and College

Skillsets often apply directly to a few different things. One of those is skillsets that you gain from on-the-job training, or mainly being in the field and gaining experience while you're in the thick of it. However, that doesn't always get to be the case for everyone, especially someone outside of cybersecurity trying to get into cybersecurity. Individuals looking to get into cybersecurity often look to college degrees and certifications to help build their skillsets and help them stand out among other aspiring (or even current) cybersecurity professionals.

This chapter is going to cover various certifications that aspiring cybersecurity professionals can achieve to help them get the job they are looking for. Additionally, these certifications are great for road mapping a plan to a particular career that an individual may want to pursue.

In this chapter, we're going to cover the following main topics:

- General security certifications

- Hacking the planet – diving into the big red certifications

- Alert! Checking out blue teaming certifications

- Checking the box – auditing certifications

- GRC/management certifications

- College of knowledge – discovering the benefits of a cyber degree

General security certifications

The title may be a little off-putting; however, general security certifications entail undergoing training and proving that a certified person understands a broad range of topics as they relate to cybersecurity. This by no means illustrates that the certified person is a subject matter expert; rather, they have become a *master of none but knowledgeable of their craft*.

Important note

As you move through your career, don't expect to *master* every subject. Technology and cybersecurity move so quickly that it is virtually impossible to master a subject. However, this does not mean that you will not be regarded as a subject matter expert or someone who is highly knowledgeable within your focused domain.

When starting out in information technology or cybersecurity, it is highly recommended that you look to general certifications to help guide you on your path to your dream career. That being said, you may be thinking, *"Why would you go general instead of more focused?"* – excellent question!

The primary purpose of cybersecurity professionals is to chase knowledge to help others, rather than be focused on knowledge or general knowledge. We, as cybersecurity professionals, want to ensure that we are getting experience for ourselves that we can use to help others.

> **Important note**
>
> Cybersecurity is about making people, processes, and systems better than they were before you got there!

The following section is going to highlight some general cybersecurity certifications that aspiring cybersecurity professionals can attain in order to help themselves, but more importantly—these certifications allow others to trust you as the certified professional to help them!

CompTIA Security+

This certification is one of the more sought-after certifications because it provides such a significant amount of knowledge, but does not go so deep to overwhelm the student in their studies and comprehension. The CompTIA Security+ exam teaches basic cybersecurity principles while also establishing the foundations for more advanced certifications later down the road.

Another perk of CompTIA Security+ is complying with ISO 17024 standards, as approved by the US **Department of Defense (DoD)** to meet directive 8140/8570.01-M requirements. This means that if you get the CompTIA Security+ certification, you're qualified to work with the government and defense systems department. For those looking to get into DoD contracting, Security+ is a certification that will open those doors for you, and is something that you can get within a short period of time!

Security+ cost analysis

One of the major benefits of CompTIA Security+ is that it is not that expensive compared to other certifications. Additionally, the exam is not that long compared to quite a few other certifications, so the cost versus the impact on the student really benefits the student in more than one way. The following is a comprehensive breakdown of what students can expect to spend on the certification and what level of effort they should expect:

> **Important note**
>
> The cost advertised reflects the price of the courses and certifications at the time of writing. These prices could be subject to change.

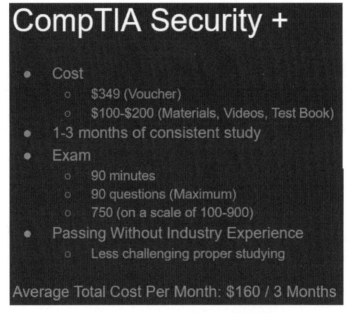

Figure 4.1 – Cost breakdown of Security+

As you can see, the cost of this certification doesn't impact your wallet too much, especially if you consider that a great-paying job could come out of getting the certification. It should also be mentioned that the certification is not entirely difficult to get, as long as you maintain good study habits of 2 hours of studying a day. Someone who studies for 2 hours a day, at least 5 times a week, should expect to be ready to take the CompTIA Security+ and pass the exam.

The next certification we are going to discuss is one of the most highly regarded certifications within cybersecurity and stands as one of the **gold standards** of cybersecurity certifications.

(ISC)² Certified Information Systems Security Professional (CISSP)

The **Certified Information Systems Security Professional** (**CISSP**) is a certification that separates senior security professionals from their junior counterparts. This certification shows that the certified individual has vast knowledge in multiple domains and that the credential holder has passed a rigorous 6-hour long exam.

The exam covers eight different domains (instead of six like Security+) and requires the test taker to have at least 5 years of cybersecurity experience before they can even sit the exam. However, do not let that stop you from taking it – you can still take the CISSP if you do not meet the requirements in terms of professional experience and earn the associate title until you have been in the field for at least 5 years.

CISSP cost analysis

CISSP is a different monster when contrasting it to Security+. This exam is going to take quite a bit more time to prepare for and is going to cost a tad more money. So make sure you have the time to dedicate to the certification and the funds to allocate to it.

The following are some cost and time points to consider with CISSP:

- Exam cost: USD 699
- Cost of materials: USD 300
- 3-4 months of consistent study
- 6 hours and up to 250 questions
- Passing without industry experience: Very challenging, even with proper study

The average cost per month for getting ready for this exam will be around USD 275. That is assuming that you stick to about 3-4 hours of studying 5 days a week and stay consistent with your studying.

Now that you understand the two different general cybersecurity certifications, we can start to move on to more focused domains and start to look at certifications that will light the way for your path toward your target career. We are going to start with what is known as the *cool side* of cybersecurity, also known as **red teaming** or **offensive security**.

Hacking the planet – diving into the big red certifications

Red certifications are something that has become quite popular in recent years. Red certifications essentially involve any certification that revolves around **offensive security**, which can include terms such as the following:

- Pentesting

- Red teaming

- Exploit development

- Application security

- Purple teaming (yes, even a different color!)

What do these mean, and why is it essential that you understand what certifications are right for you? That question can be answered by illustrating the issues that can come from taking on too many certifications – yes, this is a thing!

Offensive security certifications, by design, either teach you the fundamentals of offensive tactics or can elaborate and go extremely advanced and require you to take hands-on exams that can last days or even weeks on occasion! That's why it's best to understand what type of certifications best fit the skillset you want to build (or improve) and not get distracted by getting certifications just for the pure fact of getting them.

To start off, let's discuss different vendors and the type of certifications they provide. Each vendor offers their own unique training and exam styles while ensuring that they provide quality content to their users.

Exploring different vendors

This section is going to cover the various vendors (not certifications) that are common for offensive security-like training. The vendors mentioned provide various certifications that come with their own unique style of training, exams, and cost (important when budgeting).

SANS

SANS, also known as **SANS Institute**, is one of the most sought-after cybersecurity training providers globally. Their courses range from beginner to expert and are taught by world-class experts in the field. The courses offered by SANS can be online, such as virtual or on-demand, or are also provided on-site and in person. Most cyber professionals that you ask about SANS will tell you that the training is above and beyond (which is true!) and that the certifications are excellent validations of cyber skillsets.

The interesting aspect of SANS certifications that makes them stand out from other certifications is that they are not open book, but you can bring in the books provided by SANS to take your exam. For every course, you are given a certain number of books to study for your exam – SANS ensures that all materials needed to pass the exam are provided in the books. Individuals who have taken SANS certification exams often reference using the **indexing** technique when taking their exams.

> **Important note**
> Indexing consists of making notes within your provided textbooks to ensure that you can reference keywords in the course material during your exam.

The downside to SANS certifications is that you typically need to go through the course to pass the exam, hence indexing the material. The courses and exams usually range from USD 5,000 to upward of USD 8,000 for everything. This typically makes SANS a training provider that employers pay to upskill their staff.

> **Important note**
> If you're thinking about paying for a SANS certification out of pocket, remember that the certification should line up with a job you are looking to get. For example, if you want to become a penetration tester and make 10% more than you are currently making, you can justify paying for a SANS course because it will get you the future role and raise that will help pay for the certification

Now that we know a little bit about SANS, let's move on to the next vendor. This vendor has become extremely popular for their certifications and their mantra of *try harder.*

Offensive Security

Known as the big kids on campus, Offensive Security is a training provider with a reputation that derives from its intense and 100% hands-on certifications that challenge those who take them. Popular from gold-standard certifications such as the **Offensive Security Certified Professional** (**OSCP**), the training platform offers certifications that range from hands-on pentesting, exploit development, web hacking, and Wi-Fi hacking to advanced tactics.

Unlike SANS, Offensive Security exams are 100% hands-on and also do not cost nearly as much as SANS courses. This makes going with Offensive Security a lot more friendly on your bank account and is often the route that most professionals take due to the cost and hands-on exams.

We will discuss Offensive Security further in just a bit, so let's go ahead and jump to the next vendor. The next vendor we are going to discuss is a hybrid mix of SANS and Offensive Security. This vendor provides top-level training while also producing quality hands-on exams.

eLearnSecurity and INE

Known as the new kids on the block, INE and eLearnSecurity provide top-level training packages that range from cybersecurity and networking to even cloud training (they do not provide cloud pentesting courses).

One of the big perks of INE/eLearnSecurity is its subscription model. The subscription model allows students to pay a monthly or yearly fee that gives users and students access to quite a bit of coursework that teaches them a particular subject. Regarding offensive security (the field, not the company), the subscription platform provides training in a wide variety of topics, including the following:

- Pentesting
- Web app pentesting
- Exploit development
- Red teaming
- Advanced tactics

One of the other things that makes INE/eLearnSecurity different is paying for the certification vouchers for the certification. When subscribing to the platform, users are not given access to certification exams. This allows students to study for what they want to study and pay for an exam when they choose to do so.

Now that we have mentioned the top three vendors of offensive security-style certifications, let's get into the weeds and begin to highlight the certifications that someone can get to get in the field. It should be noted that each certification will be mentioned in the order that it is recommended to achieve it. This means obtaining the first mentioned certification first before moving on to the next one.

Discovering each red certification

Now let's start to break down the certifications you should be interested in getting if you are looking to level up, gain knowledge, or are just curious about the exam itself. The first section we are going to dive into is **pentesting-focused certifications**.

eLearnSecurity Junior Penetration Tester (eJPT)

What was once an unknown certification has now become one of the go-to certifications for aspiring penetration testers. The eJPT certification is a 100% hands-on certification provided by eLearnSecurity that lasts 3 days. Within those 3 days, students sitting the exam must answer questions by performing actions within the exam environment, and students must score 70% to pass.

The following is the breakdown and cost analysis of the certification:

- **Cost**:
  - USD 200 (voucher)
  - USD 500 (materials, labs, and four exam vouchers)
- **Preparation time**: 1-3 months of consistent study
- **Exam**:
  - 3 days
  - Real-world pentest
  - 70% minimum to pass
- **Passing without industry experience**:

  Less challenging with proper studying. When we say less challenging with proper study, we do not by any means say that this certification is easy. What it does mean is that the training resources provided are enough to have you pass the exam. So, if you study correctly (2 hours a day), you'll be set to pass the certification within a month, or, at the very least, you'll be test-ready in 3 months.

The next certification is one that has become quite a controversial certification within the pentesting field, largely due to it being a multiple-choice exam and producing individuals calling themselves hackers and pentesters, but who are unable to perform hands-on pentesting.

EC-Council Certified Ethical Hacker (C|EH)

The **C|EH**, also commonly known as **Certified Ethical Hacker**, is a well-known, but not always well-respected, pentesting certification that EC-Council offers. The certification is a 4-hour written exam that tests the student's knowledge on various pentesting concepts and even has the student look at the output of tools and scripts. While the exam is not hands-on, students who pass the exam are DoD-compliant and become eligible to pentest as a government contractor. This means that as long as you have C|EH, you have a better chance of becoming a pentester through the government than someone who does not have C|EH.

The following is the breakdown and cost analysis of the certification:

- **Cost**:
  - USD 1,199 (voucher)
  - USD 100-200 (materials, videos, and test book)
- **Preparation time**: 1-3 months of consistent study
- **Exam**:
  - 4 hours
  - 125 questions
  - 60% to 85% to pass (depends on the exam)
- **Passing without industry experience**:
  - Challenging, even with proper studying
  - Less challenging with a USD 2,000 EC-Council prep course

As you can see, this certification is quite a bit more expensive than others that we will talk about and has an *average cost of USD 450 per month* while studying for the exam. However, as mentioned, this certification provides numerous benefits, including being certified to pentest for the government (within the US), thereby potentially offsetting the cost with potential employment.

The next certification we will discuss is highly regarded but, like the C|EH, is a reasonably expensive certification that can take a hit on your bank account if not appropriately planned.

GIAC Penetration Tester (GPEN)

This certification is provided by SANS and costs a whopping USD 7,000 just for the course! However, as mentioned, SANS is a top-tier training provider that is highly regarded on account of its training. The GPEN course, also known as *SEC560: Network Penetration Testing and Ethical Hacking*, prepares students when it comes to understanding and being successful in engaging and executing penetration testing and ethical hacking.

The following is the cost breakdown that a student should expect when attempting to get this certification:

- **Cost**:

  - USD 1,999 (certification voucher, materials)

  - USD 7,340 (course training)

- **Preparation time**: 4 months of consistent study

- **Exam**:

  - 3 hours

  - 82-115 questions

  - 75% pass score

- **Passing without industry experience**:

  - Challenging without proper studying

  - Less challenging with proper studying

So, as you can see, this certification is going to take a big hit on your bank account if you self-fund the certification; however, that does not mean that you need to completely self-fund the certification. SANS has work-study programs that allow students to not have to pay for the entire certification. It is also always recommended that you check with your employer about having them fund the certification (the most common option).

> **Important note**
>
> Know that many companies require you to sign an agreement that requires you to stay with the company for a certain amount of time if you decide to have them fund it.

The next certification is a certification that starts to move us into the more intermediate certifications within offensive security.

CompTIA Pentest+

This next certification is an amazing certification to get once you have gotten a few fundamental and beginner-friendly certifications under your belt. The CompTIA PenTest+ is an exam that has a mix of multiple-choice questions and scenario-based questions that challenge the student's knowledge in the five different domains that comprise the exam. Students will be challenged on their expertise in planning and scoping, information gathering, attacks and exploitation, testing tools, and report writing.

Students expecting to take on the PenTest+ exam should take note that the exam is not easy because it is multiple choice; in fact, the exam executes scenario-based questions very well!

> **Important note**
> The CompTIA PenTest+ questions have been written by some of the industry's top pentesting and offensive security professionals.

The following is a breakdown of what students should expect when preparing for the CompTIA PenTest+ exam:

- **Cost**:
    - USD 359 (voucher)
    - USD 300 (materials, labs, and videos)
- **Preparation time**: 3-4 months of consistent study
- **Exam**:
    - 165 minutes
    - Maximum of 85 questions
    - A minimum score of 750 to pass (on a scale of 100-900)
- **Passing without industry experience**: Challenging with proper studying

As you can see, this certification takes a bit longer to study for than some of the other certifications that were mentioned before it. This is because this should be thought of as an intermediate certification that plays a role in prepping the test taker for other certifications (such as the ones to follow after!).

The next certification on our list is a complete hands-on certification, much like the eJPT that we mentioned earlier in this chapter. While the next certification is fundamental in nature (*with regard to being hands-on*), for those not used to being hands-on, the following certification can be challenging and present a big learning curve.

eLearnSecurity Certified Professional Penetration Tester (eCPPT)

The eCPPT is one of the most intense penetration testing certifications due to its comprehensive course material and its 100% practical (hands-on) exam that tests the student's knowledge of various aspects of penetration testing. The exam itself is 7 days long and immerses the student in a real-life pentesting scenario where the test taker has no information about the test environment. In the industry, we call this a **black box test**.

> **Important note**
>
> A black box test is a pentesting engagement where the pentest team has zero to little information on the target environment. The purpose of the black box test is to see what pentesters can discover as if they were actual cyber criminals trying to discover information about that target.

Students planning on taking the eCPPT should expect the following:

- **Cost**: USD 1,599 (materials, labs, and exam voucher)
- **Preparation time**: 2-4 months of consistent study
- **Exam**:
  - 7 days
  - Additional 7 days for report writing
  - Real-world black box pentest
- **Passing without industry experience**: Challenging with proper studying

This exam is going to require a bit more studying than other certifications. It is recommended that students prepare for the exam by studying for at least 4 hours a day and complete all the modules and labs within the training material related to the eCPPT exam. Please note that this is just a baseline assessment, and time commitments may change from student to student. Also, *while this exam is very challenging*, it should be noted that eLearnSecurity provides all the proper training to enable you to get the certification. This helps with not spending countless hours rummaging the internet, finding resources, and putting things together.

The next exam we are going to mention is one that has gained quite a bit of popularity over recent years. With a mantra of *trying harder*, this certification is the **gold standard** of pentesting certifications; however, that doesn't mean that it is simple to achieve.

Offensive Security Certified Professional (OSCP)

The OSCP exam is a challenging 24-hour exam that really tests the mettle of the test taker's ability to think quickly and under pressure. Students preparing for the OSCP exam should understand that a large time commitment is involved in order to pass this exam.

First, students will need to enroll in the PEN-200 course provided by Offensive Security. This course offers various subscription models, which can be seen in the following screenshot:

PACKAGES

PEN-200 course + 30 days lab access + OSCP exam certification fee	$999
PEN-200 course + 60 days lab access + OSCP exam certification fee	$1199
PEN-200 course + 90 days lab access + OSCP exam certification fee	$1349
PEN-200 course + 365 days lab access + 2 OSCP exam attempts	$2148

RETAKES

OSCP Certification Exam Retake Fee	$150

LAB EXTENSIONS

PEN-200 lab access – extension of 30 days	$359
PEN-200 lab access – extension of 60 days	$599
PEN-200 lab access – extension of 90 days	$799

Figure 4.2 – OSCP course price models

As you can see, there are many price options. Suppose you are not familiar with pentesting or want to get the best value. In that case, it is recommended that you go with the 90-day lab access package that will give you 3 months within a lab environment to test and improve your skills in preparation for the OSCP exam.

> **Important note**
>
> It is recommended that you use other materials to supplement your learning while studying for the OSCP. Books, hacking challenges, and other labs, such as TryHackMe and Hack The Box, are always recommended as a great supplement to your learning while training for the OSCP.

Individuals looking to prep up for the OSCP exam should take note and prepare for the following:

- **Cost**:

  - USD 150 (voucher)

  - USD 1,349 (materials, 90-day lab access, and exam voucher)

  - USD 799 (90-day lab extension)

- **Preparation time**: 6-12 months of consistent study.

- **Additional study materials**: Use Hack The Box, TryHackMe, or Vulnhub for additional studying.

- **Exam**: 48 hours:

  - 24 hours hands-on

  - 24 hours of report writing

  - 5 machines

  - Machines vary in difficulty

  - Pass score of 70%

- **Passing without industry experience**: Extremely challenging even with proper studying.

While this exam is challenging, it should be noted that it is possible with proper studying and patience. Many individuals train for months on end and still fail this certification the first, second, and sometimes even the sixth time. It is often recommended to find a study buddy to help motivate you while training for the OSCP, and ensure that you stay on the path to obtaining the certification.

> **Important note**
>
> Co-author Jon Helmus gave a talk about how to get into offensive security at DEF CON Safe Mode in the summer of 2020. You can find out more about that here: `https://www.youtube.com/watch?v=Db_w5LinhZc`.

Now that we understand some of the certifications that will help get us on the path to pentesting, let's take a turn in the other direction and look at some credentials that provide value for individuals looking to get into blue teaming and incident response.

Alert! Checking out blue teaming certifications

Before we dive into the certifications, let's quickly mention what blue teaming is. As mentioned in the previous section, red teaming is comprised of individuals who hack systems to illustrate the organizational impact based on vulnerabilities discovered and exploited in the target system. With that in mind, blue teaming can be thought of as the exact opposite.

Blue teaming consists of a team, and a department, of professionals who monitor the security of the systems they work for. This means consistently looking for alerts and determining alerts as incidents, false positives, or false negatives.

Sometimes you may hear these words and phrases used with blue teaming:

- Incident response
- **Computer Incident Response Team (CIRT)**
- **Operation la Operations (SOC)**
- Threat hunting

One of the interesting *hot topics* coming up with blue teaming is threat hunting. Threat hunting consists of a company employed to go and seek out threats within the network. These individuals look for potential **indicators of compromise (IoCs)** and dive into tracking the movements of those potential threats that may have breached their systems, or worse, are still in their systems!

Discovering each blue certification

Now, let's start to move on and learn about some of the certifications someone can get who is interested in blue teaming, or who wants to learn more about blue teaming.

Security Blue Team Level 1 (BTL1)

As one of the new vendors on the block, the security blue team provides distinctive hands-on defensive training that puts the student in the driver's seat in a 24-hour practical exam that prepares them for entry-level blue teaming positions. Students looking to get into blue teaming, or similar operations, should look to the BTL1 as a foundational certification. Students will learn everything, including the fundamentals of security and phishing (on the defensive side), and also start to understand threat intelligence and incident response.

Students planning on taking the BTL1 should expect the following:

- **Cost**: USD 685 (materials, labs, and exam voucher)
- **Preparation time**: 2-4 months of consistent study
- **Exam**: 24 hours
- **Passing without industry experience**: Challenging with proper studying

As you can see, the certification provides great value and amounts to roughly USD 171/ month for students who take the 4-month route to study. Students looking to get this certification should note that it can take up to 30 days to get their exam results back. So if you plan on taking this certification, ensure that you have patience after completing the exam.

The next certification we will mention is the follow-up to BTL1 and should be considered the second certification in your blue team-focused path.

eLearnSecurity Certified Incident Responder (eCIR)

The eCIR is a 100% hands-on certification that will test a student's ability in various domains, including the following:

- Network packet
- Event analysis
- Traffic analysis
- Wireshark, ELK, and Splunk
- SIEM searches
- Event and log correlation
- Event analysis
- Process analysis
- Anomaly detection

Individuals looking to get this certification should note that some time must be spent in the labs learning the material. Much like the other hands-on certifications mentioned in this chapter, the labs are where you will find most of the benefits in your hands-on certifications.

This is one of the few certifications where we will not provide a detailed breakdown. However, you can find more about the eCIR here: `https://elearnsecurity.com/product/ecir-certification/`.

eLearnSecurity's Certified Threat Hunting Professional (eCTHP)

This is a certification that has a cool title to go with it! eLearnSecurity's Certified Threat Hunting Professional is a certification that tests the student's ability through a scenario-based exam that puts the student in the driver's seat of a simulated threat hunting scenario. Students who take on this exam can expect to learn quite a bit about the following:

- IoC-based threat hunting
- Forensics
- Log analysis
- Data correlation
- Traffic and packet analysis

The process of taking the eCTHP exam is relatively similar to the other certification presented by eLearnSecurity. The student has 14 days to complete the exam *and* submit the final report. Once the report is sent, students wait to get their exam results back.

To find out more about the eCTHP, check out the certification here: `https://elearnsecurity.com/product/ecthpv2-certification/`.

The next certification is going to be the last on this current list. We are going to be diving into one of the more popular SANS blue team certifications.

GIAC Certified Incident Handler (GCIH)

The GCIH certification is a top-tiered blue teaming certification provided by SANS. The certificate is accompanied by its certification course, **SEC504: Hacker Tools, Techniques, Exploits, and Incident Handling**, and prepares students to be able to *turn the tables* on potential computer criminals and malicious attackers. Individuals who take on the GCIH can expect to learn **about incident handling and computer crime investigation** while also learning about exploits used by real-life hackers. Much like the GPEN certification and prep course, this SANS certificate costs quite a bit of money, totaling in the region of USD 7,000, which puts a high price on the certification. However, SANS does provide top-caliber support and trainers for the certification course. This can make the level of funds required worth the cost.

Here is a breakdown of the certification:

- **Cost**: USD 7,000 (materials, labs, and exam voucher)
- **Preparation time**: 4 months of consistent study
- **Exam**:

  - 4 hours

  - 100-150 questions

  - Pass score of 70%
- **Passing without industry experience**: Challenging with proper studying

Those looking to get this course should understand that 4 months should be the normal amount of time to commit to the certification. SANS provides a large amount of material that needs to be indexed and understood by the student.

Now that we understand what blue team certifications there are, let's move on to some other types of certifications that are not so technical, but are still required for certain areas within cybersecurity.

Checking the box – auditing certifications

This section, and the one following it, will be smaller than the ones on other certification paths (within this book and in general). However, that should not make you think that there is less significance in auditing within cybersecurity. Auditing is a process that ensures that companies are maintaining the minimum technical, operational, administrative, and ethical levels needed to operate a business or corporation. Commonly known as **checking the box**, auditing is a process that typically requires a specialist or analyst to analyze and evaluate a company against a predetermined checklist.

Let's take a good look at what is one of the most popular certifications within the auditing arena.

Certified Information Systems Auditor (CISA)

The **Certified Information Systems Auditor** (**CISA**) is an industry-standard certification for becoming a top-caliber security auditor. The CISA is provided by ISACA, a global association with an amazing reputation for providing IT professionals with top-level content and credentials. Cyber professionals and auditors with CISA against their name, or on their résumé, are regarded as the best of the best due to the pure nature of the CISA certification requirements. So what are these requirements?

To start, someone with the CISA certification must go through a vetting process when applying to take the exam. Students wanting to take the exam must show proof that they have at least 5 years of work experience as a security auditor.

Important note

Individuals typically get their start in security auditing by moving through the ranks. Most security auditors get noticed and picked up based on their technical background and what type of university degree they have.

Individuals who do not have 5 years of experience can submit waivers. Here are some of the guidelines based on waivers:

- 1 year of experience as an information systems auditor.

- A 2- or 4-year degree. A graduate degree in information security, information technology, or the equivalent gives up to 1 year of experience.

- 2 years of experience as a university professor of computer science, accounting, or information systems.

The CISA exam will challenge the student/test taker in five different sections that make up five domains in total. The exam is 4 hours long and consists of up to 150 questions. The following screenshot is a breakdown of the domains and the breakup of the questions:

Process of Auditing Information Services   21%

Governance and Management of Information Technology   16%

Information Systems Acquisition, Development and Implementation   18%

Information Systems Operations, Maintenance and Service Management   20%

Protection of Information Assets   25%

Figure 4.3 – CISA exam domains

While the CISA is the only certification we are going to discuss in this section, it should be noted that individuals wanting to get into auditing should focus on degree programs at the preferred university.

The next section of this chapter is going to dive into the last list of certifications. We are going to dive into management and GRC-style certifications that those looking to get into upper management should set their sights on.

GRC/management certifications

GRC stands for **governance, risk management, and compliance** – a practice where professionals focus on what is needed to ensure that compliance and risk management are executed successfully. In addition to GRC, management plays a key role in ensuring that risk is mitigated correctly and effectively. Those looking to have a career in management or GRC must understand that this is one of the fewer hands-on careers in cybersecurity and focuses more on strategy and compliance.

While many general cybersecurity degrees focus on compliance and high-level cybersecurity, such as governing and managing risk, it is important to note that there are certifications out there that help with this as well. The next three certifications on our list of certifications will help you with your career in GRC and cybersecurity management.

CompTIA Project+

The CompTIA Project+ certification is a certification that will help those looking to understand how to make their project management better and more effective for their teams and companies. Designed for individuals working with smaller companies or smaller teams, the Project+ exam teaches students how to manage resources, maintain proper documentation, and manage their overall project life cycle.

Let's take a look at a quick breakdown of what you should expect while prepping for Project+:

- **Cost**:
  - USD 338 exam voucher
  - USD 100 in extra resources
- **Preparation time**: 1-3 months of consistent study

- **Exam**:

  - 1.5 hours

  - Maximum of 90 questions

  - Pass score of 710

- **Passing without industry experience**: Less challenging with proper studying

As you can see, the Project+ exam is fairly inexpensive compared to many other certifications on this list and is not too difficult to attain with proper study.

Next, we are going to look at another certification that is the next logical step after Project+.

Project Management Professional (PMP)

The PMP is a certification that teaches individuals how to properly manage people, processes, and their business environment concisely and effectively. Noted as an advanced certification, the PMP certification requires that aspiring test takers have one of the following before embarking on their journey:

- A 4-year degree

- 36 months of experience leading projects

- 35 hours of project management education/training

Or:

- A high school diploma or an associate degree

- 60 months of experience leading projects

- 35 hours of project management education/training

As you can see, you are going to need to have some experience before even applying to take the PMP certification. Those who meet the requirements should understand that the certification can take anywhere from 3 to 6 months for preparation and that a certification voucher costs USD 550 for non-members and USD 405 for individuals who are members of the Project Management Institute.

Let's recap and do a breakdown of the certification:

- **Cost**: USD 650-700 (materials and exam voucher)

- **Preparation time**: 4 months of consistent study

- Exam:
  - 4 hours
  - 175 questions
  - Pass score of 85%
- **Passing without industry experience**: Challenging with proper studying

Next up, we will discuss the last certification on our large list of certifications to discover in your journey into cybersecurity. Let's take a look at what is the more advanced cyber management certification.

Certified Information Security Manager (CISM)

The last certification we are going to discuss is the **Certified Information Security Manager** (**CISM**), an advanced certification that teaches test takers how to manage information programs properly. Noted as having a 50-60% pass rate on first attempts (higher than OSCP), the certification voucher costs USD 760, not including resources, and throws around 200 questions at test takers.

Here is a breakdown of the certification:

- **Cost**: USD 1,000 (materials and exam voucher)
- **Preparation time**: 4 months of consistent study
- **Exam**:
  - 4 hours
  - 200 questions
  - Pass score of 450
- **Passing without industry experience**: Challenging with proper studying

Note that this exam's pass score is 450, and scoring is graded on a scale of 200-800. Students looking to get this certification need to understand that a fairly heavy time commitment is required. As mentioned, expect to spend around 4-5 months in obtaining this certification.

Now that we understand more of the certifications that we can get, let's pivot and start discussing another avenue for learning and achievement.

College of knowledge – discovering the benefits of a cyber degree

One of the most controversial things you will ever hear about cybersecurity is whether you should or should not get a degree in some type of technology-related program. You may be asking yourself, *Should I get a degree or should I pursue certifications if I already have a non-technical degree?* A lot of the discussion revolves around the statement *"You do not have to have a degree to be in cybersecurity,"* which is 100% true, but also not 100% true. What we are really trying to say is that studies show that degrees may not be the guarantee to get you into cybersecurity; however, they do provide you with a better pay scale and job promotions when it comes to timelines. In fact, studies show that entry-level cyber positions typically pay anywhere from 10% to 15% more if you have a degree. On top of that, many jobs in cybersecurity require a higher-level degree such as a master's, or for dedicated research positions, you may be required to have a Ph.D. or doctorate.

Getting a degree is something to be proud of, as all the authors of this book can attest to. Cybersecurity degrees provide a wealth of knowledge, experience, and help to grow your network with other peers who are in the field and also constant learners. In fact, that is one of the primary benefits of getting a degree – you get to be surrounded by others who want to research, learn, and connect. However, you must ensure that you do your homework and make sure you pick the right degree program for you.

Next up, we are going to discuss what you need to think about when exploring different degree programs, no matter what stage you are at in your life.

Exploring different programs

When looking for different degrees, you must pick one that best fits your needs, wants, and will help your desired career field. Do you want to do something that focuses more on programming? If so, you'll want to evaluate degrees that focus on computer science rather than general information technology degrees that focus on the overall understanding of IT and IT systems. But what about cybersecurity degrees? There are so many different ones to choose from when it comes to looking at what you may want to focus on. Luckily, that's where we are going next. We are going to discuss the various concentrations of cybersecurity degree programs that will allow you to take your career to different levels.

Cybersecurity

A general cybersecurity degree is going to help you understand the basics of what cybersecurity is and how it is implemented within an organization. Those who seek a general cybersecurity degree typically want to understand the fundamentals of cyber and how it can be leveraged to help their organizations or careers.

Cyber operations

Individuals looking to get into more offensive-style security should look for degree programs that focus on cyber operations. Cyber operation degrees derive from computer science programs and teach students various offensive tactics in cybersecurity such as software exploitation, offensive security, malware analysis, reverse engineering, and much more.

Information assurance

If you want to contribute to the field of risk management and assuring assets and information, then going for a degree in **information assurance** (**IA**) is going to be your best bet. Anyone looking to get a degree in IA will learn what it takes to protect the confidentiality, integrity, and availability of the systems they interact with.

Cybersecurity is a moderately new field, unlike IA, which is more established with a more extensive focus to include the protection of digital and non-digital information assets, such as hard copy records. Specifically, IA is determined as the confidence that information systems will perform as needed when needed and be accessible for authorized users only.

Cyber defense

Do you want to understand what it takes to defend networks, execute proper forensics, and set up the best defenses for your systems? If so, take a look at degree programs that feature programs with a focus on cyber defense to help you understand the concepts of what it takes to defend all things!

Before we move on to the next section, we will stop for a moment and take note that while the degree focuses mentioned will help you with your success in cyber, there are other degree focuses out there that can help you with your career. However, individuals looking to get into cyber should focus on these types of degree programs as guidance for their careers.

Now we are going to move on to the next section before concluding this chapter. The next section is going to focus on how we put all the theory and knowledge we learn into practical use. As a cyber professional, you must understand that you must have some hands-on skills to thrive (and help) in this career. So let's start discussing the basics of what you will need.

Building home labs

Many degree programs will supply you with labs to help you learn hands-on skillsets. However, that doesn't mean that you need to stop there. Being able to learn new technical concepts by understanding the theory of them and the hands-on elements will benefit you and those you work with because you will understand concepts and how to apply them (hands-on keyboard). That's why you must understand how to build your own labs from scratch to supplement your learning.

Thankfully, home labs can be built fairly cheaply with little to no computing power needed from you. It is advised that if you do not have the computing power to make a lab, you should create one in a cloud environment such as **Amazon Web Services** (**AWS**) or Microsoft Azure. This allows you to deploy services and train on them while using all the services' computing power and not your own machine.

Some of you may be able to power your own labs from home. Typically, this requires a computer with a decent amount of **random access memory** (**RAM**) and a decent processor. If you have the means to do so, it is recommended that you create labs for your focused area in a virtual environment hosted locally on your own machine. A great and free hypervisor to use to execute this is VirtualBox. VirtualBox allows you to spin up virtual machines on your own computer and gives you the discretion of allocating as many resources as you like to them.

Summary

As you can see, there are so many ways to get into cybersecurity and even more different domains on how to get into cybersecurity. You must take the information discussed in this chapter and link it to your own timeline on what certifications you want to get, what type of career you want in cybersecurity, and how you want to apply that knowledge.

To recap this chapter, you should now understand the following:

- The various cybersecurity certifications
- That different degrees build different skillsets
- The importance of building home labs
- The importance of networking with others
- Understanding that continuous learning is part of the cybersecurity journey

In the next chapter, we are going to be diving into how you can get hands-on experience without actually having to be on the job.

Further reading

Refer to the following links for more information on the topics covered in this chapter:

- General certs: `https://resources.infosecinstitute.com/topic/7-top-security-certifications-you-should-have/`

- Cyber operations programs: `https://www.nsa.gov/resources/students-educators/centers-academic-excellence/cae-co-centers/`

- Overview of cybersecurity degrees: `https://cybersecuritydegrees.org/`

5
Getting Hands-On Experience with No Experience

Jon's previous chapter on certifications and education was important because it helped educate you on the field and industry, which, in turn, helps you deliver value as you become a cyber professional. One challenge these two don't help with is the common requirement of experience.

It's the chicken and the egg problem all over again. Employers want to give jobs to people with experience, but you can't get experience without a job. Let's crack the egg in this chapter and explore getting hands-on experience in the specific area you want in innovative ways.

Hands-on experience can be more important than having a certification, especially when you first enter this industry. This chapter will provide all the guidance you need to get that valuable *hands-on-keyboard* experience, without having to have a cyber job yet.

This chapter will start off by presenting several actionable ways to get experience. You will learn about offensive security skill development through a vulnerable web application home lab. A walk-through of building and using a WebGoat system on a Raspberry Pi will be provided to help you learn about web application security and OWASP top vulnerabilities.

Additionally, you will learn about defensive skill development by analyzing actual malicious network traffic for indicators of compromise and interesting attributes.

Furthermore, from a non-technical skills perspective, you will learn about alternative opportunities from the traditional 9-5 entry-level position that allow you to apply cyber skills in controlled settings and develop cybersecurity experience, including internships, conference events, non-profit support, and looking within your own organization.

Finally, we will show you how to look inward to show how you already have cyber experience and don't even realize it and, more importantly, how to showcase it on a resume.

In this chapter, we're going to cover the following topics:

- Hacking all the things
- Guarding all the doors
- Blazing your own trail
- Looking in the mirror

After completing this chapter, you will have a clear set of actionable tasks that you can execute so that you can start adding experience elements to your resume.

Technical requirements

Check out the following link to see the Code in Action video:

```
https://bit.ly/3iaGzUk
```

Hacking all the things

This section will guide you on offensive security skill development through a vulnerable web application home lab. A walk-through of building and using a **WebGoat** system on a Raspberry Pi will be provided to help you learn about web application security and **Open Web Application Security Project** (**OWASP**) top vulnerabilities.

WebGoat

WebGoat is an intentionally vulnerable web application that is designed to educate individuals on web application security concepts through actual hands-on exploitation of web application vulnerabilities, as well as descriptive write-ups on why the vulnerabilities allow exploitation.

A great way to get hands-on experience and actually develop real cybersecurity skills and get experience is to have a home lab. *Home lab* is a fairly subjective term. A home lab could be one computer running some applications, all the way up to having physical network appliances, security appliances, and endpoints simulating an actual corporate network. The price point for these two extremes vary wildly, but for our purpose, we are looking for the sweet spot between a low price point and high skill development value.

Our red team's offensive security skill development lab will contain a Raspberry Pi and a couple things you likely have around the house. This device, plus the free WebGoat security lab software, will help you gain offensive security skills while performing web application pen testing and also help you understand some core cybersecurity concepts.

> **Raspberry Pi**
>
> Raspberry Pis are small, single-board computers that are low-cost and designed for a variety of use cases. They are ideal for home labs because they are affordable, versatile, and have a material community that supports it. I'd encourage you to spend a few minutes exploring the vast projects available that utilize a Raspberry Pi. (Once you're done with the WebGoat lab, of course!)

WebGoat is an intentionally insecure web application that contains vulnerabilities that can be exploited. Additionally, there is context and education content around the types of vulnerabilities and what you, as the student, are seeing and experiencing. It's an awesome self-study platform.

The OWASP is a non-profit organization that highlights the most common and serious web application security vulnerabilities. Understanding these top 10 vulnerabilities can make you a better security practitioner as you know what to look for when exploiting or defending. WebGoat provides lessons on the most common web application vulnerabilities, and this is why we are using it for this lab.

Raspberry Pis are low-cost, single-board, Unix-based computers that are excellent for projects and labs like the one we are going to build. They are intended to be fully functional, but at a low price point to make them accessible.

Before we get hacking and developing those skills, we have to build the lab. This is the grind folks don't see. Let's treat building out this lab like a recipe. We have our ingredients, then our steps, and finally we get to eat the delicious cake that is our WebGoat lab.

Ingredients

For this lab, we will need the following hardware:

- Raspberry Pi Model B with 2 GB of RAM

- A micro SD card (minimum 32 GB)

- A micro HDMI to HDMI cable

- A Raspberry PI case (not required but helps)

- A monitor that can receive HDMI input (for setting up the Raspberry Pi initially)

- A keyboard with USB connection (for setting up the Raspberry Pi initially)

- An SD/micro SD card reader (for imaging the SD card)

I've compiled an Amazon list of the hardware, except for the monitor and keyboard, to make it easier to find these parts. It can be accessed here: `https://www.amazon.com/hz/wishlist/ls/374BZBC86SGQ4?ref_=wl_share`.

For this lab, we will need the following software:

- **Raspberry Pi OS**: `https://www.raspberrypi.org/software/`

- **WebGoat**: `https://hub.docker.com/r/webgoat/goatandwolf`

- **Docker**: `https://get.docker.com` (you will download this from the Raspberry Pi command line and do not need to visit this website through a browser)

Recipe

Now that we have our ingredients, we just need to follow a recipe for assembling them in the right order to get this lab cooking. First, we will assemble the hardware, then load the software, and finally configure the lab.

Assembling the Raspberry Pi

If you decide to purchase a case, it will typically come with support pieces to protect your Pi. This includes heat sinks, a fan, and a shell. This isn't required, but the Pi is so powerful and useful that I would strongly encourage you to opt for the case. I guarantee you that you will find other uses for this Pi once you've finished with WebGoat.

If you chose to not get the case, skip to the *Loading the Pi OS image* section. If you did, let's spend a minute setting up our expectations. Don't worry about this assembly – it's not super complicated and can actually be fun.

You will have to apply heat sinks to the chips on the board to help dissipate heat. The included instructions will show you exactly where to apply the stick heat sinks.

The fan will be screwed into the pre-drilled holes to help pull heat out of the case. Finally, the board will screw into the case. This 5-minute process will make you feel like a mad scientist building a creation.

Now that we've got our machine, let's get a brain installed!

Loading the Pi OS image

The folks behind Raspberry Pi have made this step incredibly easy:

1. Simply access the Raspberry Pi website (`https://www.raspberrypi.org/software/`) and download the Raspberry Pi Imager application. You will need permission to install applications on the computer you are installing the Imager application on.

2. Run the Raspberry Pi Imager application with the SD card plugged into your computer. Select the Raspberry Pi OS from the selection when the imager application asks for it:

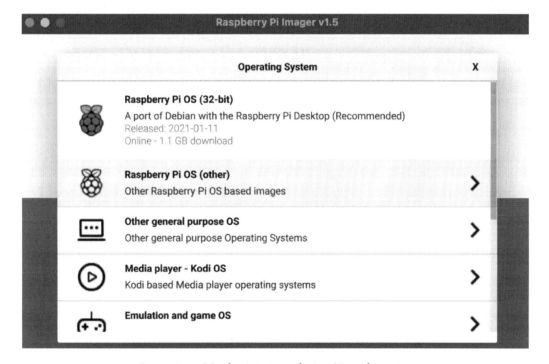

Figure 5.1 – OS selection menu during SD card imaging

3. You can preconfigure the operating system at this time by pressing *Ctrl* + *Shift* + *X* after selecting the OS. This will allow you to configure and enable **Secure Shell (SSH)** for remote access, wireless network credentials, and your local time zone. I strongly encourage you to take advantage of this feature:

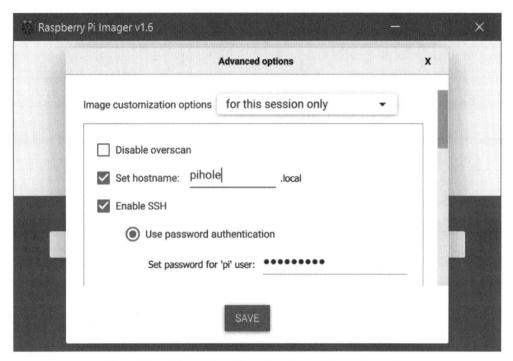

Figure 5.2 – Advanced configuration during SD card imaging

4. Finally, you must select the SD card to tell the imager application where to place this snazzy new OS you just configured. After selecting this, just write and verify to the SD card, and this part will be complete. With that, you have a full Raspberry Pi OS on your SD card. Way to go!

Raspberry Pi is so awesome. If you want help with loading the Pi OS image, they have a 45-second video that shows you exactly how to do this here: https://youtu.be/ntaXWS8Lk34.

Now, you can put the SD card into the SD card slot on the Raspberry Pi. Connect the peripherals (monitor, keyboard, and a USB mouse) to the Raspberry Pi and power it on. It's alive!

Staging the Pi

We now have a Raspberry Pi built and turned on. There may be some initial steps and configuration you will have to go through, depending on whether you pre-configured the OS. These are straightforward questions and settings that you can complete quickly and easily. I will assume you've completed that and that you are now at the home desktop, waiting to hack all the things.

Let's get our lab software installed. First, we want to make sure our environment is current. Open a Terminal by selecting **Terminal** from the top-right drop-down list. Once you're in a Terminal, type the following:

```
sudo apt-get update && sudo apt-get upgrade
```

During the update, you may be asked for additional disk space. Choose Y to proceed. This update could take up to 10 minutes. Time to grab a drink!

Loading Docker

Now that our OS is up to date, let's load Docker. Docker is a containerizing platform that allows us to install a preconfigured WebGoat *container* that contains all the dependencies, settings, and configurations we will need to make sure WebGoat runs correctly. Docker abstracts all this business from us so that we can do what we came here for – get skills!

1. Load Docker by typing the following command in the Terminal:

    ```
    curl -fsSL https://get.docker.com -o get-docker.sh
    ```

2. Once this command completes, run the following command in the Terminal:

    ```
    sudo sh get-docker.sh
    ```

    Now that our Pi has Docker, we have to add a user to Docker. This is just a good security practice.

3. Run the following command from the Terminal:

    ```
    sudo usermod -aG docker pi
    ```

4. That's it! Now, if you want to verify that your Docker instance is up and running, you can run the following command in your Terminal shell:

    ```
    sudo docker version
    ```

    This will output a bunch of diagnostic and configuration details about your Docker instance.

At this point, Docker is ready to rock.

Loading WebGoat

We are so close. Let's finish strong with this build by installing WebGoat. We will be doing this all from the same Terminal window we have been running the previous commands in:

1. Run the following command to install WebGoat:

   ```
   sudo docker pull cambarts/webgoat-8.0-rpi
   ```

   This is a WebGoat instance that works on the Raspberry Pi ARM hardware architecture.

2. Now that we have WebGoat, let's launch it. Run the following command to start the WebGoat container:

   ```
   sudo docker run -p 8080:8080 -t cambarts/webgoat-8.0-rpi
   ```

   After running this command, you will see Docker running the WebGoat instance and several outputs on your Terminal shell.

3. The final step is to verify that WebGoat is running.

   If you don't know what the Raspberry Pi's IP address is, you can open another Terminal shell and run the following command:

   ```
   ifconfig | grep "inet"
   ```

   Your IP has a high likelihood of being the four-octet value next to INET in the output of that command and will begin with 10., 192.168, or 172.

   Now, let's see if WebGoat is running. Open a web browser (Raspberry Pi comes with one) and navigate to the IP address of the Raspberry PI on port 8080. The specific URL to input is http://[raspberry PI IP address]:8080/WebGoat/login.

The following screenshot shows what the WebGoat login page looks like. This is the first page you will see when you've successfully set everything up and indicates you have successfully built your lab:

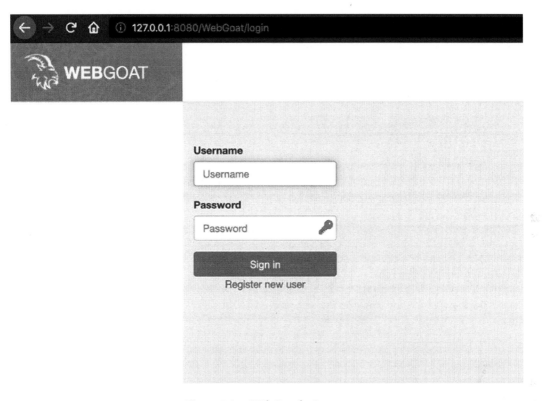

Figure 5.3 – WebGoat login page

You will have to use the **Register new user** option to begin. This straightforward process will create a user that you can use to access the WebGoat application.

Once you have logged into WebGoat, you will see that it is designed to help you learn about certain concepts and applied skills. The following screenshot shows the user drilled down into the **General** section of WebGoat, where relevant concepts are taught:

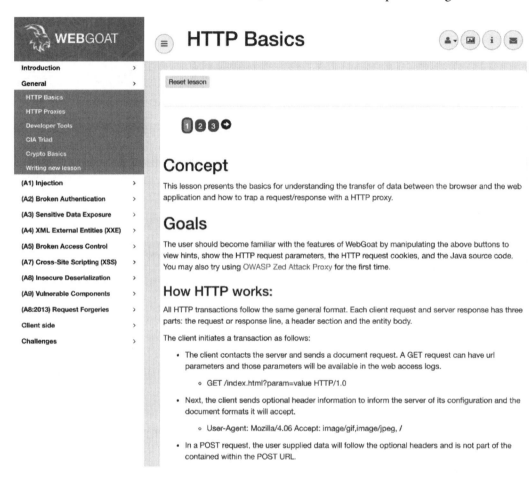

Figure 5.4 – WebGoat lab interface

Following this basic concepts section, which you can build on by undertaking future lessons from WebGoat, you will be taken to a section about offensive security skills, also known as penetration testing. The following screenshot shows information about SQL injection attacks, including examples of an attack's construction:

Figure 5.5 – WebGoat SQL injection lesson

Finally, WebGoat provides an interactive element so that you can learn about the skills you've just been educated on. The following screenshot shows the conclusion of the basic SQL injection attack section, asking you to complete an exercise:

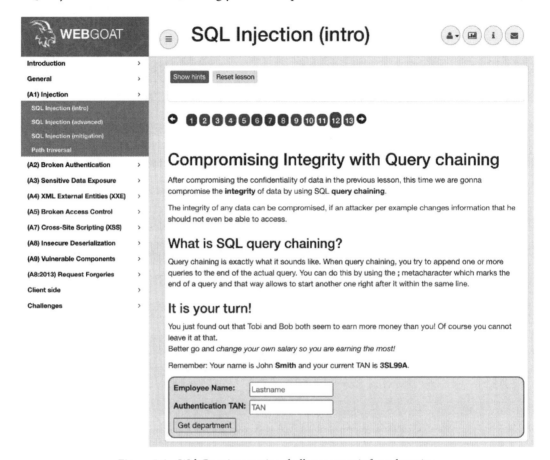

Figure 5.6 – WebGoat interactive challenges to reinforce learning

Don't worry if you get stuck or have trouble with a section. This is intended to be a learning tool, and each exercise has a **Show Hints** button to help you complete the exercise.

The WebGoat platform will allow you to learn about and practice using web application security techniques safely and thoroughly. You can leverage this at an offensive security job interview during technical screening activities. If you're asked about any of the concepts you've been taught about in WebGoat, you can not only explain what the concept is academically, but you can share your experience of having actively exploited in a controlled environment that you've built.

This is huge for both gaining experience and for showcasing your initiative to educate yourself on these hard skills.

Maybe penetration testing is not your jam. Perhaps you fancy yourself as a blue teamer (as explained in *Chapter 2, Which Career Field Is Best for You?*), a defender of systems and networks. We've got you covered! Let's check out how to get some blue teamer skills.

Guarding all the doors

There are many, many skills that cybersecurity defenders can learn about to be more proficient at their job. This section will teach you about defensive skill development through analyzing actual malicious network traffic for indicators of compromise and interesting attributes.

There are whole books dedicated to just learning about blue team skills. This section of this book covers just a few of those many skills, but it is intended to give you a good taste of that world and to give you practical hands-on experience. We will gain some experience with **Wireshark**, a network traffic analysis tool, and take a brief look at malware analysis.

Wireshark is a network analysis tool that every cybersecurity professional should be familiar with, especially if you're going to be a blue team or a security operations analyst. Wireshark analyzes network **packet capture** (**PCAP**) files. PCAP files are captured network traffic files.

Wireshark has a nice, clean graphical user interface that color codes elements and allows you, as a user, to pivot around quickly on different protocols and really analyze traffic to look for malicious behavior, such as callouts to **Command-and-Control** (**C2**) servers.

You can download Wireshark for free here: `https://www.wireshark.org/download.html`. You can opt to use the portable version of Wireshark or the full application.

When you launch Wireshark, it will not look very interesting. You will be asked to capture network traffic or open a PCAP file. You can capture your own network traffic, but this won't be as useful for developing blue team skills.

We will utilize some previously captured and interesting network traffic from a website called **malware traffic analysis**. This site can be accessed here: `https://malware-traffic-analysis.net`.

> **Important note**
>
> A word of caution on the upcoming practices: statically analyzing malicious traffic does not introduce cybersecurity risks to you or your systems. If you do *carve* out malicious files from network traffic and save them to your systems, you introduce the risk of accidently executing those files on your system, which could potentially result in a system compromise. Use caution when working with malicious files and do not carve out files unless you are comfortable handling them.

Brad, the author of the malware traffic analysis website, whose Twitter handle is `@malware_traffic`, provides a lot of materials, including a section that helps you develop and learn techniques for analyzing malicious network traffic. If you find this section interesting, I encourage you to check out the other tutorials and resources on this site.

One of the best ways to learn about Wireshark for security operations work is to actually look at malicious traffic, work through it, and analyze it. When you're done, you can add to your resume that you have analyzed malicious network traffic.

Again, if you are not comfortable working with malware or you're just kind of easing into the cyber industry, I'd encourage you just to stick to the labs that use PCAP files and not go with the ones that have the malicious executables in them.

The following screenshot shows the malware traffic analysis website training exercises section, where you can download lab materials and exercises to work through and gain experience. Additionally, **Okay-boomer** is highlighted for your convenience. These are the materials we will be using for this exercise:

TRAFFIC ANALYSIS EXERCISES

- 2021-02-08 – **Traffic analysis exercise - AscoLimited**
- 2021-01-21 – **Traffic analysis exercise - WokeMountain**

- 2020-12-31 – **Traffic analysis quiz - Pcaps for an ISC diary**
- 2020-12-03 – **Traffic analysis quiz - Pcap and alerts for an ISC diary**
- 2020-11-13 – **Traffic analysis exercise - Quiethub**
- 2020-11-10 – **Traffic analysis quiz - Pcap and alerts for an ISC diary**
- 2020-10-22 – **Traffic analysis exercise - Omegacast**
- 2020-09-25 – **Traffic analysis exercise - Trouble Alert**
- 2020-09-14 – **Traffic analysis quiz - Pcap and alerts for an ISC diary**
- 2020-08-21 – **Traffic analysis exercise - Pizza-Bender**
- 2020-08-04 – **Traffic analysis quiz - Pcap and alerts for an ISC diary**
- 2020-07-31 – **Traffic analysis exercise - Tecsolutions**
- 2020-06-12 – **Traffic analysis exercise - Frank-n-Ted (What's going on?)**
- 2020-05-28 – **Traffic analysis exercise - Catbomber**
- 2020-04-24 – **Traffic analysis exercise - SteelCoffee**
- 2020-03-14 – **Traffic analysis exercise - Mondogreek**
- 2020-02-21 – **Traffic analysis exercise - All aboard the hot mess express!**
- 2020-01-30 – **Traffic analysis exercise - Sol-Lightnet**

- 2019-12-25 – **Traffic analysis exercise - It happened on Christmas day**
- 2019-12-03 – **Traffic analysis exercise - Icemaiden**
- 2019-11-12 – **Traffic analysis exercise - Okay-boomer**
- 2019-10-05 – **Traffic analysis exercise - Tinsolutions**
- 2019-08-20 – **Traffic analysis exercise - BadBundt**
- 2019-07-19 – **Traffic analysis exercise - So hot right now**
- 2019-06-22 – **Traffic analysis exercise - Phenomenoc**
- 2019-05-02 – **Traffic analysis exercise - BeguileSoft**
- 2019-04-15 – **Traffic analysis exercise - StingrayAhoy**
- 2019-03-19 – **Traffic analysis exercise - LittleTigers**
- 2019-02-23 – **Traffic analysis exercise - Stormtheory**
- 2019-01-28 – **Traffic analysis exercise - Timbershade**

- 2018-12-26 – **Two pcaps I provided for UA-CTF in November 2018**
- 2018-12-18 – **Traffic analysis exercise - Eggnog soup**
- 2018-11-13 – **Traffic analysis exercise - Turkey and defence**
- 2018-11-01 – **Two pcaps I provided for UISGCON CTF in 2018**
- 2018-10-31 – **Traffic analysis exercise - Happy Halloween!**
- 2018-09-27 – **Traffic analysis exercise - Blank clipboard**

Figure 5.7 – A repository of malicious PCAP network traffic files

You will want to click on the **Okay-boomer** entry at `https://malware-traffic-analysis.net/training-exercises.html` and download the `2019-11-12-traffic-analysis-exercise.pcap.zip` file. Decompress (that is, unzip) the zipped file and ensure you have named your PCAP file `2019-11-12-traffic-analysis-exercise.pcap`. All files are password protected on this site. Go to the **About** page to get the password and read the disclaimer.

Open the PCAP file with Wireshark. The following screenshot shows Wireshark with the
`2019-11-12-traffic-analysis-exercise.pcap` file opened:

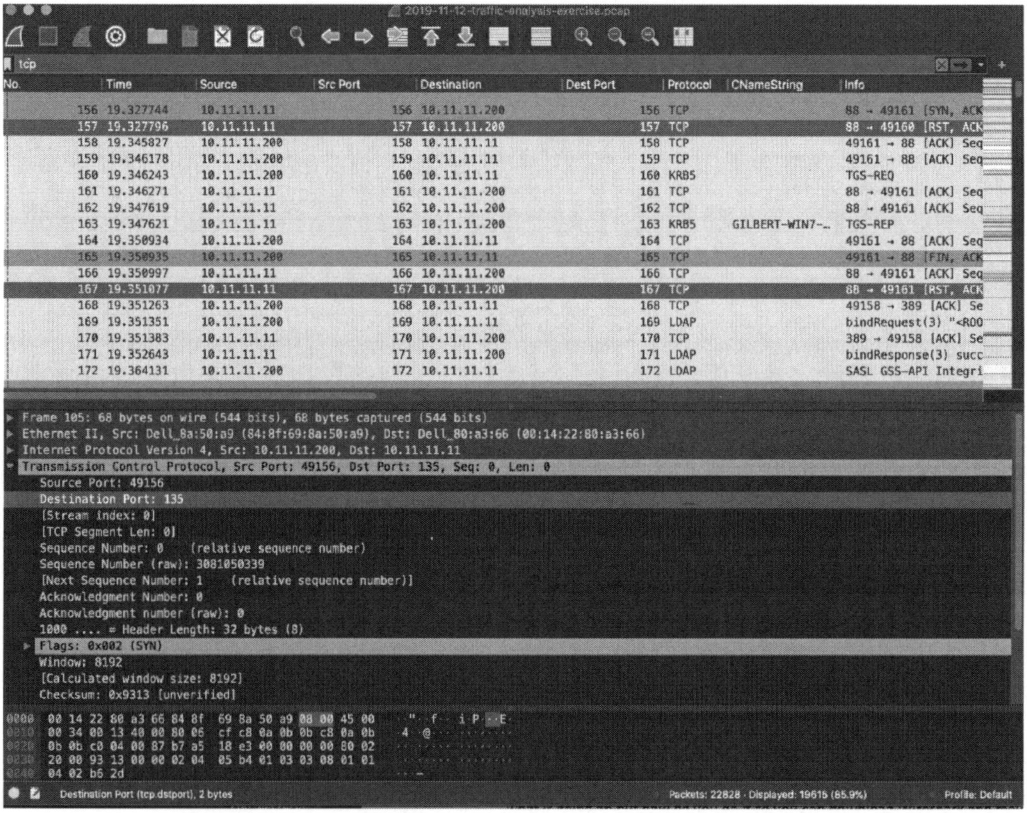

Figure 5.8 – WireShark with a PCAP file loaded and being analyzed

If you review the page where you are downloading the PCAP file from, the author
provides details about this lab scenario and tasks you will be able complete. These details
are important for analysis and make the scenario closely aligned to something you would
see in real life. These details will guide your work and make it easier for you to understand
the objectives you are learning about (so you can document them on your resume).

As a security operations analyst, if you were investigating and performing the tasks that
are provided as activities in the exercise, you would very likely need to write a report on
your findings. This report would facilitate communication with the cybersecurity office
or management. These tasks are realistic questions you would want to answer in a report
pertaining to this scenario.

Now, if this seems a bit over your head, don't worry – the author provides all the answers, along with step-by-step instructions on how you can get to these answers with screenshots of Wireshark. This allows you to try out the exercise yourself and gives you a helping hand if you ever get stuck.

The following screenshot shows the answer file for this exercise. It is 16 pages long, and the preview panel on the right shows the screenshots provided throughout the document to make it easy to understand how the answers were derived:

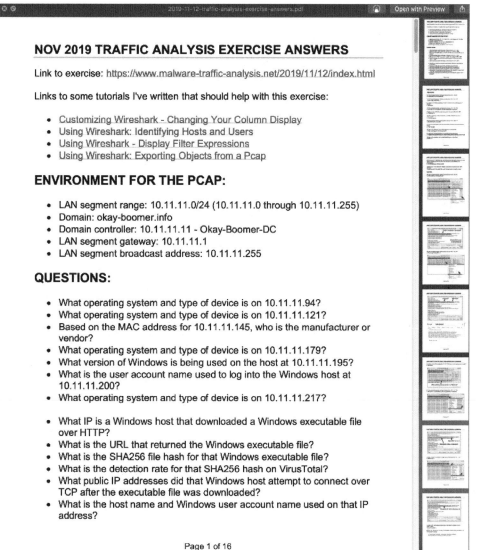

Figure 5.9 – A full walk-through lab manual is provided

If you are totally lost, I would recommend using the answer sheet as a guide. Look at what is being done on the answer sheet, then recreate it in Wireshark. This will show you the functionality, give you comfort navigating in the tool, and allow you to start demystifying what is going on with the network traffic.

Let's step through the first question as an exercise together. The question is *What operating system and type of device is on 10.11.11.94?*

Wireshark can take an IP address as a filter. Near the top, there is a text field, under the menu icons, that states **Apply a display filter**. In this text field, input `ip.addr==10.11.11.94` and hit *Enter*. You may be tempted to just put `10.11.11.94` as a filter, but Wireshark's filtering language requires you to define the argument that you are trying to filter on with the value (in this case, the IP address is represented as `ip.addr`).

Once you hit *return*, the PCAP file will be filtered on this IP address; only network traffic with this IP address is visible in Wireshark. The following screenshot shows this IP address filtered and it appears in both the **Source** and **Destination** fields:

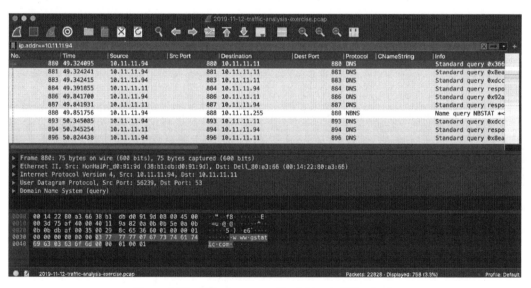

Figure 5.10 – Filtering on an IP address in Wireshark

This is great, but we are trying to identify what type of operating system and device we are using at this IP address. This information can be found at the application layer via the `User-Agent` string the web browser passes. If we add to our current filter for HTTP traffic, it will help us. This will remove network traffic that isn't explicitly HTTP. The following screenshot shows the updated filter. Note that the `&&` symbols represent an `AND` or concatenate the two filter values:

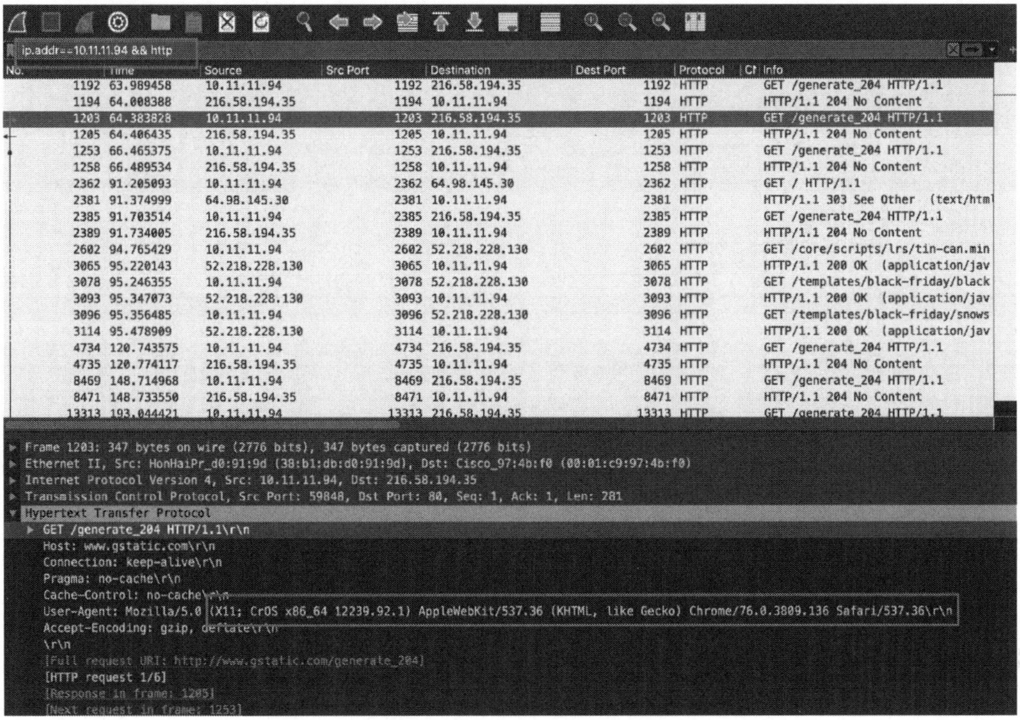

Figure 5.11 – Filtering on an IP address and web traffic

We want to view traffic where our interesting IP is the source because it will be passing its `User-Agent` string to the server. The first row meets this criteria, but no `User-Agent` is being passed. If we review the second instance (row `1203`), we will see that `User-Agent` is stating that this is a Chrome operating system and a Chrome web browser. Click the small `>` beside `Hypertext Transfer Protocol` to expand this section. `CrOS x86_64 12239.92.1` tells us this is a Chrome OS. This is the answer to the first question.

Continue through the exercises and follow along with the answer guide as needed.

More Wireshark

While you have the PCAP file loaded into Wireshark, let's explore some more interesting features. Select the **Statistics** menu option and choose **Endpoints**. The following screenshot shows where **Endpoints** is located:

| Wireshark | File | Edit | View | Go | Capture | Analyze | Statistics | Telephony | Wireless | Tools | Help |

No.	Time	Source	Src Port		t Port	Protocol	Ct	Info
1192	63.989458	10.11.11.94		Capture File Properties ⌥⇧⌘C ise.pcap	1192	HTTP		GET /gen
1194	64.008388	216.58.194.35		Resolved Addresses	1194	HTTP		HTTP/1.1
1203	64.383828	10.11.11.94		Protocol Hierarchy	1203	HTTP		GET /gen
1205	64.406435	216.58.194.35		Conversations	1205	HTTP		HTTP/1.1
1253	66.465375	10.11.11.94		Endpoints	1253	HTTP		GET /gen
1258	66.489534	216.58.194.35		Packet Lengths	1258	HTTP		HTTP/1.1
2362	91.205093	10.11.11.94		I/O Graphs	2362	HTTP		GET / HT
2381	91.374999	64.98.145.30		Service Response Time ▶	2381	HTTP		HTTP/1.1
2385	91.703514	10.11.11.94		DHCP (BOOTP) Statistics	2385	HTTP		GET /gen
2389	91.734005	216.58.194.35		ONC-RPC Programs	2389	HTTP		HTTP/1.1
2602	94.765429	10.11.11.94		29West ▶	2602	HTTP		GET /cor
3065	95.220143	52.218.228.130		ANCP	3065	HTTP		HTTP/1.1
3078	95.246355	10.11.11.94		BACnet ▶	3078	HTTP		GET /tem
3093	95.347073	52.218.228.130		Collectd	3093	HTTP		HTTP/1.1
3096	95.356485	10.11.11.94		DNS	3096	HTTP		GET /tem
3114	95.478909	52.218.228.130		Flow Graph	3114	HTTP		HTTP/1.1
4734	120.743575	10.11.11.94		HART-IP	4734	HTTP		GET /gen
				HPFEEDS				
				HTTP ▶				
				HTTP2				
				Sametime				

Figure 5.12 – Selecting Endpoints from the Statistics menu

For exercise purposes, let's revisit the first question we had for this lab by looking at the operating system and browser for the system at `10.11.11.94`. Select the **IPv4** tab and then right-click and apply the selected filter for our IP address of interest. When you apply the filter, the content in your Wireshark main screen will be updated accordingly. This is a great way to approach filtering if you are having challenges with the Wireshark filtering language's standards.

The following screenshot shows what selecting this IP address in the **Endpoints** menu will look like:

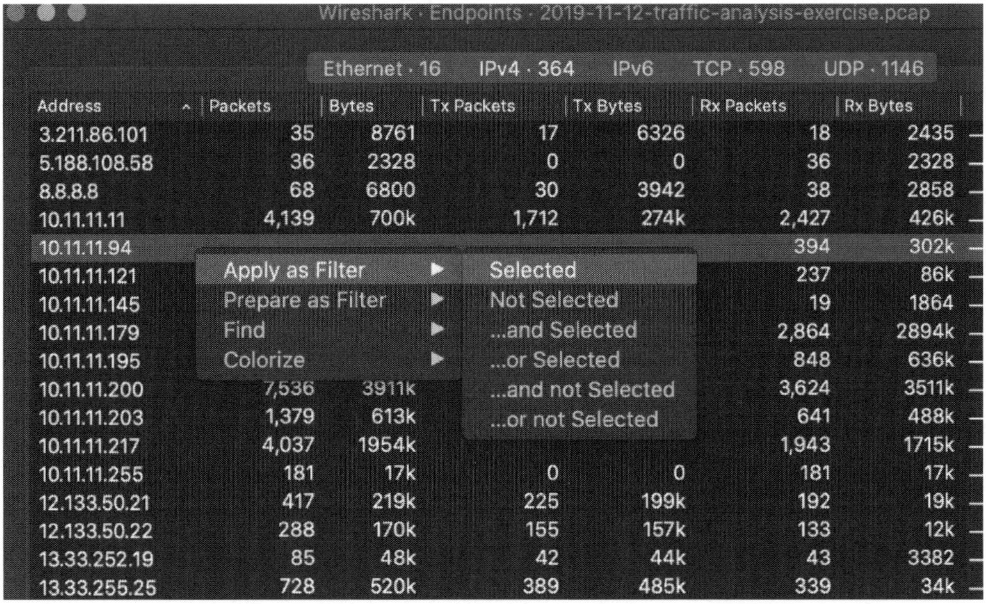

Figure 5.13 – Applying an explicit IP address filter through the right-click menu

Wireshark is now showing us all traffic for `10.11.11.94`, but we need to refine this query even further to find the answers to our questions. Again, let's go to the **Statistics** tab and go to **Protocol Hierarchy**. The following screenshot shows where you can select **Protocol Hierarchy**:

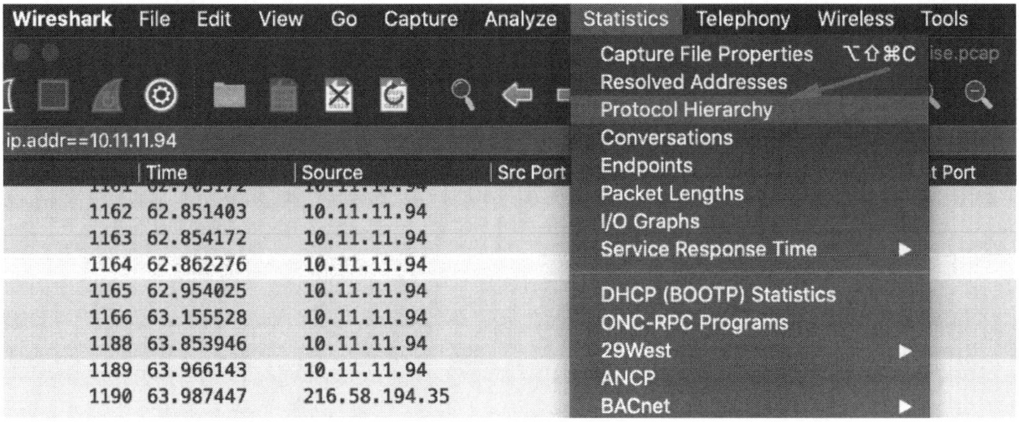

Figure 5.14 – Selecting Protocol Hierarchy from the Statistics menu

This screen is going to show all the protocol distribution statistics for this filtered IP address. All this information is interesting, but we're looking for HTTP traffic to get the `User-Agent` information. Even if you didn't know about `User-Agent`, remember that, based on the OSI protocol, the application layer is where details about the application and system will be kept. All the data below the OSI stack is focused on networking protocols and communication.

If you are unfamiliar with the OSI model, all you need to know is that it is the protocol arrangement for how network traffic traverses from one system to another. It will significantly help your cybersecurity journey if you understand fundamental concepts surrounding the OSI model. There are numerous resources on the internet that can help you learn about foundational knowledge regarding the OSI model. If you'd prefer my take on the minimum you need to know about OSI to work in cybersecurity, check out my YouTube channel, **Simply Cyber**, where I've made a video on this topic: `https://youtu.be/XgOF6GhiMuM`.

Let's filter on HTTP traffic. The following screenshot shows how to right-click and select filtering on HTTP from the **Protocol Hierarchy** screen. Be sure to select **...and Selected** as this will append `HTTP` traffic to the existing IP filter we just added. If you only choose **Selected**, you will remove the IP filter we placed in the previous step. This filter will be applied again on Wireshark's main screen:

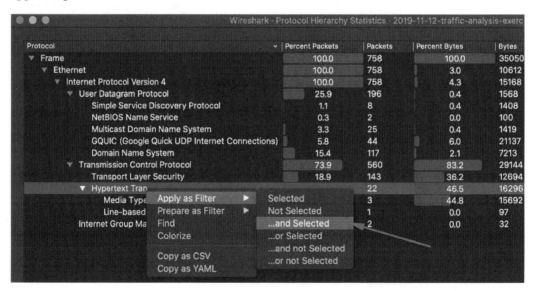

Figure 5.15 – Adding an HTTP parameter to our current filter

At this point, we only have this IP address and HTTP traffic shown on our Wireshark screen. Notice that the filter in the display filter text field is very similar to the one we manually created earlier. By using this click and select technique, you can start moving around Wireshark without knowing about the Wireshark filtering language. The following screenshot shows Wireshark after applying the two filters we discussed earlier. It shows the applied display filter:

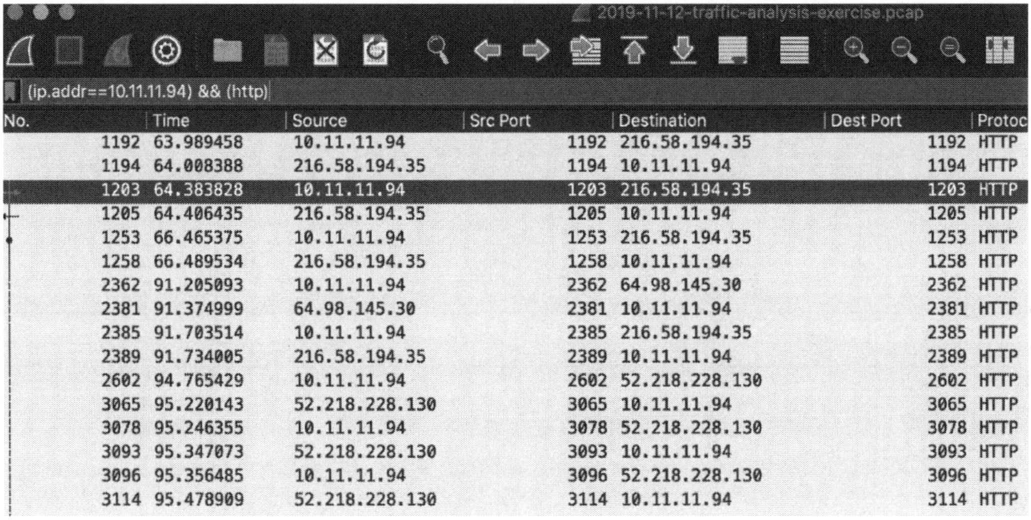
2019-11-12-traffic-analysis-exercise.pcap
(ip.addr==10.11.11.94) && (http)
No. Time Source Src Port Destination Dest Port Protoc
1192 63.989458 10.11.11.94 1192 216.58.194.35 1192 HTTP
1194 64.008388 216.58.194.35 1194 10.11.11.94 1194 HTTP
1203 64.383828 10.11.11.94 1203 216.58.194.35 1203 HTTP
1205 64.406435 216.58.194.35 1205 10.11.11.94 1205 HTTP
1253 66.465375 10.11.11.94 1253 216.58.194.35 1253 HTTP
1258 66.489534 216.58.194.35 1258 10.11.11.94 1258 HTTP
2362 91.205093 10.11.11.94 2362 64.98.145.30 2362 HTTP
2381 91.374999 64.98.145.30 2381 10.11.11.94 2381 HTTP
2385 91.703514 10.11.11.94 2385 216.58.194.35 2385 HTTP
2389 91.734005 216.58.194.35 2389 10.11.11.94 2389 HTTP
2602 94.765429 10.11.11.94 2602 52.218.228.130 2602 HTTP
3065 95.220143 52.218.228.130 3065 10.11.11.94 3065 HTTP
3078 95.246355 10.11.11.94 3078 52.218.228.130 3078 HTTP
3093 95.347073 52.218.228.130 3093 10.11.11.94 3093 HTTP
3096 95.356485 10.11.11.94 3096 52.218.228.130 3096 HTTP
3114 95.478909 52.218.228.130 3114 10.11.11.94 3114 HTTP

Figure 5.16 – Wireshark filtered on the IP address and HTTP protocol

Another great feature of Wireshark is viewing TCP streams. So far, we've been looking at traffic as singles rows of packets. It can be useful to see an abstraction at this level and see the whole communication between a client and server during a session. Right-clicking on a row and selecting the **Follow** menu item and then **TCP Stream** from the submenu that opens will show the whole session. The following screenshot shows a TCP stream, which includes row 1203 in our working PCAP file:

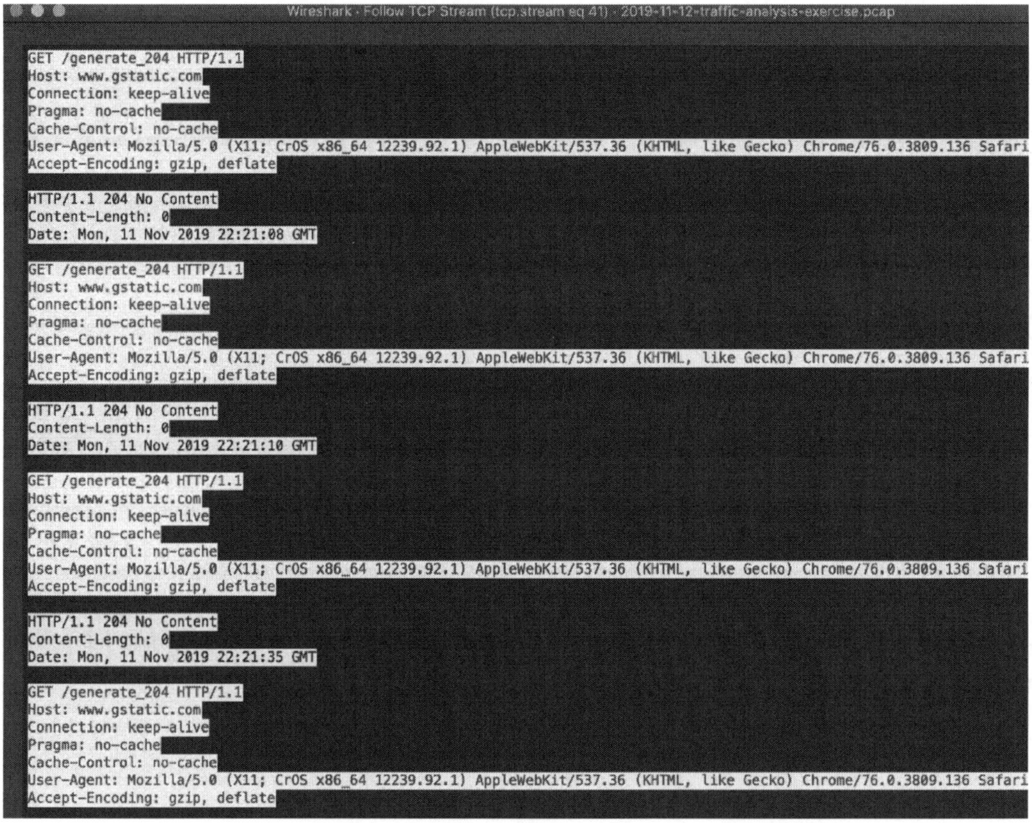

Figure 5.17 – TCP Stream assembled for easier visual consumption

Wireshark is a lot of fun to explore and can help you understand networking protocols and how traffic traverses a network. As you work through the exercises or explore, I encourage you to keep a notebook handy and document your findings. You may find something that seems interesting but not significant until later, when you have other pieces to provide context.

Documenting good notes and piecing disparate events together is a key skill of security operations analysts and can help you develop applicable skills.

At this point, you've gained some technical hands-on skills, but there are non-technical skills that you will want experience with to round yourself out as a professional. We'll dive into the skills you'll need and how to approach them in the next section.

Blazing your own trail

Building and working through labs for hands-on cyber skills is great, but there are more generalized ways of getting experience and socializing yourself within the cybersecurity community. This section highlights alternative opportunities from the traditional 9-5 entry-level position that allow you to apply cyber skills in controlled settings and develop practical cybersecurity experience through methods including internships, conference events, non-profit support, and looking within your own organization.

Conferences – more than just talks

Cybersecurity conferences offer an amazing amount of opportunities for you to gain experience, network with people who can get you experience, and to get exposure to many topics in cybersecurity that you may not naturally encounter on your own. There are many cybersecurity conferences to choose from and taking advantage of them should be accessible.

Some of the larger ones that you may have heard of include **Black Hat** and **DEF CON**, which are held annually in Las Vegas, NV in the summer. There's the **RSA** conference, **THOTCON**, **Grayhat**, and some other specific ones around niche areas in the field such as **Gartner's Identity and Access Management** summit or **CryptoCon** for cryptology. These larger conferences are attended by thousands, and also range in cost to attend and what scope of topics are presented.

There are also smaller ones that may be closer to your area. **BSides** is a loose affiliation of security conferences that are independently managed in their own areas but have a common feel and theme to them. You can check your local area by searching the internet for BSides and the city you live in or a nearby city and see if there is a BSides event. There are also local **International Information System Security Certification Consortium** (ISC2) and **ISACA** chapters, security professional member organizations, and host community events. All of these may be found in your area.

Regardless of which security conferences you attend, maxing out the conference-going experience is your best bet if you want to get that real-world experience that we're talking about getting you.

Anybody can walk into a conference, but how do you crush it while attending a conference? First off, the most obvious thing you can do is attend a conference as an attendee. Typically, there are many speakers sharing knowledge on various interesting contemporary topics in the field. Sometimes, there's multiple tracks, so you won't be able to go to all the talks, but you can choose talks that are aligned with your interest or the area that you're looking to get more information about. This affords you with awareness and knowledge about specific topics, concepts, or techniques in the field, and it also helps you identify thought leaders, public speakers, and contributors in the field.

Also, many speakers have social media accounts on Twitter, LinkedIn, and/or Discord. I'd encourage you to connect with me (Gerald Auger) on these platforms. You can follow and engage with these individuals after the conference to continue cultivating that relationship, as well as to gain information and direction from them in their specific area of expertise.

> **Bonus tip**
>
> Larger conferences typically record all their talks so that you can replay a talk you couldn't get to because of a conflict.

Attending conferences and their talks gives you a range of benefits at a job interview when you're asked how you stay current on topics (a common cyber interview question). At this point, you can reference the conferences you've attended, and you can speak about some of the particulars of these conferences. This makes you a more well-rounded, informed candidate and cybersecurity professional.

Another excellent way to take advantage of a conference for experience is by volunteering at the conference. All conferences, especially the smaller BSides ones, use volunteers to help them with crowd management, planning, setup, and speaker management. There are all sorts of opportunities for volunteering. Furthermore, if you are volunteering at a local conference, the individuals you will be networking with are often from your own community.

By volunteering, you'll get access to a lot of people and be providing a service by contributing to the industry. You'll also be able to essentially network and talk with other like-minded individuals in the industry, and you might actually find some opportunities to engage on certain topics, opportunities, and challenges that you're having, potentially get guidance, or find out about opportunities that you may not have already known about.

It's not uncommon for jobs and opportunities, whether they're for an internship or a full-time role in cybersecurity, to go unposted. It's kind of a hidden job market.

These hidden job markets are typically word of mouth through professional networking about an opportunity that an organization is offering, and they are looking for somebody who wants to fill that opportunity. If they already know of somebody or have a candidate in mind, they don't have to go through all the pain and trouble of posting, vetting, interviewing, and hiring an individual. The hiring organization can just skip to a light interview and then go straight to the hiring part. There are a lot of benefits of professional networking.

By volunteering, you are manufacturing the opportunity to network and get to know other people in the community.

A third benefit of conferences – and not all of them have this – is their **capture-the-flag** (**CTF**) events. Many conferences will host a CTF event in parallel with the conference itself.

CTF events are technical contests where players compete against each other to hack into machines, uncover flags, perform privilege escalation, and so on. This CTF contest is much more technical and it's a fun challenge, but the ability for it to help you gain experience comes from the fact that while you're doing a CTF event, you're typically interacting, networking, and learning about different types of attacks and different techniques.

Now, while these CTF events are contests and challenges, most of them are much more collaborative, and both contestants and contest organizers will provide hints, tips, suggestions, and guidance to players in the CTF that are stuck.

Some larger CTF events, such as those at DEF CON, often have vendors that will want to speak with individuals who place in the top 10 of the CTF event to discuss potential job opportunities. You have demonstrated your experience in the event to these organizations and now they are looking for people who have those skills, so it's really a win-win across the board.

Another technique that you can take advantage of with conferences – and one that was seen during the COVID pandemic – is connecting and engaging on Discord servers. Discord is a technology that provides chat rooms and engagement for certain communities. The following screenshot shows the official DEF CON Discord server. Additionally, on the left-hand side of the screenshot, you can see several other publicly available, cybersecurity-themed Discord servers:

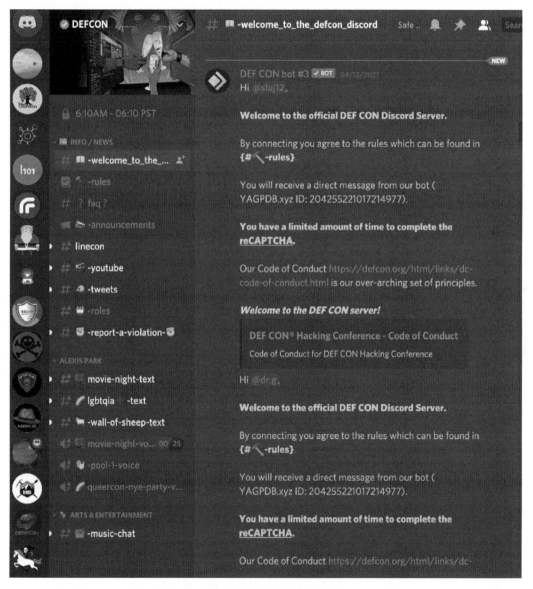

Figure 5.18 – DEF CON Discord server

Often, you will see that a conference has a companion Discord server associated with it. I believe this offering will persist even after conferences become in-person again. It's easy for communication, notification, and coordination among attendees and conference organizers.

Now, how does this give you experience? Again, there are a lot of professionals engaging on Discord servers. You're able to hear, see, and learn from cybersecurity people who are talking on the Discord server about specific techniques or resources. This may not be direct experience, but discovering a new platform, a resource, or a Git repository that has some value and interest to you is great, as you can then take advantage of it to further your own experience.

Hacking an internship

I can't say enough good things about conferences. Another really excellent way to get experience outside the traditional *having the job already* route is through internships. Internships can be very successful because you're basically working in an environment where you have low expectations put on you. You typically get assigned a mentor who helps you get acclimated and start contributing to the team.

You may think "*Oh, I have to find an organized internship that already exists, apply for it, and hopefully get selected.*" Fear not! That is a common way that most people consider the path to an internship, and don't sleep on that if you do find an existing internship opportunity in cybersecurity. I'd encourage you to apply, but we are going to give you another option.

You can get an internship in an informal way by simply reaching out to organizations. I would suggest that you target small-to mid-size organizations. Larger organizations often lack the flexibility for informal internship opportunities. Smaller organizations typically have less policy hurdles. Reach out to someone in their IT department or information security office. You can find these people using tools such as LinkedIn.

When you reach out, you should let them know you are an aspiring cybersecurity professional, as well as information about your current situation, such as that you are in college, looking for work, recently transitioned out of the military, and so on. Let them know you would be interested in helping their organization as an intern for 3 to 6 months. Share that you'd like to work alongside them in an internship capacity.

Let them know what applicable experience you have. For example, you can highlight some of the things that we've already talked about in this book, such as WebGoat and malware analysis. The point is to demonstrate that you have some cybersecurity experience and cybersecurity interest. Highlight that you'd very much like to get an internship in the industry.

Finally, finish things off by telling them you can contribute and would welcome the opportunity to get real-world experience in the cybersecurity field. Be sure to close with a call to action for the recipient. This means asking them if they'd like to have a call to discuss things further or take some other action. At this time, I wouldn't focus on the compensation status of the internship (that is, whether it's a paid internship). That is a detail that can be sorted out once you've discovered or created an internship.

Why does this work? Information security professionals want help. By capping the internship length at 3 or 6 months, the organization knows up front that they are not making a commitment to you that has no end in sight. From an organization perspective, it can be concerning if you're basically asking for a full-time job. If you say 3 months, it's easier to process and accept for the organization.

Now, here's the best part: when you get the internship, you can start leveling up your resume. You'll get work experience, so you can document that on your resume as an internship role with start and end dates. You will likely get experience with certain technologies and can capture that on your resume. This will add keywords that will help your resume navigate through HR screening and will better equip you for getting a full-time cybersecurity job.

It's important to highlight if you really are doing well with the internship. Here, you're going to demonstrate your abilities and your trust with that organization. This could potentially evolve into a full-time opportunity. As I mentioned earlier, the hidden job market is a real phenomenon. The organization you are interning at may not even have a job, but they think you're a great contributor, and they want to invest a bit more in cybersecurity, so why not hire the intern they already trust and who knows about their environment? I have personally hired three of my interns and placed them in full-time positions, in part because they demonstrated their capabilities.

You can get that experience and potentially establish a path for yourself to go on and actually get the job. I'm speaking kind of generically about what the business is that you're sending this internship request to. I did state a smaller business, but you may want to consider targeting non-profit organizations. Many non-profit organizations have difficulties funding staff and resources for capabilities such as cybersecurity, despite the need that they have for it. By offering non-profit or very affordable cybersecurity professional services as an intern, they're more likely to want to take advantage of that resource and give you that opportunity.

Note that you have to be careful because what you're offering is an individual who will effectively influence and touch all aspects of the business. Because of this reality, cybersecurity is a very sensitive role in any organization. You may want to cover this in your *how would you like me to be your intern?* letter to them.

Insider opportunities

Another excellent way to get experience is by looking at your own organization. Perhaps you're already employed and you're interested in moving on from IT, the help desk, or even the marketing department into cybersecurity. One of the best ways to get experience is contacting the information security office at your organization and telling them that you're interested in helping their office achieve their goals.

I know it sounds silly, but this has a good chance of being successful. The message to them should tell them who you are within the organization, what your interest is in cybersecurity, and what you already do that has some element of cybersecurity to it. For example, you may work on the help desk and do password resets all the time.

You should let the information security office know that you'd like to understand what the office's approach is, how it fits into the business, and that you'd like to become a security champion for the information security office in your respective area. Perhaps so that you're more informed, you can start attending some information security meetings that seem appropriate and support this idea.

Every information security office would love to have security champions embedded in their organization. The cybersecurity office will want to take advantage of this opportunity. This gives you the opportunity to become aligned and get indoctrinated with the cybersecurity office and the work associated with it. This gives you experience.

As your work engaging with the security office and becoming a cybersecurity champion begins to blossom, you will begin to establish trust and relationships with members of the information security office. You will be able to take on more opportunities within the cybersecurity office. For example, while attending these meetings, you learned that vulnerability management is difficult because the cybersecurity office has to follow up with system owners. This is communication and a manual grind. You could offer to follow up with the system owners because you have the bandwidth in your current role to also take this on. If successful, you can start to take on those experiences and then you can document them on your resume as having completed cybersecurity-related tasks.

It's important to point out you have to be willing to take on the additional work at no additional compensation other than experience. While getting experience can be great compensation for someone who needs it, be mindful not to take on too much, to manage the relationship, and ensure your primary job is still getting executed properly. I've known people who take on more and more until they are buried.

Instead of the big bang where you get the cybersecurity job, you start on day one, and from that moment on, everything you're doing is work-related experience, let's look at some alternatives that you can use to start acquiring cybersecurity experience. First, you can start building and leveling up your resume. When you do apply and interview for an entry-level position, you'll stand out among the other candidates because you already have cybersecurity experience.

These suggestions have been great, but there is another option that some folks have at their fingertips. This is leveraging the existing experience that they've already spent time accumulating. Let's take a closer look at how we can identify this experience and document it effectively.

Looking in the mirror

This section will show you how to look inward to show how you already have cyber experience and don't even realize it and, more importantly, how to showcase it on a resume. This technique is not exclusively for individuals pivoting from an IT career into cybersecurity, but it will be easier for those individuals with that work background.

One common mistake I see professionals make that are transferring into the cybersecurity field is that they think that they don't have any experience yet. I hear comments such as "*I worked help desk,*" "*I was a software engineer,*" and "*I was a networking engineer.*"

Whatever their work background is, these individuals take on the position that they have not worked in cybersecurity. In this section, I'd like to challenge you and your assumptions that you don't have cybersecurity experience. Quite often, cybersecurity skills overlay many different parts of the business, and most people have had some cybersecurity responsibilities or have developed some skills throughout their career.

If you already work in IT, you have an advantage in terms of making the transition to cybersecurity. Cybersecurity is not exclusively an IT function. There's quite a bit more than just IT-related activities, but there is an IT aspect to it. By having prior IT experience, you can take on and learn about certain cybersecurity-related skills and capabilities faster.

If you are a network engineer, you may have been executing cybersecurity tasking if you have done any of the following:

- Configured routers, switches, firewalls, and VPN concentrators.
- Configured network devices by setting access control lists on what network traffic can pass and what traffic cannot pass through the device.
- Ensured only authorized individuals can log in, validate, and authenticate, disabling accounts that aren't appropriate.

- Regularly patched your systems and applications.

- Subscribed to and made others aware of security patches for your devices and known threats that actively exploited those vulnerabilities. You may have also prioritized patch processes based on this threat intelligence.

These tasks align with vulnerability and configuration management, and you've already been doing them! These are cybersecurity competencies.

I encourage you to stop and reflect on your existing work and see if you can identify cross-skills that you execute that have a cybersecurity bend to them. Some activities to consider that may fit your background include identity and access management, encryption certificates, reading and receiving cyber threat intelligence, vulnerability management, configuration management, and risk management.

These are all core domains of the cybersecurity industry and you can capture them as experience. You have experience – you just haven't had the explicit cybersecurity job. When documenting experience on your resume, consider these elements and document them accordingly.

To continue with this network engineer example, tease out and highlight the activities that you have performed that align to cybersecurity. Maybe you managed **Public Key Infrastructure (PKI)** certificates on those network devices or generated new ones when the old certificates expired.

Perhaps you're responsible for the business's wireless network and how devices authenticate to it. If it's user accounts with passwords, and if you've configured and manage them, then you are responsible for access control – a very important domain in cybersecurity – then highlight it as experience.

Let's step away from the technical elements for a moment. As I mentioned previously, one aspect of cybersecurity that's critically important is effective communication and security awareness training.

It can be a bit boring and overlooked as important, but end user security awareness training is an incredibly important cybersecurity control that helps protect an organization. It would be invaluable to capture your experience with user training, leading workshops, or giving briefings to different audiences as work experience that can be applied directly to cybersecurity. Different audiences could be general corporate users, executives, steering committees, customers, or a specific department.

You could extrapolate and demonstrate your ability to give security awareness training to specific audiences, such as executives, on the importance or the issue of business email compromise. Alternatively, you could give a targeted talk to end users about the risk of using their personal emails for work activities.

A cybersecurity office could absolutely use this skill because they need to get their message out and communicate it effectively to different parts of the organization. Communicating the importance of cybersecurity, what initiatives are ongoing, and what activities are being planned is all necessary.

You may even have specific cybersecurity communication experience. For example, if you work on a help desk, you have likely dealt with regular security issues end users have experienced, including password resets and multi-factor authentication initialization. Having helped these users with these challenges and communicating solutions, you can demonstrate this experience. You will want to capture and highlight this communicating capability in your resume.

If you have vulnerability management experience, you can document and demonstrate if you have been responsible for patching systems, be it wholesale systems, because you work in a system administration role, or just patching a subset of systems, because you work in a certain department and you've taken on that responsibility of ownership. I mentioned earlier that you can document and capture this as relevant cybersecurity experience.

If you are doing vulnerability management in some capacity, I strongly encourage you to begin engaging in regularly receiving and digesting threat intelligence feeds. Talos is a great threat intelligence group and publishes threat intel reports that you can subscribe to at `https://talosintelligence.com/newsletters`:

Figure 5.19 – Talos provides daily threat intelligence reports

Threat intelligence informs you about the priority, urgency, and criticality of applying certain patches to affected systems. Introducing this threat intelligence aspect to your decision-making process and making prioritized decisions affords you two things:

- You're executing risk management.
- You're executing vulnerability management.

These are two critical domains within the cybersecurity space, and you may not have been giving yourself credit for this cybersecurity skill and experience.

Finally, another way to both gain experience and demonstrate experience is by making security decisions in your personal life and documenting them in a blog. In this chapter, we've talked about how to develop labs and use them to develop experience for yourself. By creating a blog, you can demonstrate your accomplishments, reinforce your learning and understanding of certain topics, and implicitly showcase your ability to communicate. There are several free blog platforms, such as Medium, where you can post and document cybersecurity activities that you have worked on. Jax will dive deeper into this area in the branding section of this book:

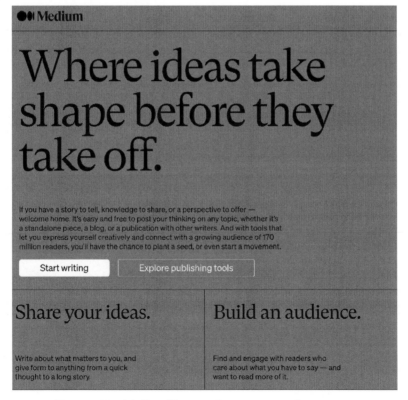

Figure 5.20 – Medium blogs are free to set up and easy to use

The preceding screenshot is of Medium's creator page, where you can start a blog for free. There are other platforms available and I recommend finding one that aligns with your workflows and values.

Summary

This chapter showed you how to build labs to gain hands-on skills so that you can experience working in cybersecurity. This will allow you to capture cyber work experience in your resume and to speak from experience during cybersecurity job interviews.

We also explored how to get a cybersecurity job and experience through internships and leveraging your current role. Internships and supporting information security offices at businesses provide you with real-world experience that is practical and helps you develop your skills.

Finally, we discussed how to take full advantage of cybersecurity conferences to professionally network, demonstrate your skillset, and learn about cybersecurity. I wouldn't blame you if you took a break to go find your socks, as I know this chapter blew them off.

Now that you have the necessary skills and experience, in the next chapter, you'll learn how to brand yourself so that you stand out among your peers and take the final steps to launching your cybersecurity career. Jax is going to show you exactly what you need to do to capture the brand that is *you*, the cybersecurity practitioner that businesses will want to help them secure their assets.

6
Time to Brand Yourself – Not the Burning Type

It's all about *you* and your brand, but what does **branding** mean? Well, I am happy you asked and I, *Ms. Jax*, will provide you with the knowledge to brand yourself successfully and professionally.

Branding is all about how you market yourself. To create a significant and cult-like following, you need a defined purpose coupled with consistency; organic followers are essential to sustained growth and follower engagement. Branding also helps with personal and professional growth. For example, branding builds a network that could lead to future employment and greater opportunities versus someone who does not have a brand or social media.

This chapter will explore and educate you on the various social media platforms and how to brand/market yourself across the various platforms. Upon completion of this chapter, you will have a clearer understanding of how and why to brand and the platforms to use for your specific branding.

The following are the sections we will cover in this chapter:

- Determining your brand and story
- Exploring the different social media platforms
- Considering a blog versus a podcast
- Engaging your audience to grow brand awareness

Determining your brand and story

Understanding your **purpose** and **vision** will allow you to understand your brand. Your brand is the **story** you want the world to see. Therefore, if your vision and purpose are not clear, it will be challenging to figure out your online presence/brand. Most people who lack vision have a social media feed that looks like an unchaperoned child in a candy store. That child is going everywhere, high on life with no path or reason. In the world of social media, more postings are not always better. Instead, the post/content should be brand-focused and consistent.

Think of your feed as a personality, and that personality is driven by what you feed it. Many people will evaluate you by your feed. Let me ask you, what do you think when you see someone who is posting cat memes, ice bucket challenges, and occasionally *save the alpacas?* I am certain your first thought is not, "*Wow, this person is really knowledgeable about InfoSec. I would love to ask them to speak at our conference or be my mentor.*" This is an extreme example but factual. More often than not, people feed arbitrary data into their feeds and the results will be arbitrary data and followers out.

This style of random posting works if you do not want to build a lucrative and sustainable brand. However, for those of you reading this book and realizing you are the alpaca person, it's okay; this chapter will save you, keep reading.

This is what I want you to do before we proceed further. Let's determine your brand.

Stop, take out a pen, and answer the following questions (take your time to ponder these questions):

- What does my current social media feed tell the world? (such as I love alpaca socks and cat memes rock). Try soliciting feedback from friends, colleagues, and family members about your social media feed.
- How do I want to be viewed by the world and my followers/future followers?
- What am I most passionate about within my life?

- What do I enjoy learning about and sharing with others?

- Does this align with how I want people to perceive me? If yes, how?

These answers will help you define your brand. Make sure you take the time to really examine what message you want to convey to your audience before you even begin branding.

Here is my personal branding journey. Before shifting my branding to where it is today, I was entirely in the space of being a special operations veteran who trained women in firearms and self-defense. I did non-profit work with organizations that combatted sex trafficking. My sphere of influence was individuals who enjoyed working in the physical security sector filled with many veterans and very few cybersecurity professionals.

When I decided to pivot into the cyber sector, I knew I needed to refine my image. I did the same thing I mentioned earlier. I sat with a pen and paper and started reflecting. I then selected people who I knew would give me honest feedback and asked for their opinion on my current branding. From that feedback, I refined my brand. My rebranding process took me a while, because I was intentional on how I wanted to shift my image.

Once I identified where my brand was and where I wanted to take it, I created a roadmap. I wanted to be viewed as a writer; therefore, I created a blog called **Beans and Bytes** and started writing cyber-specific blogs. I began by publishing an article a week, which I shared on LinkedIn. At first, I had minimal engagement around my articles.

It was after about 6 months of being focused and consistent that I begin seeing more engagement. Within less than a year, I saw traction building and my followers increasing. I quit posting on other social media platforms and I hyper-focused on LinkedIn. I did this because I had limited time, and I wanted my branding to be targeted toward executives. I did not see Instagram, Facebook, or Twitter providing me the same peer group I wanted as LinkedIn.

My personal branding decision focused solely on LinkedIn, and it has served me extremely well. Here are some numbers for you:

- **End of 2019**: Barely 600 followers.

- **March 2020**: Began building the Beans and Bytes website; followers around 700.

- **April 2020**: Refined my LinkedIn page by updating my header photo and overall data.

- **July 2020**: Began posting on my blog site and sharing articles on LinkedIn.

- **August 2020**: Began sharing more articles on LinkedIn; followers around 800.

- **September 2020**: Branding photoshoot to obtain high-quality photos for different events (headshots and lifestyle pictures).

- **November 2020**: Maintaining consistency with a daily post on my LinkedIn feed; approximately 1,600 followers. This is where my traction begins to build, and I call this compound interest with followers.

- **December 2020**: Set a goal to hit 2,000 followers by January 1 and did this by contacting more people and conducting more speaking engagements.

- **January 1st, 2021**: 2,100 followers.

- **February 2021**: 2,500 followers, maintained 3-5 posts per week, and began adding high-quality photos for increased engagement. Tagging more people in posts to increase follower engagement.

- **March 2021**: 3,000+ followers and increasing hashtags and quality photos and maintaining consistency with my other initiatives. I have an average of around 11 new follower requests per day. These requests are coming to me, I am not reaching out to them.

Keep in mind, if you want to increase your followers quickly, then it's recommended to message 50 people a day. I decided to focus my time on writing, grad school, and doing other things. Therefore, my LinkedIn growth is a little slower than others, and that's okay with me. I only spend about 5 hours a week creating quality posts, engaging with other posts, and responding to messages. I believe this is a minimum time commitment to maintain consistency and build your brand. If you put more time in, you will get a bigger reward. Do what works best for you and your lifestyle.

> **Tip**
> Another tip is when you attend a conference, seek out the other attendees by looking at the attendance roster. Find them on LinkedIn and let them know you are attending the same conference and ask them to join your network.

If someone on LinkedIn requests to connect with me, I always try and send a customized response back to them; here is an example: "*Hello X, it's a pleasure to connect and grow our networks together, ~Jax.*"

You would be surprised at how far a small, personalized message will go. Personalized messages show that you are authentic and not trying to sell something. It could make the difference between a follower engaging with your posts versus a passive supporter. Your followers are your family! When they follow you, they are entrusting you to guide them in a direction that helps them in their personal and professional endeavors.

Now it's time to define/refine your brand and the following are three simple steps to help you with this process:

1. Determining your passion.

2. What is your *why?* Create a *why* statement!

3. Leveraging social media like it's your personal marketing team.

> **Note**
> The previous three steps can be used across all platforms; the way you deliver your story will vary depending on the platform.

Let's start with the first step.

Determining your passion

I will use myself as the example with *LinkedIn* being the platform. I have a military background with experience working in *special operations* and operating a defense contracting firm. Before I understood branding, that's where I stopped, not realizing I had deeper layers I needed to share with my followers. This included my passion for cyber law and policy coupled with my executive leadership.

I created an outline of my branding layers, which are listed as follows:

- I am knowledgeable in military cyber and threat intelligence.
- I have a passion for academia and am pursuing my master's in cyber.
- I am a small business owner and an executive leader.
- I am a public speaker.

Take out your notebook and pen and spend a few minutes identifying 3-5 layers for your personal brand. Once you have identified your brand layers, you can add that to your brand.

I will teach you how to leverage *all* your experience, not just the most recent accomplishments. What you did 10 years ago is viable today. It's all about how you package and present it to your followers.

If you are new in the cybersecurity industry or have never done any branding, you have a clean slate. This means any content you begin publishing will be *your* brand. On the other hand, if you are the alpaca socks person, there is a plan for you as well. Both strategies need to start with clear intentions, goals, and consistency. With time, your followers will begin engaging with you in the manner you desire. Keep in mind, if you rebrand yourself, you may lose followers, but that's okay. When you adjust a branding story, it's natural to lose followers. The followers you have today may not want to learn about cyber.

> **Note**
>
> If you are unsure what field you want to specialize in or you're transitioning career fields, keep it simple; review cybersecurity news and share your personal thoughts on articles.

Writing like an expert

If you decide you want to write more, starting as a tech blogger can be intimidating. When all else fails, stick to the basics. If you don't feel confident with sharing your unique thoughts about a cyber topic, then share the original article. It's about audience engagement while showing your personal passion related to your brand. When you do share articles, a good rule of thumb is to write at least 1-2 sentences about the article. When people share articles with no context, it can appear as spam instead of convincing someone to read what you shared.

Here is an example of writing some context around a shared article : "*@ZDNet wrote a detailed article about remediation techniques to reduce the likelihood of being impacted from the most recent Wastedlocker ransomware. I am anxious to hear anyone's thoughts on these remediation techniques.*" The following is an example of a post from a ZDNet article I shared on my LinkedIn page:

Jaclyn (Jax) Scott
Founder ■ Managing Partner ■ Podcaster ■ Cyber Expert ■ Tech Blo...
1mo · 🌐

This is the second law enforcement intervention to remove malware from compromised machines without users notifications.

The first reporting happened around April 13th. I shared an article about the FBI having a court-approved order to remove web shells from compromised US-based Microsoft Exchange services without first notifying the servers' owners. Article: https://lnkd.in/ehTyUaK

Anyone else concerned about privacy? What cyber law covers this type of intervention?

Josh Jackson this is your lane. Can you shine some light on privacy versus security and the law which supports agencies intervening without organization's approval?

#privacy #cybersecurity #technology
https://lnkd.in/ekDZHJq

Emotet Malware Destroys Itself From All Infected Computers

thehackernews.com · 3 min read

Figure 6.1 – Example of sharing an article on LinkedIn

Sharing your thoughts on current cyber news will engage your audience while not needing to write a complete article. Another recommendation is to add a question. You can see where I did that in *Figure 6.1*, which created a great discussion among my followers.

You do not need to become a blogger to have a successful brand. You can easily share data and add personal insights to make an impact. However, blogging does help increase brand awareness and followings, and we will discuss blogs in the *Considering a blog versus a podcast section.*

Branding is a fluid process. You may go down one path and realize it's not for you. For me, writing an article every week became too cumbersome. I adjusted my approach by sharing other articles or writing mini articles on data I found through my daily research.

Once I began seeing traction on my blog site and other articles, I started to redefine my *why*. My *why* has changed a few times and in the next section, I am going to help you find your *why*.

What is your why? Create a why statement!

Your *why* will change as you move through this process. Finding your *why* will keep you focused; your *why* is your passion.

Before I launched my new brand, my *why* was not fully declared. It became clearer as I took steps by writing articles and engaging with more experts in the field. If you cannot clearly define your *why* from the very start, it's okay. In the military, we have a saying: *a 75% solution is better than no solution.* Don't get stuck on perfection then never make a move. Sometimes, 75% is enough, because you will find the answers when you move forward:

"Perfection is the enemy of progress."

– Winston Churchill

My initial *why* was to become a better technical writer and writing helped me learn. At first, I wanted to be viewed as a writer, then writing turned into a personal passion for me to dig more into cyber law and policy. My *why* then changed into being an expert within cyber law and policy. Eventually, I want to be a contributor at Forbes and consult at the congressional level.

Right now, as I write this chapter, my *why* statement is this: "*My why is to become an influencer within the cybersecurity sector who educates, mentors, and leads those less experienced while continuously bettering myself as a leader and expert in my field.*"

Your *why* should be your everything; it should be what drives you every day to become a better version of you.

So, let's find your *why* statement by answering the following questions:

- If you could be anyone/anything, who/what would that be and why? (such as a paid public speaker, pentester, and/or incident responder)

- What motivates you today to achieve better things for yourself and your life? (This could be your child or financial goals.)

- When you think about your answer to question *number 2*, how does it make you feel? (Alive, successful, or I made it!)

- *Number 2* is your *why*; it's the thing that motivates you to achieve number 1, to read this book and better yourself.

These next questions will help you understand your goals that are influenced by your *why*:

- What is stopping you from becoming the person you wrote down in question *number 1*? (This could be anything; write it down.)

- What can you do now to reduce or eliminate what is blocking you from becoming this person? (Only pick 1-2 things you can get rid of now.)

- Let's say all those barriers and fears were gone; what would your ideal title or job be?

- How will this position or title better support your *why*?

The answers to these questions will help you define your end goals and your *why* will support it. Both your *why* and purpose are key in understanding how to brand.

Next, let's review the purpose of social media in branding yourself.

Leveraging social media like it's your personal marketing team

We live in extraordinary times where we can connect in seconds with millions of people around the globe. Not all of us can afford a marketing firm to manage our branding and social media feeds. Therefore, learning how to leverage social media as your personal marketing team is essential for branding.

Branding and marketing on social media take time and commitment. A good rule of thumb is to give a new brand around 6 months to 1 year before expecting increased engagements from your followers. Unless you are an overnight sensation like the *skateboard Kool-Aid guy*, it takes time. Consistency and quality posts are key.

Each platform is different in their marketing tools. Make sure to research and figure out what works best for you. I have used the marketing tools for both Instagram and Facebook, and they worked well. What I found that worked best on LinkedIn were **hashtags** and **data consistency**.

I would not pay for marketing for at least 6 months. Let your brand develop and resonate for a bit. Get to know your new brand before jumping into spending money on marketing. You will be thankful you waited.

Next, we will discuss the most utilized social media platforms and provide insights on how to leverage them for your branding.

Exploring the different social media platforms

> *"In today's world, social media is the primary platform for digital marketing, thanks to the 3.80 billion social media users as of January 2020. That is more than a third of the earth's entire population!"*
>
> *– TechMagnate.com*

Is it just me, or does it feel like every week or month there is a new social media app? I cannot keep up, and neither should you. I will teach you how to be strategic in your branding by picking one, maybe two, platforms to focus on and then expanding.

First, we will review some of the leading social media platforms. There are many, so we will focus on the ones we recommend for cyber branding

In this order, we are going to review **Twitter**, **Discord**, **Instagram**, **LinkedIn**, and **YouTube**. This is not an all-inclusive list.

At the end of this section, you will be provided with a social media summary to help you decide on the best 1-2 platforms that fit your brand and audience.

Twitter

Twitter is a more relaxed platform to engage with other cybersecurity professionals:

Figure 6.2 – Twitter

This platform is great if you want to have a brand that is a little more laid back, with puns, humor, and memes; Twitter may be your pick.

The infamous 280-character platform changed the way we communicate in many ways. Between 2016 and 2020, Twitter was a means of communication by the US president (Donald Trump). Our country was informed by the former US president using only 280 characters, showing how this platform can spread information quickly.

> **Note**
> I am not judging the content of the former president's messages. I am using it as an example of how impactful Twitter has become in reaching millions of people.

The example of former President Trump shows us how powerful social media platforms can be for distributing information. So, how do you leverage it for your brand?

Twitter was designed to allow its user to post short posts with the idea to provide followers brief updates. Twitter does not have a recommended posting limit. On Twitter, you may see someone posting a dozen times in one day, especially if they are posting updates about a current breach.

This platform is excellent for providing real-time updates. Twitter was the first platform to offer near-real-time updates and it gained popularity quickly.

> **Note**
> The streaming access through Periscope was discontinued in March 2021. As of now, no announcements have been made for another platform to replace Periscope.

Twitter aligned its mission to become a central, go-to app for communication. There are new integration features that allow tweet sharing to Snapchat stories and eventually tweets on Instagram.

Here are key points I would encourage you to consider when developing a Twitter account:

- Have a good cover photo; avoid using a selfie. The more professional your photos, the more professional you will be viewed. The photos do not need to be done through an expensive photographer. Use the timer on your phone. Set up an area in your house or outside with good lighting and start taking photos.

- The cover photo is a piece of real estate you can use to market yourself. I would encourage you to use another photo of yourself but with data about what you do. See the following example of my Twitter home page:

Figure 6.3 – Example of my Twitter home page

- I have seen both a company photo and an individual photo used as the main photo. It really depends on the story you want to convey to your audience. If you want it to be about your company, then your logo might be the better.

- The *about* section is a great place to share more about yourself. Look at others for ideas, then create an about section that aligns with your brand and personality.

- Always try to cross-link, such as sharing your other social media platform data. You can link to Snapchat, a blog site, and other relevant pages. This is a great way to save time while growing your followers on multiple different platforms.

- Your Twitter handle can be whatever you pick. I have seen everything from someone's name to sed syntax. Be creative!

Twitter is a great place to meet others in the industry and still share your favorite cat memes.

Next, we will discuss the very popular chat platform called Discord. It's a VoIP platform designed to bring gamers together.

Discord

I am *not* a gamer. However, I am on this platform because it's an excellent tool for communication and collaboration. For many, Discord has replaced online forums; its VoIP design has become popular for digital distribution and instant messaging. You can use this platform for voice calls, text, and media/file sharing. It has become extremely popular among gamers and is used in some cybersecurity training platforms as the primary means of communication.

> **Note**
> Discord has recently added Stage Channels, which is similar to the Clubhouse app, described later in this section.

Figure 6.4 – Discord

Discord is growing quickly because of their marketing to gamers and the free voice-to-text chat app. Today, Discord is the most popular voice-to-text chat app. The app is free but there is a membership-based subscription. You can subscribe to Discord either monthly or yearly. Then you have access to the community. This platform is beneficial for gamers as well as networking. More cyber experts are using this as their communication platform while giving online classes, making it a great place to meet other pentesters, threat hunters, and more.

This is not a platform to provide daily updates. You can direct your followers from this platform to your other platforms.

If you are entering the cyber community and you don't have a Discord, it is likely you will eventually have an account. It's good to have a general knowledge of this platform.

In the next section, we will walk you through Instagram and the best way to leverage this platform for branding.

Instagram

Insta-famous is the hot thing. Instagram is all about photos. This is a great platform if you love photos. It's also a great platform for **direct messaging** (**DMing**):

Figure 6.5 – Instagram

If you don't have an Instagram, I would encourage you to create one for DMing and live streaming.

This app is great for live streaming. You could, for example, live stream a podcast recording session and use this app to field questions from followers during the podcast. I have used this app in conjunction with the Clubhouse app for the DMing features.

Figure 6.6 shows an example of a good cybersecurity Instagram profile. You can check out others like this and decide how you want to format your page:

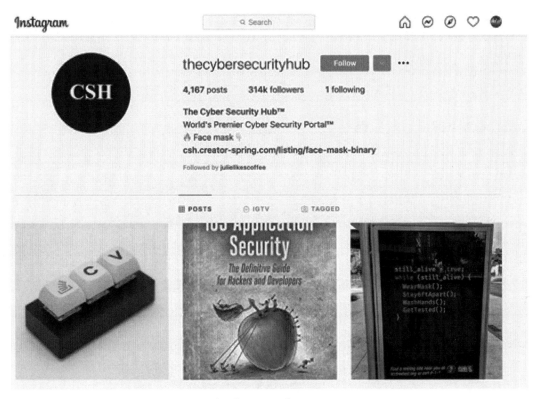

Figure 6.6 – Example of a great cybersecurity Instagram page

Daily posts are very important to gain and maintain followers. You could look into other outside apps to help with posting, such as Hootsuite.

Next, we will cover LinkedIn, a platform that is known for its professional essence.

LinkedIn

Prior to the pandemic, LinkedIn was a decent social media platform:

Figure 6.7 – LinkedIn

It had a steady following. Then, in 2020, COVID-19 hit and LinkedIn engagements grew exponentially. This is because of LinkedIn's mission for users, which is as follows:

1. Grow your professional skills.

2. Develop your professional network.

3. Make a career move.

In 2020, LinkedIn added more recruiting features for finding talent and for talent finding recruiters. One of the changes included new banners you could add to your profile photo. Initially, they started with *Open to Work*, then they added *Hiring*. See *Figure 6.8* for an example of these LinkedIn banners:

Figure 6.8 – Example of LinkedIn banners

This is a wonderful platform if you are seeking to grow a professional network within cybersecurity. If you are new to LinkedIn, I would start by building your profile and looking for others in your industry.

When you ask to connect with others, make sure you add a customized message to your follow request. If someone doesn't know you, they may not accept your request and you may come off as spam. Be clear on why you want to follow them and why you want them as part of your network.

Here is a template of a message you can send to someone you want to add to your network:

> "Hi, Their Name
>
> I love what you are doing at X Company. I am looking to connect with people like you to build a network of like-minded people supporting each other. It would be great to connect with you.
>
> Enjoy your day,
> Your Name"

Figure 6.9 – Example of a LinkedIn message to a new follower

On LinkedIn, it's recommended to post at least three times per week. The best days to post are between Tuesday and Thursday and the best times are between 8 A.M. and 10 A.M. and noon and 2 P.M. The worst day to post is Sunday.

LinkedIn, like all platforms, works off an algorithm. Your post will be pushed to the top depending on your posting time, consistency, and overall engagements.

Here are a few hacks you can use to get more engagements:

- Be the first to like your own post. I know this sounds strange, but most people don't want to be the first to like a post.

- Second, tag someone in the comment section. The reason you want to tag in the comments and not the post is it shows you have a *comment* on your post.

- Third, make sure you add suitable hashtags to your post to increase the number of viewers.

- Doing all three will increase your overall engagement and help boost you in the feeds.

To receive the most engagements you need to share your own insights and content. Keep in mind that this is a professional platform so keep the photos of yourself and selfies tied back to your business. The woman who I believe does this well is the CEO of Spanx, Sara Blakely. She is all about the inspirational coffee cup pictures as she sips coffee. Then she writes something about her journey as a CEO and closes with inspiration:

Figure 6.10 – Example of how to use a selfie while branding on LinkedIn

LinkedIn is wonderful for building a professional brand and using this as a starting point for other platforms.

The final social media platform we will discuss is YouTube.

YouTube

YouTube is hands down the most popular online video app, with over 126 million unique monthly viewers. This platform is fantastic for videos. You can upload videos and embed them on other social media sites making sharing content extremely easy. You also have a live stream option.

When you create your YouTube channel, make sure you fill in as much data as possible. The about section is your largest area to tell your viewers about your channel and brand. You can add other personal/professional pages, which will allow your followers to connect with you on other platforms.

You can pin a video at the top of your channel, so your viewers see it immediately when they enter your YouTube page. This is a great spot to have an intro video about you and your brand. The following is a great example of Dr. Gerald Auger's YouTube page:

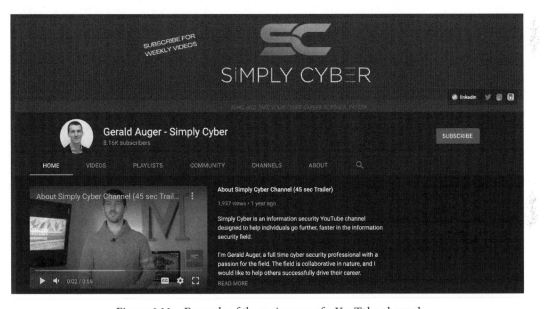

Figure 6.11 – Example of the main page of a YouTube channel

The following is an example of Dr. Gerald Auger's **ABOUT** section on his YouTube channel. All the screenshots in this chapter showing followers/subscribers are from February 2021. If you visit any of these author profiles now you will see their followers/subscribers might have doubled due to these branding techniques. Dr. Auger's numbers might have doubled or even tripled by the time this book is out in the market:

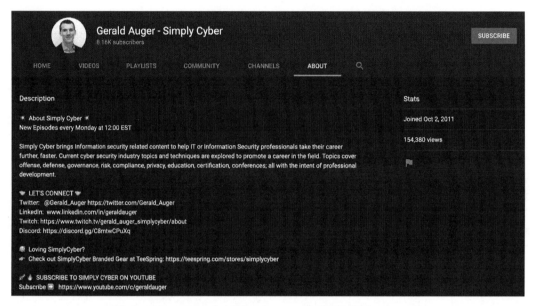

Figure 6.12 – Example of the about page of a YouTube channel

With social media, there is not a one-size-fits-all process. You need to research and identify what is best for you and your brand. Each of us writing this book use different approaches to our branding.

This section provided a summary of various platforms to assist you with understanding the difference between each platforms

Next, we will briefly talk about the Clubhouse voice app.

Clubhouse

As I write this section of the book, this app is still in the beta phase. Clubhouse looks promising and will likely have continued growth:

Figure 6.13 – Clubhouse

This platform is wonderful for all ages. Many people are integrating their podcasts and other media streams to connect with other like-minded professionals. This app is voice-only and works by creating chat rooms that draw in targeted conversation. Only the hosts are allowed to talk and be on "stage" while everyone else is a viewer. I really enjoy this app and believe it's a fantastic resource to grow your cyber network.

The following is our summary analysis of the eight most-used social media platforms.

Summary of the primary social media platforms

The following are eight different social media platforms and we will briefly review their overall target demographics and use:

Figure 6.14 – Eight different social media platforms

Let's start with Twitter:

- **Twitter**: Great for puns, humor, and short videos. You can cross-post onto Snapchat and soon Instagram. You can link other accounts in your bio section. The age demographics are young adults, millennials, and Generation Z.

- **Discord**: This platform is great for networking and communication if you are a gamer. A lot of young kids are on here. Great platform to build a following and connect followers to other accounts.

- **Instagram**: The age group is between 18 and 35 with over half being women. The platform is used for live streaming and photo content. The age range is still young adults and Generation Z. You can cross-post to Facebook and Instagram, live stream, and share stories.

- **Facebook**: More of an older age demographic; however, surveys show roughly 75% of users are between 18 and 44 years of age. Nonetheless, most young kids under the age of 35 don't use this app as much. You can live stream and share stories.

- **LinkedIn**: Over half the user base is between the ages of 25 and 34 years old. Great for building business connections and your brand as a business professional. You cannot cross-post; you can post videos and photos. You can live stream on this platform.

- **TikTok**: 62% of users in the US are between the ages of 10 and 24 years old. This is a great platform to engage the younger generation. The platform focuses on entertaining and short videos. After you have 1,000 followers, you can live stream.

- **Snapchat**: This platform is focused on the younger generation and 73% of the users are between 18 and 24 years old. This is a great platform that allows you to engage the younger generation; typically Generation Z and millennial users are on this app. It's also a great way to connect and draw users to other platforms.

- **YouTube**: The demographics of this platform may surprise you; of the primary US users, about 72% are between the age of 15 and 25. This is still a good all-around platform to connect with all demographics. YouTube is very good if you want to develop a lot of video content. If you begin to do more public speaking and online teaching, I highly encourage you to set up a YouTube page to share your recordings through your YouTube channel on your other social media platforms.

As we wrap up this section on social media platforms, we want to remind you that if you are seeking more integration or cross-posting capabilities, there is likely an application to support your needs. If the app itself doesn't do it organically, research different tools and you will likely find software to support your marketing endeavors.

The last two topics we are going to cover are blogs versus a podcast, two things that are growing rapidly within the cyber industry.

Considering a blog versus a podcast

These platforms and approaches are diversely different, and I will explain their differences to help you decide which platform might be best for you.

Blog

Blogging is an expressive platform and very individual-based. You may interview people as part of your blog article, but as a blogger, it's about you and what/how you write.

Blogging is a remarkable platform for new cybersecurity professionals to hone their skills and technical writing. I would encourage anyone who is entering this field to write more. Cybersecurity is just as much a science and technology as it is an art. When you write, you tap into the right side of your brain, which is your creative side that helps you as you research and develop products.

Get familiar with some other cybersecurity bloggers and their work to decide whether you want to blog. There are different platforms to express your writing but the best I have found for new writers is Medium. You can join for free by using either a Google account or Facebook. They have a small 5-dollar monthly fee if you want access to all the features:

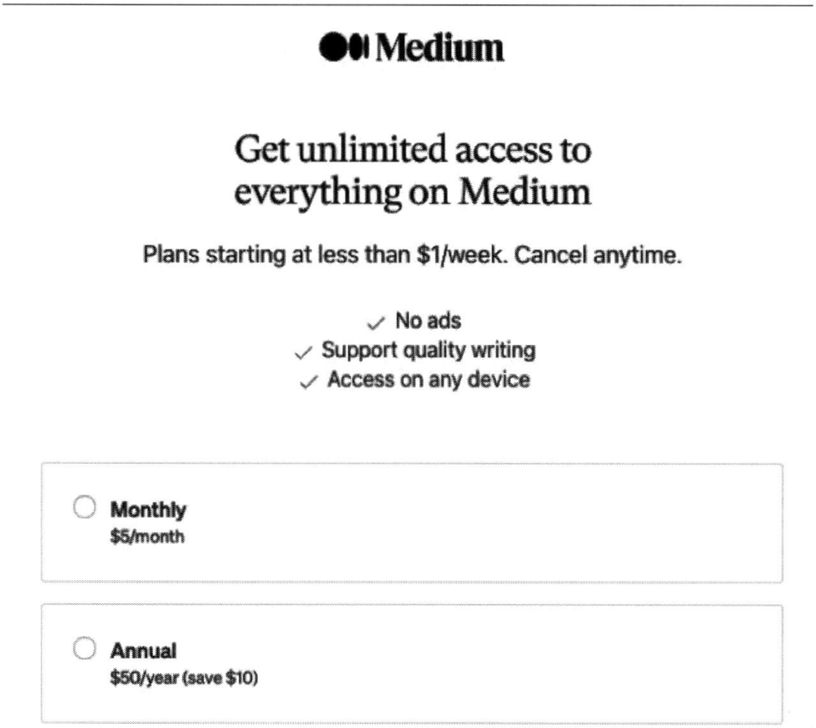

●●| Medium

Get unlimited access to everything on Medium

Plans starting at less than $1/week. Cancel anytime.

✓ No ads
✓ Support quality writing
✓ Access on any device

○ **Monthly**
$5/month

○ **Annual**
$50/year (save $10)

Figure 6.15 – Medium monthly/annual memberships

Medium makes integration to your other sites and platforms very easy, allowing you to cross-post to other sites with a few clicks.

Once you begin writing articles, if you feel like this is a niche you enjoy, then you can contact larger blogs such as ZDNet and The Hacker News to become an author on their platforms.

Here is a list of blogs and news sites with editors and staff writers we recommend:

- **Krebs on Security**: In-depth security news and investigations – `https://krebsonsecurity.com/`.

- **ZDNet**: Great all-round cybersecurity news impacting us globally –`https://www.zdnet.com/blog/`.

- **The Hacker News**: Latest hacking news, cyber-attacks, and general cybersecurity news – `https://thehackernews.com/`.

- **SANS**: Great all-around information about cybersecurity – `https://www.sans.org/blog/`.

- **FireEye**: Excellent intel source on threat actors and IOC data – `https://www.fireeye.com/blog.html`.

- **Dragos**: Very robust blog site with additional outside resources to help with research – `https://www.dragos.com/resources/`.

- **Talos**: Another very robust site that provides articles and podcasts to fit your research needs – `https://blog.talosintelligence.com/`.

- **ThreatWire, also known as Hak5**: Great for cybersecurity news in video formatting – `https://www.hak5.org/category/blog`.

I would start with the preceding blogs/sites to get familiar with the sites and news. I created a browser tab folder labeled **News** and added all the preceding links. Then, every morning, I spent 30-60 minutes reviewing a couple of the sites. Doing this will help you become more aware of current threats and with content creation.

Podcasts

Podcasts are different in their approach. Unlike a blog, your podcast is not all about you. It's about a list of topics, the vision, and any guests you have on the show. A blog site can vary with articles. A podcast is not as forgiving; you must know your mission for the podcast prior to launching.

Podcasts usually take less time overall to develop and publish than writing a blog article. However, podcasts take longer to launch than a blog. Most podcasts, unless you need to complete a lot of editing, are half finished once you hit *end recording*. Generally, article editing can take another 1-2 hours depending on what needs to be edited and what data needs to be uploaded. For podcasts, you will add a prerecorded intro and outro, do some minor edits, add the show content with guest information, and then you are done.

My recommendation is to have about eight episodes recorded prior to launching. If you have a backlog, there will be less worry if you cannot record one week.

With a podcast, you must be consistent. The recommendation is to post one episode per week. Maintain the same day and time that you post so your audience knows when you are publishing your new episode.

Here are some recommendations for podcast software depending on if you have a Mac versus Windows system:

- **StreamYard**: Very good for recording and you can also stream live up to three different RSS feeds on the basic plan: `https://www.streamyard.com`.

- **Alitu**: For compressing audio: `https://alitu.com/`.

- **Buzzsprout**: For hosting audio and sending it to audio platforms: `https://www.buzzsprout.com/`.

- **Spreaker**: For hosting audio and sending it to audio platforms: `https://www.spreaker.com/`.

- **Lightworks**: For video and audio editing: `https://www.lwks.com/`.

- **GarageBand**: This is standard software build into every Mac. It's a great tool I use and there are a ton of free "how-tos" on YouTube about podcast editing. No link because this is standard software on Macs.

- **Royalty-free sounds and music**: Great for your intros and outros: `https://www.bensound.com/`.

If you use a recording tool such as StreamYard, for example, you can record the video and use it on other platforms such as YouTube.

Before concluding this section, here are a few really good cybersecurity podcasts:

- **The CyberWire Daily**: Really quick 20-minute segments talking about the most recent cyber-attacks and global news

- **WSJ Tech News Briefing**: Less technical and more high-level news about technology impacts and growth

- **Hacking Humans**: Weekly episodes that take a deeper look at social engineering scams, phishing campaigns, and exploits that are making headlines.

- **Darknet Diaries**: This is a podcast that is longer than most (60 minutes) and does a great job of telling a story of real-world hacks, hacktivism, and cybercrime.

- **DanielMiessler, Unsupervised Learning**: Great podcast for top news reports while digging deeper into understanding the attacks.

- **Smashing Security**: Weekly podcast that runs about 50 minutes and provides relevant cybersecurity news in a humorous manner.

- **The Social-Engineer Podcast**: This podcast is monthly and connects cybersecurity with human psychology.

- **Hackerz and Haecksen**: This is an inclusive cybersecurity podcast designed to educate and break the stereotypes of cybersecurity professionals.

I would encourage you to pick 1-2 podcasts and listen to them a couple of times per week. Work into this slowly; you don't want to burn yourself out. As you do this, you will begin to learn and understand the industry terms, helping you with your journey into this industry.

A summary of this chapter is knowing your audience, then knowing your platform. Decide which approach is best for you and your brand, then focus and maintain consistency. In time, your engagement will grow.

Next, we will discuss how to engage your audience.

Engaging your audience to grow brand awareness

The techniques provided in this section are not all-inclusive; these are foundational steps to help you grow brand awareness on any platform.

If you are reading this and have been publishing content and doing all the *things* we mentioned earlier, yet your followers and engagements aren't increasing, here are a few possible reasons why:

- You may not be engaging your audience in a way that resonates with them. For example, if you are rebranding from your alpaca socks, the current audience may not be interested in your thoughts on cybersecurity.

- It may mean you need to refine the content to become more engaging, such as adding more graphics or content to engage your followers.

- You may not be on the right platform. Review the summary of platforms in the last section and make sure you are on the right platform for your brand and target demographic.

Here are some general ways you can better engage your followers:

- Use more photos and graphics.

- Share 60-second or shorter videos.

- Share more personal articles with high-quality photos.

- Re-share friends' posts and tag them and others in your posts.

To build a following, you must be consistent, intentional, and strategic in your approach. Your followers need to trust you. Create and stick to one strategy for at least 3 months and watch your followers increase. If you start and stop too often, then your followers lose trust in you and your brand.

Here are the key things to remember when branding:

- Know your *why* and your purpose.

- Determine the 1-2 platforms you will target.

- Know your platform demographic, method, and rhythm to post.

- Be consistent; give it at least 3-6 months before you change your marketing plan.

- When you don't know something, research and ask for help.

Make sure to review the social media summary report we provided as part of the social media section. This is a great resource as you create your media/marketing plan.

Summary

In conclusion, in this chapter, you should have learned more about your *why* and branding story while obtaining a foundational understanding of the different social media platforms available. You should also have a better understanding of picking between a blog versus a podcast with resources to assist in your cybersecurity growth and branding.

A final note before I hand you over to Kim; if this chapter helped you find your purpose and refine your *why*, we would love if you shared that information with us. It has been a pleasure leading you on this journey. Best of luck as you move on to *Chapter 7, How to Land a Jay-Oh-Bee!*, in which you learn about finding a job, preparing your resume, and mastering your interview.

Questions

This has been an amazing journey. Here's a quick recap:

1. What was the number one thing you learned from this chapter and why?

2. What is your purpose?

3. Did you define your *why*? If yes, what is it?

4. Which platforms are you going to focus on for the next 6 months?

5. What is the number one thing to branding? (I said it multiple times.)

6. Do you know how many times I wrote alpaca in this chapter?

    A. 3

    B. 5

    C. 8

    D. What are alpacas?

Please reach out to any of us on our social media platforms. Also, reach out to me if you want the answer to the alpacas question.

7
How to Land a Jay-Oh-Bee!

In the previous chapters with Jax, Jon, and Gerald, you learned how to prepare your technical knowledge, as well as brand yourself. In this chapter, we'll land you your first cybersecurity *jay-oh-bee*!

I, Kim, am excited to join the ride with you again in this chapter. I will be providing tips and tools to help you find your first job or your next career pivot. I will provide guidance to help you set realistic expectations by using metrics within the job market. Résumé and interviewing tips to assist with getting past the gatekeeper will be provided in this chapter as well.

In this chapter, we will be covering the following main topics:

- When and why to pivot
- Understanding the cybersecurity job market
- Preparing your résumé – tips and tricks
- Landing an interview (and acing it)
- Extra resources
- Entry-level myth busting

Remember that list of dream jobs you created in *Chapter 2, Which Career Field Is Best for You?* Check it again and make changes if needed based on the knowledge you have gained between *Chapter 2, Which Career Field Is Best for You?*, and now. Make sure you have that list handy, as we will bring it to use again during this chapter.

Before moving on, keep in mind that everything you are about to learn in this chapter can only be mastered through consistency and repetition. Since the cybersecurity industry always changes, you should keep your profile fresh to adapt to this agile environment. Thus, to keep standing out from the crowd, keep perfecting your portfolio by revisiting the resources, tips, and tricks provided in this chapter frequently. The methods provided in this chapter are hands-on practice friendly, so feel free to try them as you read along.

The advice in this chapter is meant for people from different backgrounds and skill levels, regardless of whether you are an international student, a US citizen, a seasoned cybersecurity professional, or entry level.

Enough with this chapter's forewords – let's look at the first section.

When and why to pivot

Whether you are new to cybersecurity or currently in this field and looking for a change in career, there are questions to consider before making a career pivot. In this section, we'll look at some career pivoting aspects to help you decide when and why to pivot in the cybersecurity field. First, let's look at some *whys*:

- **Need a career change or improvement**: If you are already working in the cybersecurity field and not satisfied with your current position, consider a change in position, focus, level, or even company. Sometimes, it is the nature of the job that's not challenging or interesting enough for you, or you are ready to move up to managing positions, or the culture of the current company does not fit you. Whatever the situation might be, analyze it carefully to find the root cause of your wish to career pivot so that you can make the right decisions.

  If you are from other fields, trying to transition into cybersecurity, expose yourself to different options and required skills and poke around to see if this field is really for you. Changing career is a big deal, so make sure you find something you can be passionate about.

- **Cybersecurity provides a respectable salary**: This is another reason many are attracted to cybersecurity. Being driven by money is not necessarily bad, but working without any passion can't really lead you to a satisfying career. Thus, besides the good income, do learn about cybersecurity and its different aspects, and then find something about it that entreats you and keeps you happy while working. For example, cybersecurity is science, so if you are a curious person, you are in the right place.

- **You are passionate about cybersecurity and/or something technology-related**: This is great – you started off having what it takes to have a successful career in cybersecurity. Throughout the journey of getting the right job, there will be obstacles and challenges; just make sure you remember what got you excited about cybersecurity in the first place, and you will get there.

These points are some common reasons why you might wish to pivot into a cybersecurity career. There could be many other reasons, but whatever they are, when is a good time to pivot into cybersecurity?

The answer is: any time is a good time to join cybersecurity! As mentioned in previous chapters, cybersecurity is always growing, changing, expanding, and needing more talent. Thus, more professionals joining the field is always welcome – especially in recent years, where the working culture has been moving toward working from home more and more, making the importance of cybersecurity clearer.

On the other hand, if you've transitioned from a different position or field, before completely leaving your current occupation, make sure you have some test drives for some cybersecurity activities, courses, and so on, to ensure that this transition is right for you. Changing career will take time, so don't rush the process.

In this section, the main takeaways I want you to have are as follows:

- Determine the root cause of your career pivot, to make the appropriate decision.

- Cybersecurity always welcomes new talent, so don't rush your career pivot process, and make sure you test-drive your target position to verify that it's the right job for you.

Let's move on to the next section, where we will deep dive into the cybersecurity job market!

Understanding the cybersecurity job market

In this section, I will show you how to use **open source intelligence** (**OSINT**) to find the right cybersecurity jobs, companies, and other aspects that require research when you're looking for a job. To get started with this, let's take a look at the different employment platforms you can use to search for jobs. Then, we'll look at what information to search for when job hunting.

Employment platforms

First things first, to land a job, we need to find one. There are many online and free job search platforms out there, such as Glassdoor, LinkedIn Jobs, Indeed, Google, ZipRecruiter, CareerBuilder, and so on. These platforms are a good start for you to get familiar with what job search engines look like. At the same time, check out other platforms that are cybersecurity job focused, such as `infosec-job.com` or `cybersecjob.com`, and so on.

In the beginning, expect to spend some time registering for accounts with those platforms, and making your profiles look appealing. Remember, these websites are where employers go to find their next hires, and there is a chance your profile will be viewed at any given time. If that is the case, your profile should always be ready to impress employers if they happen to come across it. In the next sections and subsections, we will look at how to make your profile attractive.

Note that there are many other hiring websites or applications out there besides the ones mentioned here, so don't limit yourself to only the ones that were recommended in this book.

Searching techniques

Now that you know about some different employment platforms, it is time to do a lot of job searching based on the list of dream jobs you created in *Chapter 2, Which Career Field Is Best for You?*. If you have not noted any position down, pick out several cybersecurity fields or activities that caught your interest and slowly drill down along the way. From there, go on the hiring platforms and start searching away. But wait a minute – what exactly do you need to search for? The answers are in the following diagram:

Figure 7.1 – Job market research components

Let's take a detailed look at the different components of this diagram.

Searching for job postings

Having some positions you would like to work in is a good start, but you also need to make sure those positions are in demand. Thus, searching for job postings for those positions is essential. The results can give you an indication of what the employers are looking for. Expect that several scenarios might happen: no job posting was found, many postings were found, or some job postings have been listed, but the number of postings is not so promising. Based on the results of these searches, you will have more insights into the current job markets, which can help you make better critical decisions for your cybersecurity path.

However, searching for every single position in the cybersecurity field until you find the most promising ones is not necessarily the most efficient way to go about this. Fortunately, there are resources available that have already done all the statistics for you. **CyberSeek** is an example where demand and supply data for cybersecurity jobs all over the US is provided.

The following screenshot shows some statistics of the cybersecurity job market as of May 2021:

Figure 7.2 – Cybersecurity demand-supply heatmap

Spend some time to learn the heatmap, to find out which positions are most in-demand, which states offers more job openings, and to discuss the importance of job locations in the **Searching by Region** and **Searching by Living Expenses** sub-sections. For now, let's move on to the next section.

Searching by keywords

The position you want to apply for is the searching keyword you should use. For example, if you want to be a Network Security Engineer, try searching for Network Security, Security Engineer, or Network Security Engineer; several job postings should show up. The following screenshot shows an example of a search for Network Security Engineer on the LinkedIn Jobs site (as of July 2021):

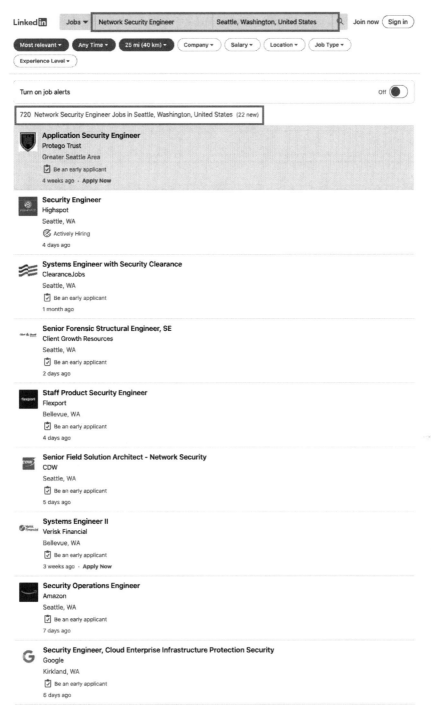

Figure 7.3 – Job search sample

Notice that by using only one set of keywords, we are able to find 720 positions open in a single city (Seattle, WA). Keep trying relevant keywords and even more results will show up.

Searching by region

In the screenshot shown in the previous section, we saw that searches can be done for a specific city or state. Depending on the position you are targeting, check for it in the heat map provided in *Figure 7.2*; you should be able to find the states that have the most job openings for the position you desire. You might be wondering, *"Why do we care about the location?"*. There are several reasons this location factor might be important to you:

- The region you are in is not the most in-demand market for the job title you desire. Thus, based on this, you can choose another position, consider relocating, or look for remote work offers.

- Different regions have different pay scales for the same job titles, so knowing the market price will give you an idea about your future job outlook.

Searching for living expenses

If you are willing to relocate for the job you like, make sure you know what you are getting yourself into. For example, a Software Engineer position in San Francisco might get higher pay than the same position in Seattle; however, there are other factors, such as housing and living expenses, to consider. Overall, living in San Francisco can be much pricier compared to Seattle, so if you get paid twice the rate, but must pay rent that's twice the price, will moving still make sense? As a result, knowing the living standards of different regions could also help you make a critical decision.

Searching by pay scale

As mentioned in the previous subsection, the same position gets different pay in different areas. Thus, it is worth considering the same position in different regions, or different positions in the same regions. So, where can we research salaries? There are several good resources out there, such as ziprecruiter.com, glassdoor.com, and more. Let's take ziprecruiter.com as an example. The following screenshot shows the national average of yearly income in the cybersecurity field, as of June 2021:

Figure 7.4 – Average cybersecurity yearly compensation

The preceding screenshot shows the average income of the whole industry, nationally and in the Seattle region. However, keep in mind that many factors can impact the salary of different positions, such as regions, company sizes, years of experience, and more. Let's get more particular results by specifying states, company sizes, and years of experience, as shown in the following screenshot:

Figure 7.5 – Average cybersecurity compensation based on industries,
company sizes, and years of experience

The previous screenshot is a sample search that was performed on `glassdoor.com` as of June 2021. Besides specifying company sizes, years of experience, and industries, you can investigate the salary based on specific companies, as shown in the following screenshot:

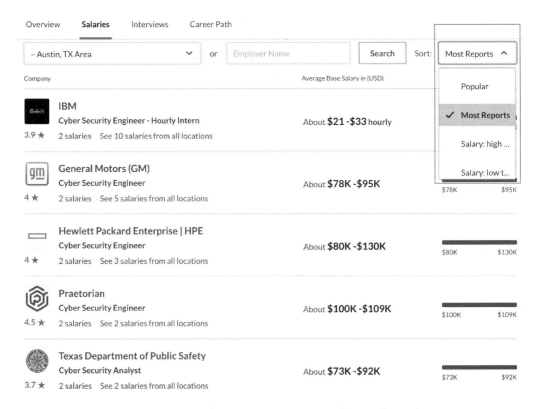

Figure 7.6 – Average cybersecurity compensation by specific employers

Note that the salaries found on this website are submitted anonymously by current or previous employees, so the numbers can change over time. Now, let's look at a survey that was done by Cynet in the following screenshot, on a specific position such as Security Analyst/Threat Intelligence Expert, and see how different factors can impact the salary:

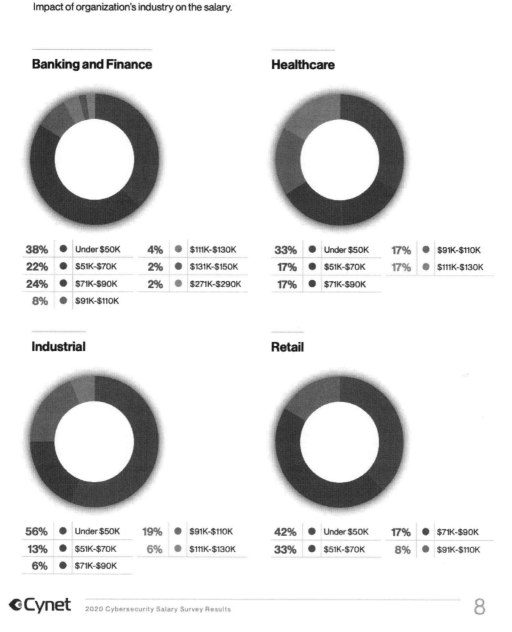

Industry

Impact of organization's industry on the salary.

Security Analyst/
Threat Intelligence Expert

Banking and Finance

38%	Under $50K	4%	$111K-$130K
22%	$51K-$70K	2%	$131K-$150K
24%	$71K-$90K	2%	$271K-$290K
8%	$91K-$110K		

Healthcare

33%	Under $50K	17%	$91K-$110K
17%	$51K-$70K	17%	$111K-$130K
17%	$71K-$90K		

Industrial

56%	Under $50K	19%	$91K-$110K
13%	$51K-$70K	6%	$111K-$130K
6%	$71K-$90K		

Retail

42%	Under $50K	17%	$71K-$90K
33%	$51K-$70K	8%	$91K-$110K

Figure 7.7 – Security Analyst/Threat Intelligence Expert compensation by industry

As shown in the preceding screenshot, some industries offer higher pay than others, for the same positions. For example, Banking, Finance, and Healthcare tend to provide higher compensation than others, such as Industrial or Retail:

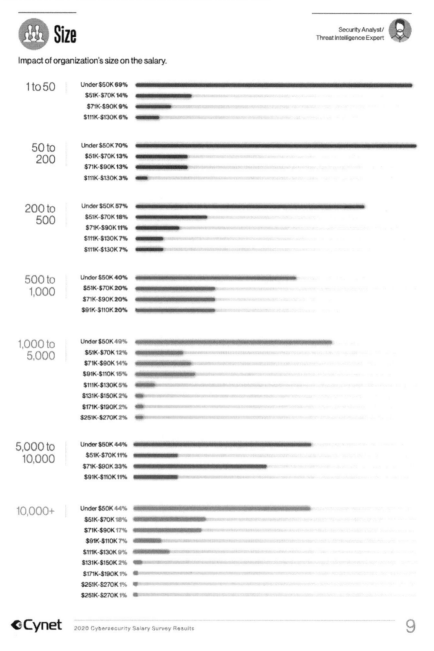

Figure 7.8 – Security Analyst/Threat Intelligence Expert compensation by company size

In the previous screenshot, we can see that the company's size affect the salaries as well. As the size of the company grows, there are fewer people getting paid under $50,000. Furthermore, bigger companies tend to have more salary ranges compared to smaller ones:

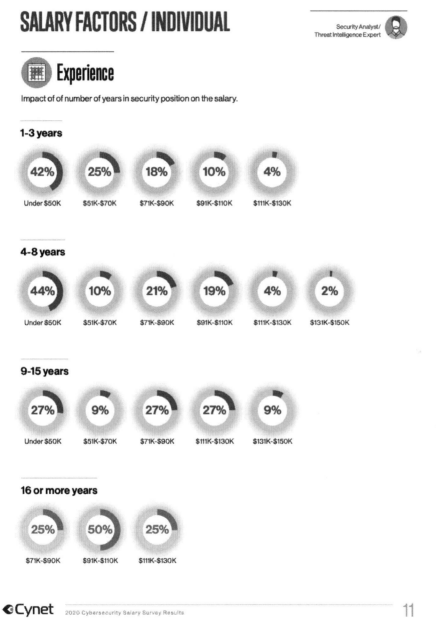

Figure 7.9 – Security Analyst/Threat Intelligence Expert compensation by experience

In the preceding screenshot, we can see that the compensation for the same position of Security Analyst/Threat Intelligence increases based on years of experience. The more years of experiences on hand, the higher pay employees can get:

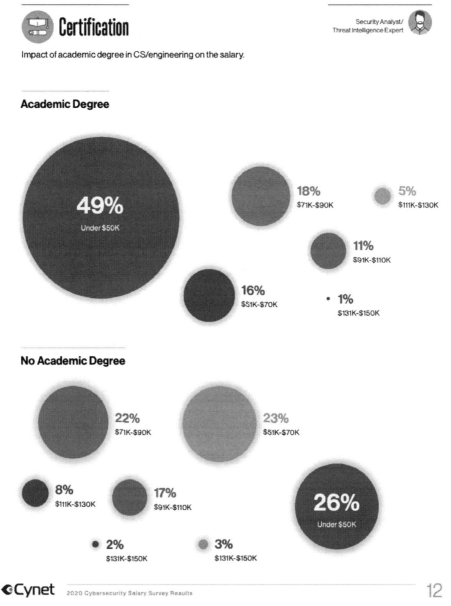

Figure 7.10 – Security Analyst/Threat Intelligence Expert compensation by certification

Lastly, the previous screenshot shows that generally, having an academic degree does not promise a better head-start in terms of compensation. Remember, even without a degree, so long as you have the skills on hand, your work will be valued. However, do not get set back by these figures if you are pursuing an academic degree. The takeaway here is that a degree becomes a meaningless piece of paper if you have no technical skill. Thus, instead of only focusing on getting the degree, learning, and strengthening your technical skills is as equally important.

As shown in *Figure 7.7* to *Figure 7.10*, many aspects add up to salaries for different positions. The survey that was conducted in those figures was done in 2020, but these numbers can fluctuate over time or based on demand. So, keep checking salary reports and surveys frequently to stay up to date about the salary trends and expectations of the cybersecurity industry.

Searching for peers

Let's assume you have several positions that you are interested in working in. Go on the internet and search for other people who are already working in that position, see what they have on their profile, how they brand themselves, and what skill sets they have – sometimes, you can even find their résumé publicly available. Why do we need to do this? Because if they are hired, it means they have what the employers are looking for. Thus, learning from them will give you a head start.

After researching several profiles, you will start to see the same patterns from the people working in the same position. For example, pentesters' profiles tend to have certificates such as Pentest+, OSCP, and so on and they may have attended hands-on practice platforms such as Hack the Box, Try Hack Me, and more. Based on these patterns, you can start building your profile accordingly, to match what employers are looking for. One of the platforms that is user-friendly to start this search is LinkedIn.

Searching for employers

Working culture is essential if you want to have a supportive and healthy working environment where you and your career can thrive. Therefore, spend some time investigating the cultures of companies in the industry, and find some that would fit your characteristics and work ethics. This research can be done in many ways: talking to people who are already working in the field, reading the news; performing internet searches, and more. For example, searching for `best companies to work for` could return thousands of articles, which will provide you with lots of insights, as shown in the following screenshot:

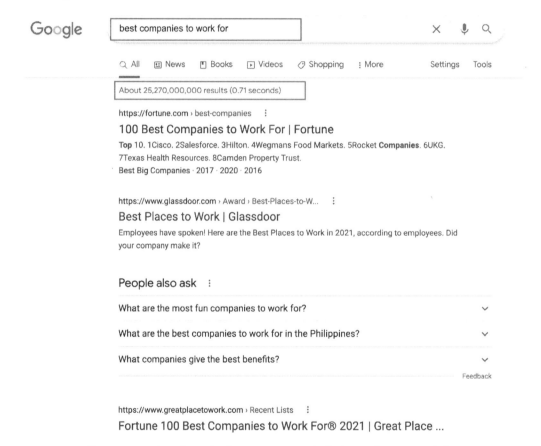

Figure 7.11 – Search results for companies with the best culture to work for

Several credible resources are glassdoor.com, fortune.com, businessinsider.com, forbes.com, and many more. Take fortune.com, for instance – as of May 2021, the top 10 best companies to work for are as follows:

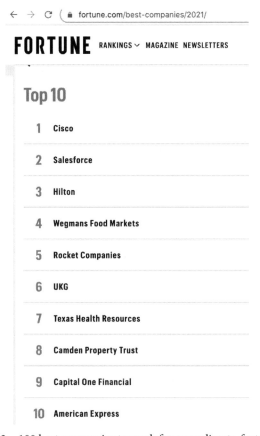

Figure 7.12 – 100 best companies to work for according to furtune.com.

Up until this stage, you should have a good amount of information at hand that gives you an overall update of the field's current situation. In this subsection, we have learned how to find the current insights of the field and hiring situations, to help direct your job search in the right direction. The following is what we have learned about:

- Demand-supply rates of different jobs in the cybersecurity field.
- The pay scale of different positions in different regions.
- Living expenses to bring into consideration in case you need to relocate for the job.
- Profiles of currently employed individuals who are working in your desired positions.
- Companies with the best working cultures and environments.

In the next subsection, we will look at why and how to document all the searches we did here, for future reusability and continuous improvement.

Ranking the searches

Job hunting is not a simple and straightforward process – it requires lots of study and trial and error, and it's easy to forget some things easily. Thus, we need to keep track of our findings. Although there are many options out there in the job market, not all fit our needs. As a result, ranking our preferences will not only help us plan, but will also be beneficial for interview preparation. In this subsection, I will provide details of what you need to rank and how they will benefit your job search journey.

Ranking your list of dream jobs

It is time to bring back the list of dream jobs you have created since *Chapter 2, Which Career Field Is Best for You?*, again! Check this list – has any of the information we've learned about in the previous subsections of this chapter and other chapters make you want to modify your list? If so, go ahead and make changes to the list before moving on: remove positions you think do not fit you anymore, or add more positions you think are promising. If no changes are needed, that is good too. Either way, let's move on to the next step!

Now that you have a list of dream jobs you like, let's rank them and put them into groups. Group A should contain the list of your most favorite positions, group B should contain the positions that are of second choice, and lastly, group C should contain the list of jobs you are willing to take on; you do not love them, but they are affordable. Make sure list A and B have no more than three positions in each of them. The following table shows an example of ranking job positions:

A list
Security Engineer
Cloud Engineer

B list
Security Architect
Cybersecurity Analyst
Penetration Tester

C list
Network Engineer
Cybersecurity Consultant
Software Engineer
IT Support

Figure 7.13 – Dream job ranking example

Why do we need to rank these jobs? Besides being organized and make things easier to track, there are three main reasons why I highly recommend ranking and listing desired job positions:

- The first reason is because we want to give ourselves plans A, B, and C, leaving us more chances to be flexible and open up to opportunities. Oftentimes, people found a position they think they love so much and put all their energy into getting that position. However, in the end, either they could not get that specific position, and must plan everything all over again, or they get that position, but only realize in the end that the job they hoped for was not what they imagined. Thus, let's keep our options open and put ourselves in an active place where we are not locked to only one target.

- In addition, while ranking your list of dream jobs, you have a chance to slow down and really think about each position you will put into the list. This is a very important process, where you will have a critical conversation with yourself by trying to figure out why and which job you truly enjoy doing. There are many factors for deciding on a *dream job*, but the most important thing is your passion. Thus, make sure you choose the ones that can keep you happy and motivated to go to work every day!

- The last reason is that you do not have enough time to learn everything. Each job requires a specific set of skills, and a decent amount of time and effort must be spent to achieve such knowledge. Thus, limiting the number of desired positions will give you more time and opportunities to focus and deepen your skills for those jobs.

Ranking your list of dream companies

A similar concept to ranking your list of dream jobs applies to ranking your list of dream companies: group A contains your most favorite companies, followed by B, C, D, and E, respectively. Be picky for the first two groups (A and B) since they are the most appealing companies you want to work for. Groups C and D can be companies you have heard of or know about that have decent working cultures and environments.

Group E can contain companies that you do not mind getting rejected from; they could be companies you found while looking for job postings, where there are several open positions, but you don't really know who they are, or cannot find much information about them. Notice that with the list of dream companies, we have more than three groups. I will show you the usefulness of the extra groups (D and E) and how we should work with the rest of the groups in the *Landing an interview (and acing it)* section, later in this chapter.

In this subsection, I have shown you why and how you should create lists and rankings for desired companies and positions. You do not need to perfect the lists right now, but keep in mind that these lists will keep changing the more you work on the job hunting processes.

More searching

In the previous section, we learned how to create and rank lists of dream jobs and companies. In this section, we will do more searching based on those lists and make changes to them accordingly along the way.

Searching by employers, again

This time, let's tailor your search to be more cybersecurity field focused, by looking for leading cybersecurity companies or the best cybersecurity companies to work for and learn about them, including what they do, their employees' satisfaction rates, and so on. If you found any that caught your interest, add them to your list of dream companies and rank them using the same ranking rule we introduced in the previous section.

Searching by employees, again

In the previous subsection, we searched for the employees that are working in the positions you like. This time, let's change the search up a little by searching for people who are working in the same position *and companies* you want to be in. Pay attention to how they express themselves and what specific skills they have, and then repeat the same search for several people in each organization.

For instance, one company tends to have more than one Security Analyst, so try to find as many profiles as you can to draw out some commonalities in their portfolio. This way, you will have more of an idea of what your favorite companies are looking for in someone who wants to apply to certain positions. Once you have found those employees, look for their teammates as well, and try to confirm if their team dynamics and culture are what you expected.

Lastly, if you find a team you like, reach out to a member of the team directly and ask if their team is looking for a new member, or if they are willing to refer you into the company. Most of the time, people are willing to respond to you. However, sometimes, it is a hit or miss scenario, so do not be discouraged if you receive *no* as the answer, or do not receive any answer at all.

While searching, there might be some outstanding profiles that catch your attention. If that is the case, save their profiles for later reference. Later, in the *How to prepare for your résumé* section, you can pull up their profiles again and mimic the wordings they used.

Searching by job description

So far, we have lists of companies and positions we want to work for. We also have a list of people we might want to be our future teammates. Let's analyze job descriptions for the positions you like in detail, to find out which technical skills are required or desired. Look for job postings for the same position in different companies, including the ones in your dream companies list, to find similar patterns and requirements. Let's take Penetration Testers as an example. The following screenshot shows the required skills for Penetration Testers from four job postings from different companies, where all the similar technical requirements are marked in red:

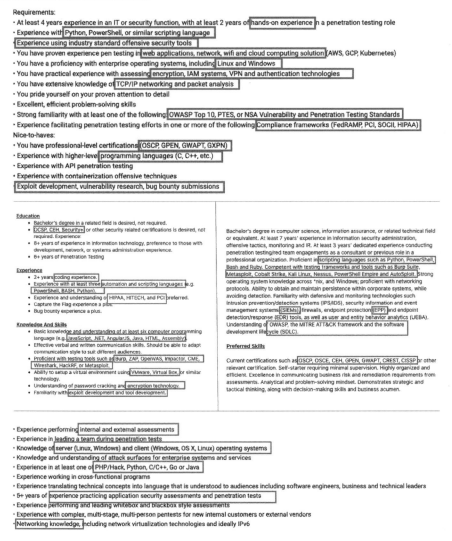

Figure 7.14 – Job description and requirement examples

In the preceding screenshot, based on only four postings, we can find out a fair number of common requirements for Penetration Testing positions, including, but not limited to, the following:

- Experience in programming/scripting languages such as Python, C, PowerShell, and more

- Understanding of networking

- Hands-on experience in pentesting

- Certificates such as OSCP, CISSP, and more

These required or desired skills, certificates, and knowledge are what you should ensure you have before the job interview. Thus, note them down and start learning as soon as possible. Some skills might require more time than others to master; consequently, the earlier you start, the better you can be. In terms of certificates, several of them were introduced in *Chapter 4, Exploring Certifications and College*, so feel free to revisit that chapter if needed.

One thing to note when looking at the job descriptions is that some companies might require more years of experience than others. This depends on their standards and needs. Therefore, do not let the required number of years of experience scare you. If you really have the skills, knowledge, and willingness to learn, companies will want you!

Good job! You have made it to the end of this section, where we learned how to use OSINT to collect information from people, platforms, companies, and job postings, to prepare our profile. In the next section, we'll showcase what you have learned in this section through your résumé.

Preparing your résumé – tips and tricks

To land a job, there are many gates you must go through, including preparing, applying, interviewing, and so on. A résumé is a ticket to get you through the first gate. Each day, companies receive hundreds of applications, and if viewed, each résumé only gets a couple of seconds viewing time. So, your résumé should be concise, crisp, and attractive to catch the employer's attention at first glance. We'll look at how this goal can be achieved in this section.

Keep the résumé short

Unless you have years of experience in the field, your résumé should be no more than a page, especially if you are a new graduate. Always keep in mind that the hiring person only has around 6-7 seconds to look at your résumé. Therefore, if you are applying for an entry level and submitting a three-page résumé, chances are the second and third pages will not be viewed. If you really need to use more than one page, make sure the most important information is listed on the first page.

Include only relevant and important information

As mentioned previously, employers will skim through your résumé in a short period of time, so only leave the most relevant information in it. For example, some people like to put their personal activities, such as *playing sports in their free time*. This information is not valuable to the employers at the résumé review stage. Understand that at the stage of scanning résumés, employers are mainly looking for the technical and soft skills, education, and technical projects. However, as a new graduate, if you have extracurricular activities, such as attending competitions or joining student clubs, this would be beneficial as well.

Sometimes, unrelated work experience is acceptable

As mentioned in the previous section, you should try to avoid as much irrelevant information as possible. This includes work experience. If you are applying for a position in the Information Technology field, positions in other fields such as Customer Service may seem to be unrelated. For instance, listing waiter/waitress experience in a Cybersecurity Analyst résumé should not be your first choice. Instead, choose the experiences you have that are more related to the job you are aiming for.

Experience does not have to be work only – it can be personal projects, volunteer work, courses completed, student clubs, or others. However, if you do not have any related experience, instead of a blank résumé, having any experience is obviously better. In this case, describe those experiences to make them as related as possible. For example, as a waiter/waitress, you are exposed to online and instore transactions, which can be subjected to cyber attacks or frauds. Thus, you have cybersecurity experience as a user, who knows how to handle secured transactions. Try to make the most out of what you have on hand, and never leave a résumé blank.

Utilize keywords

In most cases, before your résumé is viewed by an actual person, it must past the automated screener, commonly known as the **Applicant Tracking System (ATS)**, where AI is used to match your résumé with the specific job posting you applied for. This process is done based on keywords. Let's use the example in *Figure 7.14* again, for if you applied for a Penetration Tester position, and in the job posting, keywords such as Python, TCP/IP, OWASP, security assessment, and penetration test showed up – you should try to have those keywords in your résumé as well. The more keywords in your résumé that match the job posting, the more chances you will have to get past the machine screening route. However, *do not* lie in your résumé. Things you list in your résumé might be asked for by the employers during the interview, so, for example, if you do not know anything about Python programming, it is better not to put Python in your résumé.

There are resources available that can help you check if your résumé is ATS-friendly to specific job postings, such as `resumeworded.com` and `skillsyncer.com`. These systems show you the percentage of critical keywords that were met, the likelihood of your résumé getting passed the automated screening route, suggestions for improvements, and more. I highly recommend that you run your résumé through these systems before submitting your application.

Prepare several versions of the résumé

Start off by creating a general version of the résumé that includes as much information as possible – it does not matter if that information, experiences, activities, and education are relevant or not to the field you are applying for. This résumé acts as a record keeping sheet, and only you should have access to it. Let's call this version our **master résumé** for now. For this master résumé, it is acceptable to have more than one page. From here, create other versions for specific positions in your dream job list by selecting only the experience and information that relates to that job.

For example, I would create a master résumé where all my experience, activities, and education is included, relevant or not. Then, I would check my list of dream jobs, which contains several positions, such as software engineer, cloud engineer, and mobile developer. I will then, based on the master résumé, create a résumé for software engineer positions, another résumé for cloud engineer positions, and another résumé for mobile developer positions.

Instead of having only one résumé and trying to fit that into several positions, have several versions, as suggested. That way, your résumés will look very concentrated and clean. While creating these several copies, you might notice that you have more experience in some positions than others. This is a good sign and hint to you about which position you need to strengthen or increase your knowledge on.

When applying, make sure you modify your résumés so that they match the specific job posting you are going for. For example, just because you have a Cybersecurity Specialist résumé does not mean you should use that same résumé to apply for all the Cybersecurity Specialist positions, as different companies have slightly different requirements for the same job.

Along the way, every time you have any new achievements, make sure you note them in the master résumé, as well as other versions if appropriate. Keep in mind that a résumé is never *completed*; updating résumés is a constant process, even if you are currently employed, so the things you do or achieve at work should be updated in your résumés as well – you never know when they might come in useful in the future.

Quantify and qualify your achievements

When describing your experience, projects, or activities, provide as much quantified and qualified data as possible. For example, if you have helped a company improve their system's security issues, stating *Improved organization A's system security* can underrate your achievements, while not providing any helpful information to the hiring person. Instead, provide the quantity and quality of your work by changing the statement to something like *Implemented a security automation system for organization A, which reduced the risk of cyber attacks by 70%.*

Notice that after adding quality and quantity into the description, the achievement provides much more helpful and realistic data: the problem you have solved, the quality you brought to the organization, and the software/technology/practice you have used. At the same time, make sure you use words for actions, such as implement, design, collaborate, mentor, create, and so on, to add more value and context to your descriptions.

Be honest

As mentioned in the previous section, employers might ask about anything you list in your résumé, so make sure you really have knowledge on the skills and technologies you've described. If you have listed several skills but some of them are not very solid, you should let the employer know that too, which can help clarify their expectations. For example, if you list known programming languages such as Python, C, and PHP, but you are best at Python and do not know much about C or PHP, you can add your level of knowledge to those languages, such as Python (proficient), C (beginner), and so forth.

Soft skills are important

As mentioned in previous chapters, technical skills are not everything in the cybersecurity field. Communication, mentorship, leadership, and teamwork skills are just as essential. Consequently, make sure you include those skills alongside your experience with them in your résumé.

Less is more

Sometimes, people are tempted to describe each past experience or project with lots of details, which can be overkill for the résumé reviewer. For each project, experience, or activity, include no more than three to five bullet points, and each bullet point should be a maximum of two lines. Anything longer than that can look like clutter and hard to read. Overall, keep the number of experiences and projects to two to three each.

6-second test

As mentioned earlier, each résumé tends to be read in 6-7 seconds. Thus, put yourself in the perspective of the hirer, and try to read your résumés in 6-7 seconds by yourself, to find out what information stands out the most and what needs improving. Keep going back to edit the résumé and do the 6-second test again and again. This will help you produce an impressive résumé.

Cover letter

Some companies require a cover letter when applying for jobs. A cover letter gives employers a quick summary about you, the quality you can bring to the company, and why you are a good fit for their company. Additionally, similar to a résumé, a cover letter does not get so much reading time from the employer, so make it short, straight to the point, and show the quality and quantity of your skills, experience, and knowledge.

It is also a good practice to have several copies of cover letters, where each version is tailored toward a specific position.

In this section, tips and tricks on how to create an impressive résumé were provided. At the same time, some insights about the résumé screening process were provided. Keep in mind that the advice provided in this section should be looked over again and again to achieve better and better quality. More importantly, it is necessary and helpful to have others review your résumé, especially people from the industry. You can start by talking to friends and acquaintances from networking to ask for their feedback on your résumé. In fact, there are available open source or paid resources that provide résumé and cover letter samples and reviews. Details about those resources can be found in the *Extra resources* section.

Landing an interview (and acing it)

Previously in this chapter, guidance on job hunting and résumé preparing was provided. In this section, we will move on to the next step: getting ready for an interview!

Generally, there are several routes that are included in the whole process of landing a job, as shown in the following diagram:

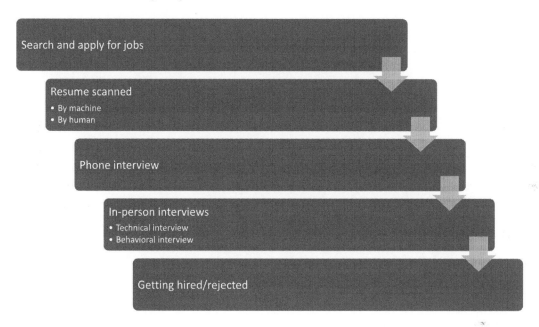

Figure 7.15 – Hiring process

As there are many steps involved, and the pressure can be overwhelming, you should start applying for jobs as early as possible, to get familiar with the whole process and master it over time. This is where groups D and E in the list of dream companies we created in the *Ranking the searches* section come to good use. Start by applying for the companies in groups D and E and try to gain as much interviewing experience as possible with those companies. Then, slowly try with companies in group C. This can be great practice for the future, when you are ready to apply for your group A and B companies.

Looking back at the previous diagram, searching for job postings, applying for jobs, and résumé scanning were covered earlier in this chapter. We'll look at phone and in-person interview steps in the upcoming section.

Preparing for the phone interview

Once your résumé has passed the screening stage, the hiring teams will start reaching out to you, starting with a written notice, letting you know they are interested to learn more about your skills, and to schedule a time for a phone interview. If, in fact, you get an interview, this means your résumé is working out. However, if you have applied for many positions, but only receive rejection messages or receive no reply at all after several weeks from applying, this means you should go back to work more on your résumé before moving on. If this is the case, it is beneficial to try out the résumé review services provided in the *Extra resources* section, later in this chapter.

Now, let's assume your résumé is good and you have earned a phone interview – what do you need to know? These phone interviews tend to last about 15 to 30 minutes in general. The contents of the interviews depend on certain situations and the interviewers themselves.

Sometimes, the interviews will be non-technical, where interviewers just want to verify your status, availability to work, and to communicate more about the position, as well as the future team you might be working with.

Other times, interviewers will ask you more technical questions that are related to the details listed in your résumé and the job posting.

Regardless of which scenario it might be, you should take the phone interview seriously, as it is the ticket to getting onto the next route. The following are some suggestions to help you prepare for the phone interview:

- **Keep records of all the job postings you have applied to**. Why? Because having a detailed description of the job postings is helpful for you to prepare your résumé and interviews. After applying for several positions, chances are you might forget the details of the postings, which means you may show up in interviews, not remembering what you applied for. This is never good. So maintain a record of all the job postings you have applied for. Do not save the URLs of the postings; instead, copy and paste the contents into a document. Why? Because the URL might become unavailable in the future, which means all its contents, too.

- Once you know a phone interview is coming up, **look for the job description you have saved** and make sure you understand the details listed in there, especially for the requirement section. If there is a technology you are rusty with, it is time to brush up on it. If there is anything you do not understand from the job description, note it down and ask the interviewer later.

- **Go over the résumé you used for that application** and make sure you have enough knowledge to talk about the technologies and skills you listed in your résumé.

- **Learn more about the company and team you applied for** – look for what they do, their mission, vision, cultures, and so on. This will give yourself a chance to impress the interviewer by showing them how much you really understand, care, and want to be a part of their team.

- **Be in a quiet place with internet access** and make sure you are in an environment where no distractions could occur. At the same time, choosing a quiet place, instead of sitting in a noisy coffee shop, shows the employer that you are taking this opportunity seriously and are being respectful. How about the part where you need internet access? The phone interview gives you the advantage that employers cannot look at you, and during the interview, there might be some questions where you are not sure of the answer. If that is the case, do a quick Google search and try your best to answer the questions.

  However, do not lie – do not read off the internet word for word and claim you are an expert in that subject – that is not a good thing to do. Instead, you can be honest and explain that you do not have a lot of knowledge about this certain topic, then share what you just learned from the Google search (without mentioning that you just searched about it seconds ago) and show the interviewer your willingness to learn more about this topic later.

- **Ask questions**, as this will show the interviewer that you are proactive and engaging. Always prepare some questions prior to the interview; this could be about something from the job description, future work expectations, future team, and so on. During the interview, you might come up with more questions, so note them down and ask them as well. Try your best not to close the conversation with a *No* for the answer to *"Do you have any questions?"*.

That's it for the phone interview! Let's say you nailed it and the employer wants to move on with an in-person interview.

In different companies, technical and behavioral interviews might be combined or separated into different routes. Either way, expect to be tested on both.

Preparing for the technical interview

Some companies offer take-home assessments, while others require you to be on-premises. Either way, this is the time where your technical knowledge will be tested. These tests are time-sensitive, and you are given between hours to days to finish the project.

The first couple of times you have an in-person interview may be overwhelming, but the more you practice, the better and more comfortable you will get. Do not be discouraged if you cannot pass some technical interviews – it is part of the process. Note down the topics you need reinforcement in and keep trying. As mentioned at the beginning of this section, having interview practice with the companies in your dream company list will be very beneficial.

If you are doing the technical assessment on-premises and being proctored by technical interviewers, make sure you communicate with them before, while, and after solving the questions. Do not dig right into the questions without clarifying the tasks needed to be completed. Remember, interviewers want you to be a part of a productive team, not a robot who just works without thinking. Thus, communication is important.

While tackling these questions, if you get stuck, do not hesitate to ask the interviewers for a hint. Be straightforward and nice; most of the time, interviewers would not say no to a polite request such as *"hey, I want to implement this method, but I'm not sure how to get there. Could you give me a hint?"*.

Once you have completed the assessment, keep communication going by summing up what you have done, what you think could have gone better for the solution, and check if the interviewers have any questions.

By keeping constant communication, interviewers get the impression that you are easy and effective to work with, which, in many cases, allows them to be more forgiving about your technical skill shortage. By asking for guidance and clarification, you are showing your willingness and eagerness to learn and to be coached, which is a very positive strength to have. In most cases, companies prefer to hire an employee who can work well with others and is willing to learn as they go, rather than someone who has a lot of technical knowledge but no teamwork ability.

Preparing for the behavioral interview

Behavioral questions are meant to help employers understand more about your behaviors and soft skills at workplace situations. Thus, questions to be expected could include, *"Talk about a time when you solved conflict with other team members"*, *"What would you do if your team leader does not agree with you?"*, *"What are your top strengths and weaknesses in the workplace?"*, and many more. To best prepare for this route, consider the following suggestions:

- Search for **common behavioral questions asked by big tech companies** and practice answering them at home. You can even record yourself answering those questions and review the recordings later, to find areas for improvement.

- Search for **suggested answers for behavioral questions**. There are many videos on YouTube and other social media channels that suggest how to best answer behavioral questions to impress employers.

- **Talk to people who are working in the field and the companies you want to work for**. Ask them about the behavioral questions they have faced and how they handled those questions.

- **Keep records of situations you have faced at work and school**; note down how you have handled those situations, what you have done well in those situations, and what you could improve on. This will be great material for you to talk about when you go the behavioral interview route.

- Additionally, this is another chance for you to **show your willingness to learn and that you are a coachable team member**. If possible, include details to indicate your enthusiasm to learn from others and to share knowledge with others. A humble and supportive team member who can work well with others is preferred.

- More importantly, **express your leadership and mentorship potential**. Companies like to see you grow and move up after working for a while, and if you are in such positions, you need to be able to mentor and guide others, letting the whole team grow together. Thus, do not hesitate to share that you would love to move up to management after working for a couple of years.

- Lastly, **be authentic** – remember that there are no correct or wrong answers for behavioral questions. These questions are meant to find out if you are a good fit for the organization you are applying to. As a result, while trying to perfect the answers, to best describe yourself and to impress the employers, do not lie; instead, be transparent.

Before moving on to the next section, I want to leave you with another suggestion: keep records of all the companies you have applied to – when, which position, and the progress of your application (accepted, rejected, no response). Why? Because some companies keep records of all your applications, generally for about 3 – 12 months. When reviewing your applications, employers tend to pull up all your applications in the system and, for instance, if they see that you applied for 5-6 positions at the same time, or you applied to 2-3 positions that are totally irrelevant, employers might feel that you are not serious about the positions you are applying for; instead, you were just spreading your luck everywhere. This is not the impression you want to give your future employers.

Additionally, if you have recently failed an interview, during the time frame of 3-6 months, where your previous applications are still on their system, it is better to wait for this time frame to pass so that when you reapply, your new application will come in fresh, which can win you a better chance moving forward. In fact, depending on your skills and performance, companies in the **Facebook, Amazon, Apple, Netflix, and Google (FAANG)** group might ask you to wait between 3 to 12 months after your last interview to reapply.

As a result, you should keep track of the dates you have applied for the positions, to avoid having too many applications coming in within too short a period of time.

In this section, you learned about different interview routes, including phone interviews, technical interviews, and behavioral interviews, and how to prepare for as well as handle them. Depending on companies and situations, the order and/or number of those interview routes might not be the same. Yet, you should expect to face them regardless. Additionally, since COVID-19 and the increase in working from home, many interviews have moved to 100% online. If this is the case for you, make sure you still show up in polite and appropriate attire, as if you were in person. Furthermore, don't forget to prepare a quiet environment with good internet access for your interviews, as mentioned in the *Preparing for the phone interview* sub-section; background noise and an inappropriate location can cause distractions and give off the wrong impression to employers.

Keep in mind that it is perfectly normal to feel nervous when taking interviews, but the more you do them, the more comfortable and experienced you will get. Make sure you note down what you have done well and not well after each interview so that you can learn for future experiences.

In the next section, extra resources and tools will be provided to help you prepare to land your next cybersecurity *jay-oh-bee*!

Extra resources

In the previous sections, many guides and resources were introduced. However, there are still many available resources out there you can utilize. In this section, some other open source and paid resources will be brought to your attention. It is impractical to list all the available services in the market, so keep researching and looking for others, even if they are not mentioned in this book.

Employment platform

If you wish to work for the US government, usajobs.gov is the place to go. This is where federal jobs can be found. Besides, usajobs.com also provides different hiring paths for individuals from different backgrounds. The following screenshot shows various hiring paths on `usajobs.gov`:

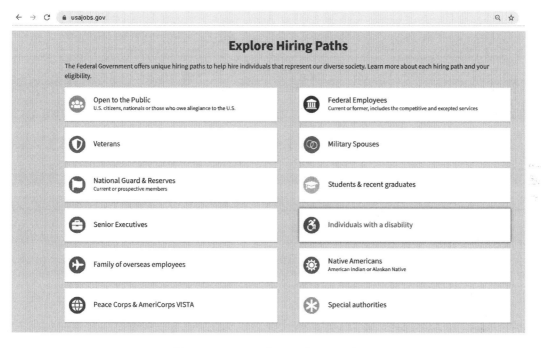

Figure 7.16 – usajobs.com hiring paths

Résumé preparation

The following services can help you with preparing your résumé:

- **LinkedIn résumé builder**: If you have LinkedIn Premium, or have signed up for LinkedIn Learning, you will get LinkedIn Premium as well. With LinkedIn Premium, you can access LinkedIn résumé builder, where you can upload your résumé to get feedback. Your résumé will be checked against popular keywords that are used for the job title of choice and the format of industry standard **applicant tracking system** (**ATS**).

- **Rooftopslushie.com**: This a platform where you can connect with people in the industry, specifically to have them review your résumés. The price for each review is offered by you, so even though the service on this platform is not free, it is affordable. Besides, you can find services such as interview tips, negotiation guides, career advice, and referrals on this website.

- **ResumeGenius.com**: This site provides free résumé and cover letter samples for different cybersecurity and information technology positions. If you struggle with producing quantitative and qualitative statements in your résumés, this is a very good resource to learn from.

Interview preparation

The following services can help you with preparing for interviews:

- **Rooftopslushie.com**: As mentioned earlier, this resource provides mentoring and interview preparation services, with a fee offered by yourself. There's no fixed price.

- **Interviewing.io**: This is another platform that lets you connect with industry professionals and book mock interviews with them. Other side services include job boards and referral. Although this platform is focused on software development, you can still utilize the behavioral mock interview service. Note that it is free to have mock interviews with peers, but you must pay to have mock interviews with industry professionals.

Job hunting

Job hunting is a hideous process, and the following services can help make it easier:

- **Cybersecjobs.com**: This is a platform specifically for job postings in the cybersecurity field. You can search for jobs on this website based on a sub-field of interest.

- **Ninjajobs.org**: This is another job platform that focuses on cybersecurity positions. The interface is fairly easy to use – only the job's title and location is needed to get you started.

- **Dice.com**: This acts not only as a job posting platform, but also provides a salary predictor, career development resources, tech salary reports, and more.

- **Whitetruffle.com**: This site matches your profile with employers and automatically notifies you once a position is found.

- **Angel.co**: This site provides job postings from start-ups. If you do not have a lot of experience, working for start-ups is a great way to learn and, oftentimes, easier to get accepted.

Referral services

Besides getting referred by friends and acquaintances, going for paid referral is worth trying as well. Hence, try using to the referral services of some of the resources introduced previously. Bear in mind that getting a referral does not mean getting a job. Referral makes it easier, but you still need the skills and knowledge to get in.

Salary guide

Besides the websites provided in the *Search by pay scale* sub-section, there are other resources available that provide salary ranges and insights, such as LinkedIn Salary or payscale.com. For example, the following screenshot shows the salary range of Security Engineer positions in the Seattle area from LinkedIn salary site:

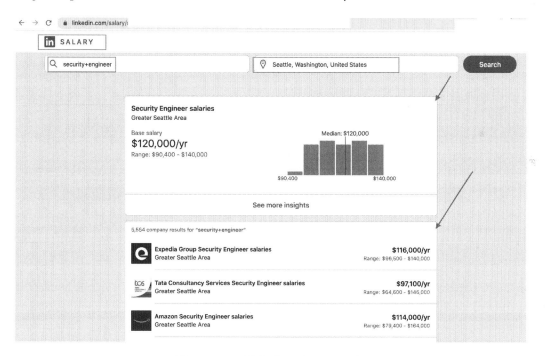

Figure 7.17 – LinkedIn salary example

The following screenshot is another example from payscale.com, where the salaries of Cybersecurity Analyst positions have been provided. With payscale.com, if you wish to have more specific numbers, you can provide more information, such as years of experience, level of education, certificates held, and more:

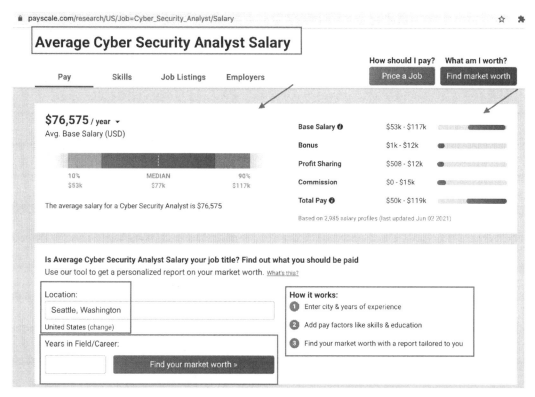

Figure 7.18 – payscale.com salary example

In this section, several paid and free services, websites, and resources were provided to assist you in résumé preparation and interview preparation, including the job-hunting process, recruiting platforms, and a salary guide. Try to utilize these resources as much as possible before going into actual interviews, and don't be set back by some paid services that have pricey fees. Think of these as another form of education and investment for your future career, and hey – investments in education are never lost!

Entry-level myth busting

So far, many aspects of the cybersecurity job market have been analyzed to give you a holistic and just view of its current trends. However, if you are a newbie to this field and still have some doubts, don't worry – let's bust some cybersecurity entry-level myths:

- **You must be technical to enter the cybersecurity field**: This is one of the common misunderstandings in this field. In fact, cybersecurity contains lots of individuals who transitioned from different fields, many of which were non-technical. Like I mentioned in *Chapter 2, Which Career Field Is Best for You?,* and in this chapter, employers look for people with an eager to learn and positive attitude to work with, which in many situations outweighs years of experience. Skills can be learned over time, so if you are new to the field, just keep learning and improving your knowledge, and opportunities will come along. Cybersecurity welcomes people with different backgrounds, skill sets, and skill levels.

- **Women are not welcome in cybersecurity**: It is fair to say that there is a shortage of women in the field. However, many efforts are being made to increase the number of women in cybersecurity. Companies, schools, organizations, and the cybersecurity community itself offer scholarships, support, and much more to encourage women to join cybersecurity. If you are a woman and new to this field, you will be able to find lots of support as you go along, so no pressure!

- **Cybersecurity people don't welcome newcomers**: There are knowledge hoarders in every field, and cybersecurity is not an exception. Don't let that discourage you from joining the field, as cybersecurity always opens its doors for newcomers, and most people in this field are very supportive. So, welcome to cybersecurity!

- **You must have years of experience to be hired**: As mentioned in previous sections, it is nice to have prior experience; however, it is not a must. As the field offers many levels for each position, there are plenty of chances for you to get hired, even if you are fresh out of school. Again, don't forget that your own personal projects can be counted as experience too!

- **You must have a ton of certificates to be hired**: Certificates can help you get ahead; however, without it, you can still get hired. In fact, having one or two is already great, so don't pressure yourself on having three or more when applying for entry-level positions. On the other hand, if you do not have any certificates, often, companies are willing to sponsor you to have one after hiring you. Either way, getting certificates is good in the long term, but do not pressure yourself into having them all at once and in the very beginning.

These were some common myths about entry-level cybersecurity and newcomers. There are many more out there. Nevertheless, do not get caught up in them and discourage yourself out of this field. Keep in mind that cybersecurity is a place for individuals with various backgrounds, skills, knowledge, and abilities. Emerge yourself with others who are already working in this field and look for advice and guidance whenever you can!

Summary

Landing a job is not an easy process – it requires many steps, preparation, and strategies. All the resources and guidance that was provided in this chapter can help you set up your portfolio and prepare for the hiring process ahead. In this chapter, we learned the following:

- When and why to pivot to a new cybersecurity career

- How to determine the right job and company for you

- How and what to look for when researching the job market

- How to prepare for your résumé

- Interview types, processes, and what to expect during each of them

- How to land and ace each interview route

- Different platforms for job searching, interview preparation, résumé building, referrals, and salary guides

- Several myths about entry-level cybersecurity and newcomers

As mentioned previously, not every resource can be listed in one book, so keep researching and do not limit yourself to the ones that were introduced in this book only.

Lastly, before closing this chapter, I want to leave you with a reminder that all the guides in this chapter should be revisited constantly to bring the best results. Put this advice into practice, review what you have done for improvement, check back on the provided advice, edit and prepare some more, then do more reviews, and repeat. Even if you have landed a job, keep practicing these skills to keep your knowledge fresh. This is one type of learning, and learning should never be stopped.

In the next chapter, Jon will introduce the outlook of continued education in cybersecurity. For now, good luck landing your next cybersecurity *jay-oh-bee*!

Section 3:
Now You're in; Time to Level Up!

This section will wrap up the book. You will receive final guidance on how to set goals and maintain momentum without hitting burnout in your career.

The following chapters will be covered under this section:

- *Chapter 8, Giving Back to Others and Yourself*
- *Chapter 9, Trusting the Process*

8
Giving Back to Others and Yourself

Alright, so now we get to the part of your journey where you need to figure out what you need to do to continue developing and learning throughout your career. Up until this point, we have discussed different careers, how to get skills for those careers, and also helped you plan your way to getting that first cybersecurity job. However, the story continues even after you land the ideal job that you patiently and diligently worked so hard to get.

This chapter is going to discuss what you need to do after your successful appointment, as well as things to look out for. When all your hard work pays off, that does not mean you stop working. However, you can take frequent breaks and start to settle into your career. It's time to start learning how you can continue your information security path in the direction that you desire. This chapter is written to help you understand how continuing your growth will help influence your success, as well as make you a better cyber professional. After all, being a continuous student will allow you to both learn and teach!

In this chapter, we're going to cover the following main topics:

- The "How-To" of public speaking
- What burnout is and how to avoid it
- Indicators of toxic environments

The "How-To" of public speaking

To begin this chapter, we will discuss topics to consider when it comes to public speaking or giving lectures to other cybersecurity enthusiasts. This entails submitting proposals to conferences and events that are based on relevant topics of interest to you, or research areas that you want to discuss with folks in the industry. This is a great way to teach yourself to still be a student, while also giving back and teaching others. It is also a great way to showcase yourself as a professional! Think of public speaking as a way to have a live resume, where you discuss your history as a cybersecurity professional, and also the topics that interest you.

> **Important note**
>
> There is an old saying that goes *"To teach, one must maintain the mind of a student. A student continually learns and strives to obtain new knowledge. A teacher must do the same, but share that knowledge to enlighten those around them."*
>
> In information security, we can all be teachers, because we are all continuous learners at heart. We all have knowledge and wisdom, so be that pivotal influence in someone's career and share your knowledge with them.

So, how does someone find out where they can speak, and how do they go about it?

This is a fairly common question we see when someone is trying to highlight a topic of interest and discuss it with others in a presentation setting. To be honest, there is no wrong way to go about it. Most conferences and lecturing establishments have a straightforward process on how to go about things. However, the following will help you with a general idea of how you can accomplish this:

1. Think about some of the research you have been working on lately, or even past experiences that taught you important lessons. Think about how you can turn these ideas/research into actionable learning objectives that could be discussed in a presentation.

2. Once you have your research idea in place, start writing it out on a physical or digital medium. This means writing out the rough draft of the outline using pen and paper, or a digital document such as a Microsoft Word or Google Docs document.

    When you're writing out your first draft, think about how it will benefit the audience. Imagine you're an audience member who will sit in on the presentation – think about what you would want to walk away knowing.

3. Find some conferences with **Calls for Papers** (**CFPs**). There are quite a few, which we will list later in this chapter.

4. Submit your rough draft to a few different talks – and cross your fingers!

The four steps mentioned here will help you with understanding what you need to do in order to get a talk submitted. Of course, this doesn't mean that your talk will actually get accepted. Typically, talks go through a review board where various board members of different backgrounds review your work and evaluate it with other presentation submissions. If accepted, you would get a message from the board advising you that your presentation has been accepted.

Now that you understand what is needed and the process of submitting for CFPs, let's start to move to the next portion of this chapter. As mentioned previously, we will discuss some places where you can submit your talks, such as various different conferences and universities.

Introducing different conferences

There are many different conferences that occur throughout the world all year long. Different conferences bring in different crowds from different backgrounds and career fields. As we have mentioned throughout this book, there are many different fields within cyber that you can go to, so it is essential to know which conferences are the best for you to attend.

The following sections mention different conferences that occur throughout the world, though many take place within the United States.

DEF CON

DEF CON is a hacker convention that occurs in Las Vegas every year, typically around late July or early August. The conference, which started in 1993, is commonly known as the **hacker summer camp** and has talks that cater to various research styles. The conference also has villages, which are sub-conferences within the conference that host targeted areas of cyber such as red teaming, industrial control center, internet of things, social engineering, and much more! The DEF CON banner is shown in the following figure:

Figure 8.1 – DEF CON banner

DEF CON is one of the largest hacker conferences. Now, let's take a look at a conference that is known for its high-level training, amazing vendor selection, and overall "professional appearance." This next conference may not be one to speak at, but is most certainly an amazing opportunity to level up your training and networking.

Black Hat

Black Hat is an international security conference that is given on different continents. For example, there is Black Hat Asia, a security conference held in the Asia region. Black Hat is commonly known as the **professional security conference** and has attendance from vendors and speakers worldwide. In fact, Black Hat is very similar to DEF CON – except that Black Hat is seen as the professional version of DEF CON. The Black Hat banner is shown here:

Figure 8.2 – Black Hat banner

As mentioned, though Black Hat might not be the best choice to do your first speaking engagement at, it does provide an opportunity to network with other cybersecurity folks, meet professional vendors, learn more about cybersecurity products, and acquire amazing training provided by top-level cybersecurity professionals.

The next type of conferences are small, yet mighty. The BSides conferences are organic, small, and humble conferences held in their respective areas, and are generally coordinated by local cybersecurity professionals.

BSIDES

BSides conferences happen all over the world. Essentially, a BSides conference is a smaller conference organized and run by folks within a local community. Submitting papers to local BSides conferences is a great way to get started in public speaking due to the fact that BSides events typically get fewer CFPs. This makes your chances of getting a presentation accepted considerably higher. While the conferences mentioned here are wonderful to explore, we advise you to do some of your own research and discover other conferences in the cybersecurity field. Other great avenues to explore for speaking engagements could also be a lot closer than you think. Possibly even your local school!

Universities

Speaking at your local university is another great way to get experience speaking about technical topics in front of people. Chances are, if you're reading this, you are going through a time where you are looking to transition. You may even be in school. The great thing about being in school is that you are already used to giving presentations. Doing it in a conference setting isn't much different, only you are doing it on a topic (technical/non-technical) that interests you.

If you are able, it is always preferable to start by giving talks at a local university. Crowds tend to be more forgiving, and the stress is not nearly as high as when talking to a group of folks in a setting such as DEF CON. Additionally, being able to speak at a university allows you to network with other folks who are just starting out in their career.

You should now have a concrete understanding of where to start when thinking about what conferences are available to you for speaking purposes. Next, let's discuss potential topics that you can think about presenting. The next section will discuss topics to present, and how you can present them!

Discovering topics

When it comes to topics, there is plenty to discuss. As mentioned before, one of the most common issues with folks looking to submit talks is that they think their topic is not technical enough, or that people won't be interested in it. That should never be the case.

If you look at some of the conferences mentioned within this book, you'll notice that they cover a large variety of topics. Additionally, these topics are often illustrated at different skill levels and geared toward other folks in their security journey. Essentially, this means they can be beginner-friendly, with introduction topics or low-level subjects. Other topics can include advanced issues that look at very technical subjects.

So, what topics interest you? What topics do you think would benefit others? Do you have something to share that you think would have an impact on someone else?

As you can see, we do not need to worry if the topics we are presenting are seen as "cool" or "technical." We only need to consider whether we wish to share them. If the topic will only have an impact on two people, you should still do it! Two people benefiting from your topic means you still made an impact.

The following list gives general ideas for topics for talks at a conference:

- **Introduction talks**: A talk that introduces the audience to a field is a great way to help those looking to break into cybersecurity.

- **Tools and tactics**: There are lots of tools and new tactics being updated within the cybersecurity field. Find a new technique or tool to talk about and educate the audience on how to use it!

- **Niche expertise**: Do you have experience within a niche field? Something like cloud computing, exploit development, advanced tactics, or artificial intelligence? Making a presentation on one of these topics is a great way to give back to the community!

As you can see, there are plenty of different topics to present, even more than this shortlist mentioned. The list should act as a primer for potential talks that you could do.

Now that we have a better understanding of how to navigate everything before your speech commences, let's take a look at a couple of other key factors: **what to expect during the talk and after the talk.**

During the talk

So, you have been accepted to talk at a conference on a topic that you are really passionate about. While this in and of itself sounds extremely exciting, you will want to ensure that you consider a few things to prep up on, things that will probably occur during your presentation. Remember that preparation affords 90% of your success, and poor preparation can lead to poor performance.

During your talk, something to keep note of is to ensure that your transition between slides is smooth. This means ensuring the talk moves in an organic and easy-to-follow manner. For example, you wouldn't talk about ethical hacking on one slide, and then talk about plants on the other. You would talk about ethical hacking on one slide, followed by a buffer slide that leads into the slide about plants. The point of the buffer slide is to allow your audience to adjust to the next topic, and have their brains shift accordingly.

Imagine watching a movie that you are *super enthusiastic* about watching. Imagine, mid-way through, the movie makes a shift without prepping the viewer. This can leave the viewer in a state of disarray and even potentially affect the way they see the film. *Treat presenting talks the same way.* You want to ensure your audience is not left confused, as this could mean they potentially walk out of your talk (yes, that happens).

Something else that is extremely important during your talk is to ensure that you take breaths that will allow your brain to catch up. Taking breaths ensures that you stop and think before moving to the next slide or word. If you get nervous during your talk, that is a good indicator to take a breath. If you feel you are losing track of where you are in your presentation, you should definitely take a breath. Most importantly, if you feel you need to take a breath, you should take a breath!

One last thing to think about while you're up there giving your presentation is to celebrate the topic and your own expertise! Ensure that you talk about your background and how it lead you to present. Ensure that you sound excited to give a talk to such an amazing audience. Your job is to motivate those listening in by selling yourself and celebrating the topic being discussed.

> **Important note**
> Ensure your last slide contains your contact info on where folks can find you. This means providing LinkedIn, Twitter, and other public information.

So, now that you have been advised on what to expect during your talk, let's pivot into what to expect after your talk.

What to expect after your talk

So, you have completed your talk. First things first, give yourself a pat on the back! Giving a presentation is a huge accomplishment that many never do, but you did!

After you have given your talk, it's best to have some time to yourself. You may see a crowd of supporters rush you, which is excellent! However, it would help if you let yourself relax a bit and reenergize. This relates to the principle of *stress + rest = growth* that will be mentioned later in this chapter.

After your talk, take a moment for yourself and celebrate. Once you're ready, go out and network with folks. Chances are you are going to have some new followers that will want to follow up with you about the content you spoke about. Ensure that you are fully open when discussing the topic after the talk, unless there is a non-disclosure agreement preventing you from discussing some aspect of the information you presented. Folks will be interested in finding out more about you or the topic – so be sure to make them feel included.

> **Important note**
>
> When thinking about ways to cut into the industry, know that lots of recruiters and directors go to conferences to listen in on new talent, and recruit that talent. Use your conference talks to promote yourself like you were presenting a resume, while also making an impact in the field.

Remember, after the talk is really the time to connect with others. You never know who will want to connect with you. You could meet someone who would like you to talk at another conference, speak to an organization, or potentially ask you to come interview for a job! The ideas are limitless here, so be ready!

With public speaking can come a lot of motivation that can quickly overwhelm you if not handled correctly. The joy of getting to share information with others can become addictive and exhilarating. However, it can also become exhausting if not handled properly. The next section of this chapter is going to discuss burnout and how you can handle it to ensure continued success in your cybersecurity journey.

What burnout is and how to avoid it

You know that feeling when you are passionate about something, and then you start to lose interest in it – even though you still really want to enjoy it? Often, this type of *lifeless* feeling can make us feel exhausted and be unable to participate in what we love. For example, perhaps you really love playing chess, but you have dived so deep into playing the game with no breaks that it has made you feel exhausted. Additionally, perhaps you have played through the exhaustion and used substances to help push through.

This example of the chess-playing scenario is an indicator of **burnout**. Burnout is a phase of emotional, physical, and mental exhaustion caused by extreme and extended stress over a period of time. It happens when you feel defeated, emotionally drained, and powerless to meet endless demands. In the case of the chess scenario, the game was played over a prolonged period of time, without any breaks. This could cause mental exhaustion.

When we think about burnout in cybersecurity, it can come in many different forms. Typically, burnout means being exhausted due to prolonged periods of working on many projects at once. This happens quite a bit to high-functioning folks who work 60-80 hours a week on different projects. While 60-80 hours is doable, it is not maintainable without breaks.

> **Important note**
>
> There is an article written by Jon Helmus that details the stress and balance of burnout. You find the article here: `https://medium.com/@ jonathanchelmus/screw-cybersecurity-avoiding- technology-burnout-c71ba5d5261`.

So, how do we avoid burnout while still maintaining efficiency? How do we ensure that we take sufficient rest to complement our growth and success? The key is to learn how to avoid burnout.

Avoiding burnout

Avoiding burnout is not rocket science. You need to ensure that you have a balance between your cybersecurity life and your personal life. This seems pretty straightforward in theory. However, putting this into action can become quite an issue. If applying principles was easy, everyone would live a healthy and happy life. However, this does not seem to be the case.

So, how do we find the perfect *zen* and balance? The following are things to consider to avoid burnout:

- Take breaks *away* from your computer. Do this a few times daily to ensure you reduce screen time and don't get screen fatigue.

- Go outside (with no technology). This one sounds pretty straightforward, but you'd be surprised how difficult it can be to form it into a habit.

- Don't bite off more than you can chew. This means not taking on more projects than you can handle. A good rule of thumb is to *never* take on additional work if your current work is already making you tired.

- Take a vacation if you can. It's essential to enjoy the love of your labor, so celebrate with a trip, even if it's a staycation in your home!

As you can see, it's pretty simple – take breaks to give yourself some time to heal. The brain is a muscle, just like any other muscle, and needs to rest when under long periods of stress. Just like going to the gym, you need to have rest days to allow your muscles to grow. The brain needs to rest to grow too!

Always remember that *stress + rest = growth*!

Now that we know what to look out for in terms of burnout, we need to understand something else that is extremely important and can take a physical and mental toll on us. The next section of this chapter is going to discuss toxic environments and how we can avoid them.

Indicators of a toxic environment

Toxic work environments can leave you feeling tired, unfulfilled, or even worthless (harsh but true) when it comes to your professional and personal life. This tends to take a toll on us physically, and can even affect us mentally. In today's cyber work environment, it is easy to get overworked because there tends to *always* be a problem that needs solving, and never enough time to solve it:

Figure 8.3 – Toxicity

Toxicity in the workplace may not look like someone constantly yelling at you or giving you unrealistic deadlines. In fact, a lot of toxicity within the workplace is very subtle and may not even impact you in the way you think. The following are some indicators of a toxic work environment and how you can remove yourself professionally without burning any bridges.

Exclusion and gossip

We have learned over the years that there is no room for gossip within the workplace. This doesn't entail banter between co-workers about their weekend, or discussing recent politics (though it is advised not to talk about politics within the workplace). Gossip and exclusion typically takes the form of cliques within the work environment. This means looking out for large groups of folks at your company that typically stay isolated and never invite anyone to gatherings outside their immediate group members, showing a general disinterest in doing anything with anyone else outside of their group.

To avoid this, simply do not interact with these toxic groups and report them to leadership. It is the leadership's job to ensure that things like this do not occur, and provide increased awareness of the problem so it does not occur in the future.

Toxic leadership

There is a saying: "*people don't leave bad jobs, they leave bad leadership*." This means that companies sometimes cultivate bad leadership within their organization, and that faulty leadership can have a severe impact on those they lead.

> **Important note**
> Narcissistic leadership is when leadership demands that you always agree with them and does not allow you to ask questions or challenge them. They expect everyone else to be perfect while they meet lower standards.

Bad leadership comes in many different forms, so it's good to know what it may look like. Here are some things to take into account:

- **Micromanager**: Someone who is always telling you what to do about every little detail of your job and your duties. It is a boss's job to lead, not dictate.

- **Blame game**: Someone who will continually blame you for your mistakes at work. It is the leadership's duty to take the blame for their employees – not the other way around.

If you think or feel that you are experiencing bad leadership, report them to human resources immediately. If the issue persists, it is an indicator of a toxic culture within the workplace. It may be time to send your resignation or find another position with a new company.

Recognizing lazy co-workers

This one sounds interesting, right? Lazy co-workers are typically an indicator that folks who have been at the company longer feel they can get by doing less work. This is because they often feel they can offload the work to new and junior folks within the company. For those of us who have been in the industry for quite some time, we have all seen this on occasion and understand that this is not due to bad or lazy employees – it is due to the culture within the company allowing them to be lazy employees. Everyone in the company has a responsibility and duty to carry out work that aligns with their job requirements, and last we checked, being lazy is never one of them.

> **Important note**
> Part of being a new employee or junior employee is to understand the way your company works, the systems and tools it uses, and integrate within the culture – not be tortured by it.

If you see or experience something like this, it is important that you report it to leadership or human resources immediately. If it does not get resolved, this is an indicator of cultural issues and might indicate the time is right for you to start looking for a different company.

High turnover – employees quitting often!

This is a touchy thing to mention because cybersecurity has a high turnover by design. The typical length of a cybersecurity employee's time with a company is around 1.5 to 2 years. This is not that long compared to most careers. However, that doesn't mean that it may also not be something to take note of when thinking about turnover due to toxic work environments.

When looking for jobs and filling out applications, check sites such as LinkedIn for employees that have worked within that company. How long did they stay? Was it a year? Was it less than a year? It could be argued that if you were to survey 10 previous employees of a company you're interested in, and collectively they have an average of a year spent with that company, this may be a good indicator of a toxic company.

Lack of work/life balance

Our careers give us purpose and drive. However, they also provide wealth and health for our families. It is important to ensure that the company you work for takes note that you are a human being with wants and needs that revolve outside of the workplace. This means not exerting yourself when there is no need to, working unnecessary hours, or having to miss copious family events for work-related things.

If you start to see a lack of work/life balance, you need to talk with leadership as soon as possible. Your family can often see indicators of a lack of work/life balance. Family is the first one to notice and advise you that *perhaps you are working too much*, or *the family would like to see you once in a while*!

Outside of family, other indicators of lacking work/life balance include not having time to do things outside of work. Life is full, long, and beautiful – so ensure you take time to enjoy it!

It is about time to wrap up. However, before we do, let's finish off with a quick summary.

Summary

This chapter talked a lot about different things that we need to think about when speaking with others in a conference or mentor setting. As discussed, there are lots of ways to give back to the industry, and quite a few different roads to take when attempting to help others. Remember that it doesn't matter how you help or make a positive impact – it matters that at some point, you find your own way to make that positive impact.

The next section is going to discuss how you can trust yourself, the industry, and the overall process of getting into cybersecurity. Remember that your cyber career is not about the destination, it is about the journey!

Further reading

Refer to the following links for more information on the topics covered in this chapter:

- Avoiding burnout in cybersecurity: `https://www.securitymagazine.com/blogs/14-security-blog/post/93890-five-tips-to-avoid-cybersecurity-burnout`

- Cybersecurity conferences repository: `https://github.com/santosomar/virtualseccons`

- DEF CON: `https://www.defcon.org/`

9
Trusting the Process

As we conclude this book, Gerald and Jax want to leave you with some final thoughts on **goal setting**, **mentorship**, and **networking**. This final chapter will explain the importance of *goalsetting* and why goals are critical for career growth. We will explain the importance of mentorship and networking and how both can help with personal and professional growth.

We will be covering the following topics in this chapter:

- Understanding the SMART goalsetting framework
- Learning about the mentor and mentee relationship
- Exploring different ways to network with impact

Understanding the SMART goalsetting framework

Have you ever felt like you are working hard but spinning your wheels? That you have big dreams but cannot seem to reach them, no matter what you do or how hard you try? Goals are the steps to dreams, and they are critical for long-term and sustainable success. This section will help you take a step back and refine your goals by developing, prioritizing, and being specific. In this section, we will review the **SMART** goalsetting framework to provide guidance on how to create personalized goals to fit your career desires.

Proper goalsetting addresses time-sensitive and important goals first, then moves downward to other goals that are still important to your overall vision.

The following diagram provides a visual depiction of this framework:

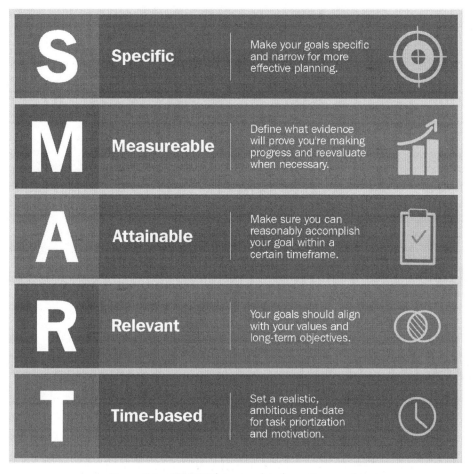

Figure 9.1 – SMART framework information graph

SMART is a mnemonic acronym that stands for the following:

- **Specific** (what, who, where, and why)
- **Measurable** (motivational)
- **Attainable** (realistic)
- **Relevant** (in line with the overall dream)
- **Time-based** (end date and time-driven)

The SMART framework is a way to create criteria to guide the users in realistic objectives to reach longer-term growth in every aspect of their life. You can use this framework in business, school, or family life. Let's look at each in more detail.

Specific

You should be as specific as possible with your goals. This is also where your *why* statement from *Chapter 6, Time to Brand Yourself – Not the Burning Type*, will be placed. During this initial step, take a moment to think about your *W's*; that is, what, who, why, and where. Use the following questions to help determine your 4 Ws:

- What am I looking to accomplish with this goal?
- Who are the key players needed for this goal to succeed?
- Why do I believe this goal is important?
- Where in my life does this goal impact me? (that is, work and/or family)

Here is an example: let's say you are a senior manager wanting to become a director. A specific goal could be "*I want to gain the necessary skills to become a director in my organization to progress in my career, provide for my family, and continue to lead large, successful teams.*"

In this section, be specific – you could even include the color of the shirt you will be wearing the day you accept the director role.

Measurable

Measurable helps with the sustainability of goals. Let's use weight loss as an example of sustainability goals. Weight loss is hard, and many people dislike taking those necessary before, during, and after photos. However, during the process of weight loss, there will be times where you will not see any weight loss for a few weeks. With photos, you have more than a number on a scale to tell you that you are making progress. The progress photos could be the one thing that will make or break you reaching your end goal.

Measurable goals help you track progress to keep you accountable and motivated. The following is a list of questions that you should ask yourself to help you determine the measurability of your current goals:

- What do I need to put into place or do to accomplish this goal?
- Who do I need to call or talk to about this goal?
- How will I know when I have accomplished my micro-tasks for my bigger goal?

Let's use the director analogy from earlier. Your goal may be to pick two or three different leadership, technical, or analytical courses to help you prepare for a director position. Your measurable goal would be to set the first and most relevant class with a micro-tasks and timeline to contact the school, and then determine how soon you can take the course, study, and take the exam.

These smaller steps/goals of studying and taking the exam will keep you focused on your bigger goal and motivated to keep pushing forward.

Achievable

When we get really excited about our dreams, we sometimes set unrealistic goals. An example is having a specific goal of becoming a director in 1 year, yet you are a tier I analyst. This could be seen as an unrealistic goal. There is a difference between having big goals versus unrealistic goals.

Becoming a director is realistic. Becoming one in a year when you are a tier I analyst could be very unrealistic, especially if this is your first year in the industry and working for this company. Setting unrealistic goals will deflate your motivation and thus impact your overall career progression.

In this section, we'll determine what is achievable for you and your current situation. The following are two questions you should ask yourself to help you determine if this goal is achievable and realistic:

- How realistic are my goals based on my overall life situations, such as family, finances, experience, and education?
- How can I accomplish this goal?

In this section, you need to be very honest with yourself. Do you have the time and funding to get the necessary training for the next position up? What resources do you have that can support this goal?

> **Tip**
> When focused on a goal that someone else has power over, this can be a little tricky. The example of becoming a director is not only dependent on your experience and education, but also on who else applies for the job and the hiring officer.

Relevant

In this section, you will determine if the goals you want to set actually matter to you. Yes, of course they matter, but do they really matter to your bigger dream? A way of determining if your goals support your current dream is by working backward. Start by identifying your dream, and then work backward to your goals.

An example could be a student currently going to school for their masters. However, they are a Vice President of a large organization and without the degree, they still have over 20 years' experience. The CEO has already talked to them about moving into a higher executive position. Therefore, the goal to obtain their masters could be a personal goal and no longer something needed for career progression. In this example, you could work backward from your current dream and identify your current position to see if your dream aligns with your goals and vice versa.

Don't get stuck in a goal just because it's something you thought you needed. The master's degree is nice to have but isn't always necessary for that next promotion. Many times, it's hard to let go of such goals because of ego or another reason. Be honest with yourself. Here are a few questions that can help you determine if this goal is relevant to you:

- Is the time right for this goal?
- Does the return on investments seem worth it?
- Is this a legacy goal that I need to revise and revisit as part of my new goals?

Using the example of the director position, the issue here could be that your significant other is about to have a child. The time you will need for taking the courses, and then the extra time you will need to give to the new position, may not be best for your current life circumstances. However, in a couple years, it could be a perfect time to revisit this goal.

Time-based

End dates are critical for anything we do in life. In military school, when I was attending a really difficult school, we use to count the days backward to help us stay motivated. You may hear someone say, *"25 days and a wakeup."* This means we only had 25 more days of hell; then, we would wake up and go home.

When you have the finishing line in view, it helps you maintain motivation as you move through the challenging times. Not every goal will be smooth and sometimes, those longer-term goals, such as a master's degree, can be very daunting. But you will know that if you keep pushing forward, you will be done in 2 years, for example.

Goalsetting timeframes can vary between short, medium, and long-term goals. The time frames will be determined by the dream. Remember in the previous section that I talked about working backward from the dream? Doing this will help you determine your timeframe. If your goal is to get a master's and you know it will take you 4 years, then this would be a long-term goal, but you could also have short and medium goals. A short-term goal could be finishing each semester with a B+.

Here is a list of questions to help you develop a time-based goal around a 12-month period:

- When do I realistically think I can finish this goal?
- Where will I be with this goal in 3 months from now?
- What can I do right now to start working on this goal?
- What can I accomplish in 8 weeks?

If you are seeking to become a director in a year and you know there are certain courses you need to take, the first step could be to determine how long each course is, and then how long it will take to attend the course, study, and take the exam. Once you've figured out a realistic and not rushed date, then purchase your exam voucher and set your date.

> **Tip**
> It's a good practice to put goals and goal dates on a whiteboard or around your house. Big goals require constant reminders and motivation. I sometimes post reminders on my bathroom mirror and other spots in my house I know I will see.

Use the following list to help develop goals specific to your needs:

1	Specific
	Answer the what, who, where, and why of the goal.
2	Measurable
	How will you know when you have reached your attended goal?
3	Achievable
	What micro goals and actions will you take to reach your goal?
4	Relevant
	Is this aligned with your bigger role as an X?
5	Time-Bound
	What is your finish date and realistic timeline?

Table 9.1 – Develop your goals using SMART.

Upon finishing this section, you should have a clear understanding that goals are critical for long-term success. The framework we provided in this section will assist you with anything you decide to do in your life. When you start setting goals, reach out to us and share your goals so that we can support you.

Another important factor within the cybersecurity community is mentorship. In the next section, you will learn about the importance of mentorship and what it means to be a mentee.

Learning about the mentor and mentee relationship

The concept of **mentoring** has such incredible value, especially within the information security community. It's a practical means for sharing knowledge and networking with like-minded professionals. These relationships can have various forms and lifespans, but there are techniques you can employ to find and maximize their utility.

First, let's explain the difference between a **mentor** and **mentee**. Everybody was a beginner at some point in any skill. Experienced people have acquired knowledge and can share it with those that do not have it yet. They can mentor a mentee to transition them from knowing nothing on a topic or skill to becoming proficient.

"Those that fail to learn from history are doomed to repeat it" is a famous quote by Winston Churchill and very applicable here. A mentor can guide a mentee to avoid pitfalls and mistakes the mentor has already made. Hopefully, you can see the immense value as a mentee; that is, you save time, avoid pain, and develop a skill.

Relationships defined

Now that we know about the roles. let's talk about the relationships. You can seek out a mentor for very niche, specific skills that might be for a short-term relationship, and you can seek out a mentor for long-term items, such as a career mentor. For a short-term skill example, I sought out mentoring on how to better use Instagram to engage the cybersecurity community. Regarding longer-term items, I myself have a career mentor I speak to every few years or when I'm planning a big career change to seek his advice on my decisions.

The point to take away is that there isn't a one-size-fits-all definition for what a mentor-mentee relationship looks like. Remove any preconceived notions you might have and be open-minded. They are fluid and defined by the people involved in the relationship. They are not defined by age, but rather expertise in most cases. These relationships are symbiotic with each person sharing and growing from each other's experiences.

Be accountable

A critical element of any mentor-mentee relationship is that both parties must be accountable. This means that if you agree to take some action by some time, then you do it. If your mentor is missing deadlines or not delivering on their commitments, you may consider moving on from that mentor.

It's not personal, but the intent of the relationship is to help you (the mentee) develop. Missed commitments are not helping you develop and, arguably, are wasting your valuable time.

SMART goals are measurable and achievable, right? Use them when working with a mentor to hold each other accountable. For example, if your mentor is going to review your résumé for feedback, you should both agree on when you will send them your résumé and when they will send feedback. Commitments need to be consensus-driven and agreed upon. Once you agree, stick to it.

If your mentor is missing deadlines, you should have an honest conversation about accountability. It's not malicious intent in many cases, but it could be a busy time in their life, and they don't have time to commit, or they have made commitments they can't keep. Regardless, openly and objectively discussing accountability and meeting deadlines will set the terms of the relationship and make sure you are getting value.

Put in the work

The workload of a mentor-mentee relationship is not evenly distributed. You, as a mentee, will need to put in closer to 80% of the work. As the mentee, the goal is for you to develop, and that happens by putting in the work. The mentor will be providing guidance and direction for the mentee to take action. For example, the mentor may tell you, *"here are three techniques to look at"* or *"here's a lab to work on that will develop web application security testing."* It's now the mentee's responsibility to be accountable and go off and work through the activities the mentor provided.

You can come back after to the mentor with issues, concerns, and lessons learned and have a productive conversation with them.

If you have the mindset that you're just going to be spoon-fed and the mentor is going to do all the work to develop you, you should realign your expectations. There is no shortcut and no easy button to get skills. You've got to put the work in.

Objective and constructive conversations

Every kind of interaction between mentors and mentees must be honest, objective, and constructive. Honest conversations will drive the most satisfying experiences. If a mentee is working on some items a mentor gave them and they are way too hard, you should have a conversation about it. You don't want to miss deadlines (you want to stay accountable, right?), and you definitely want to get value out of the experience, so if you aren't honest, then the other person in that relationship is going to assume things that aren't being said.

Another common topic of conversation in these types of relationships is if the mentor or mentee isn't meeting their commitments. Nobody wants to get frustrated, passive-aggressive, or have the relationship turn sour. Having an honest conversation about wanting to continue the mentoring and the ability to meet deadlines can help clarify expectations and if both people have the time, interest, and ability to be involved. It would be better to figure out early that a mentor cannot commit than wasting months not knowing.

Find a mentor

What's the best way to find a mentor? If you are following the lessons in this book, you will have been networking and engaging with individuals in the industry. I've always advocated that mentors should be organically discovered, and those relationships nurtured. Sometimes, this can be from someone in your office who is a professional colleague and may have different skill sets than you.

If someone is being assigned as your mentor, that can work, but as we've already mentioned regarding commitments and accountability, the best mentors are the ones that want to do it. Engage with people online, LinkedIn, cybersecurity Discord servers, and conferences to build a network and discover individuals that are contributing back and helping guide people in the field. These are ideal mentors!

It's also probably a good idea to map out your goals and direction before looking for a mentor. Don't expect a mentor to define your goals for you. As outlined previously, make sure the mentor is providing growth in a direction that supports your long-term vision.

You will naturally start having conversations and identify or align with certain individuals. Ask them questions and seek out their knowledge. If they are receptive to your requests, it's the beginning of a mentoring relationship. These organic relationships will grow, and you will have a rewarding experience.

The capability to have natural and fluid conversations with others will help you build your impactful network. The next section will provide you with tips on how best to approach networking, both in person and virtually.

Exploring different ways to network with impact

I read a book called *Never Eat Alone* by author Keith Ferrazzi, and there was a description in this book that stuck with me. The book is based around using your time wisely while still finding time to network. The author explains that there are three ways of launching a successful business, as follows:

- You have a lot of wealth, which affords you the ability to finance your company.

- You are an expert in a specific field, such as an attorney or doctor.

- You have a healthy network that comprises wealthy influential people who trust you and would be willing to invest in your business.

I pondered about which one of these would be the most realistic for me to accomplish in the shortest period. I decided to focus on number three and develop a strong and influential network.

Building followers is different than building a network. In the *Chapter 6, Time to Brand Yourself – Not the Burning Type*, we talked about building a brand and followers. This is one aspect of networking. Networking is about building relationships – it's about depth, not width. People assume that because they have 400,000 followers, they have 400,000 people who trust them and would give them investment money. This is not an accurate assessment. Instead of focusing on a large number, focus on smaller numbers while fostering and developing depth. You will notice that once you do this, your network will grow and naturally support you in your endeavors.

In the following sections, we will discuss seven tips to help you start building your network.

Tip #1 – find common ground

When reaching out to new contacts for which you don't have a soft introduction, find a common ground. Maybe you both work in the same sector in the cyber field.

An example could be introducing yourself and sharing a report you wrote, or even something you saw online, you believe would benefit this person in their career. Always take the stance that you are there to assist them in their endeavors, not the other way around.

You never want to come off pushy. You should have a structured plan and know "why" you want to become connected with this person before you reach out.

Tip #2 – it's about them, not you

When you take the mindset that it's about them, not you, it takes away the context of having a parasitic relationship.

Instead, a networking should be symbiotic, where each party gains and grows from each other. This is how trust is built, and your network creates depth instead of width.

Tip #3 – create depth, not width

To create a flourishing and deep network, you must dedicate time and consistency to your network. This is more than daily posts or snapchats. It's about writing personalized emails, text, voice messages, and/or calls.

Consistency is key. It's okay not talk to someone every single day. However, it's not okay to go a year with no contact. Yes, this does happen, and its okay, but it should not be the norm across your network. You cannot expect your network to support you when you don't support them and check in regularly.

A quick call to ask how someone is doing will easily start a conversation and allow you to know what is going on in their circle. This can also ignite a call about their problems and challenges. Knowing when to listen and commiserate and when to offer possible solutions is a fine art. But just because they are talking about their challenges, this may not mean they want to hear about yours.

Tip #4 – be smart when networking

Maintaining a strong network can take a lot of time if not managed correctly. A good approach is to find a way you can multi-task while calling someone. Driving is a perfect time to call and catch up with someone.

I found that a commute is the best time for making calls and catching up with my network. Also, another great way is by sending a quick text. We are lucky that we live in a world where we have so many means of communication. So, instead of having 30-minute calls, dinners, and other social events, you can also use text, instant messaging services, and email.

Another example could be meeting at a golf course. If you don't like golf, find another sport that would be fun and slow enough that you have enough time to talk. This is also a great way to invite multiple people to the event, allowing you to effectively meet with a small group of likeminded people to have fun and still catch up on current events.

Tip #5 – taking networking virtual

Prior to COVID-19, most networking was done in person. One of the positives from COVID-19 was the necessity to move online. This forced creativity in different ways when it comes to networking and conducting business.

Today, there are a plethora of networking events you can find online. Simply research online networking events and you will find different genres and vendors. Find the one that best suits your needs and start networking.

This is a great way to create relationships without even leaving your home.

Tip #6 – leverage social media and brands

Think back to *Chapter 6, Time to Brand Yourself – Not the Burning Type*, where we talked about branding. Your brand can be a huge help with networking. Most of the time, your first impression will be your social media page. A great way to leverage a good brand is by reaching out to people using your social media platform.

An example of this is using LinkedIn to build your network and reaching out to others in your field. You can use the example message template provided in *Chapter 6, Time to Brand Yourself – Not the Burning Type*, to reach out to these new contacts. Make sure to personalize the message so that they will accept your invite.

Next, follow this up and set up a quick 15-minute connect with them. Just connecting on your social media is not enough. Connect for 15 minutes so that you can learn about what they are doing and identify better ways to support their endeavors. Remember, networking is symbiotic, and you must show your value; otherwise, you may come off as just another person trying to take up their time. Once they start seeing your value, they will be interested in protecting and nurturing that value.

Tip #7 – follow up after a first meet

Following up is powerful! So many people do not follow up that when someone does, it places you above the rest. Be considerate of the person's time. If the person you would like to meet with is extremely busy, doing an initial follow-up is always good. If they don't respond right away, it's best to wait a week or two before doing another follow-up. But always follow up.

Depending on the message platform you are using, may it be a social media platform or email, messages do get lost. Depending on how busy that person is, they might miss your message because it was buried. A friendly follow-up is a great way to be at the top of their inbox or messages.

The key to successful networking is knowing your target audience and being polite, consistent and authentic. It takes time, but in a year, your network will mature, and you will have a trusted circle of likeminded people.

Summary

As we come to the end of this book, we want to remind you that the cybersecurity field is very diverse. In this chapter, we provided you with the final tools for your toolkit so that you can be as successful as possible.

Having a clear vision of your achievable and supportive goals is critical for success. If you don't have one yet, find a mentor. The mentor/mentee relationships in this industry are vital. It's the backbone of growth. Finally, build your family and your network. Consider your network a reflection of your morals and desires.

At this point, you should have a clearer picture of cybersecurity, the different career paths available, and how to create and set goals. We encourage you to take a few minutes and write down where you believe your skills and passion best fit within the industry. Create goals around that career path and begin taking the steps to reach your dream. If you have questions or need additional guidance, please reach out to any of the co-authors of this book for additional help.

We wish you the very best in your cyber career and look forward to hearing your comments on this book. We are here to serve you in your journey.

Assessments

Chapter 1

1. The CIA Triad in cyber means Confidentiality, Integrity, and Availability. These are the core pillars of information security (InfoSec) a subset of cybersecurity.

2. Distributed Denial of Service (DDoS), Man-in-the-Middle, and Drive-by attack

3. The first significant data breach happened to Yahoo in 2016, when hackers stole approximately 500 million accounts dating back to 2014. This breach then sparked the need for data protection and next came the Consumer Privacy Protection Act of 2017.

Chapter 2

1. C
2. B
3. B

Packt.com

Subscribe to our online digital library for full access to over 7,000 books and videos, as well as industry leading tools to help you plan your personal development and advance your career. For more information, please visit our website.

Why subscribe?

- Spend less time learning and more time coding with practical eBooks and Videos from over 4,000 industry professionals

- Improve your learning with Skill Plans built especially for you

- Get a free eBook or video every month

- Fully searchable for easy access to vital information

- Copy and paste, print, and bookmark content

Did you know that Packt offers eBook versions of every book published, with PDF and ePub files available? You can upgrade to the eBook version at packt.com and as a print book customer, you are entitled to a discount on the eBook copy. Get in touch with us at customercare@packtpub.com for more details.

At www.packt.com, you can also read a collection of free technical articles, sign up for a range of free newsletters, and receive exclusive discounts and offers on Packt books and eBooks.

Other Books You May Enjoy

If you enjoyed this book, you may be interested in these other books by Packt:

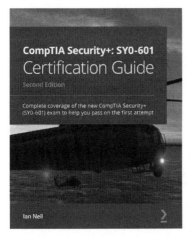

CompTIA Security+: SY0-601 Certification Guide – Second Edition

Ian Neil

ISBN: 978-1-80056-424-4

- Get to grips with security fundamentals, from the CIA triad through to IAM
- Explore cloud security and techniques used in penetration testing
- Discover different authentication methods and troubleshoot security issues
- Secure the devices and applications that are used by your company
- Identify and protect against various types of malware and virus

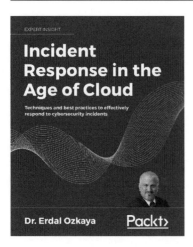

Incident Response in the Age of Cloud

Erdal Ozkaya

ISBN: 978-1-80056-921-8

- Understand IR and its significance
- Organize an IR team
- Explore best practices for managing attack situations with your IR team
- Form, organize, and operate a product security team to deal with product vulnerabilities and assess their severity
- Organize all the entities involved in product security response

Packt is searching for authors like you

If you're interested in becoming an author for Packt, please visit authors. packtpub.com and apply today. We have worked with thousands of developers and tech professionals, just like you, to help them share their insight with the global tech community. You can make a general application, apply for a specific hot topic that we are recruiting an author for, or submit your own idea.

Share Your Thoughts

Now you've finished *Cybersecurity Career Master Plan*, we'd love to hear your thoughts! Scan the QR code below to go straight to the Amazon review page for this book and share your feedback or leave a review on the site that you purchased it from.

https://packt.link/r/1801073562

Your review is important to us and the tech community and will help us make sure we're delivering excellent quality content.

Index

IDS – Intrusion Detection System

IPS – Intrusion Prevention System

APT – Advanced Persistent Threat

SIEM – Security Information & Event Management

    ⌐ collects + analyzes security alerts, logs, past + present data

    .. to detect attacks early

DLP – Data Loss Prevention –

    ⌐ stops sensitive data from being stolen or escaping a network

    (data in use, data in motion, data at rest)

ISE – Identity Services Engine / enforce user access (role-based control)

TrustSec –

Printed in Poland
by Amazon Fulfillment
Poland Sp. z o.o., Wrocław